*Routledge Revivals*

# Policing 'Domestic' Violence

Violence in the home, particularly assault by a man on his wife or girlfriend, is an everyday phenomenon. What should the police and law courts do about it? In *Policing 'Domestic' Violence*, first published in 1989, reissued here with a new preface, Susan Edwards draws upon her extensive research into their actual responses, both before and after recent initiatives towards reform at the time, to address the practical and theoretical issues for criminology and feminism.

Examining police and court practice, the author exposes the ways in which the patriarchal ideology enshrined in the law, and the masculine ethos of the police and legal profession, ensure that women receive less justice and less protection. She documents in detail the processes by which crimes against women are trivialized.

The book combines a review of international research with the author's own five-year exploration of policing in the UK through interviews with officers, observation and a review of record-keeping practice. It covers the introduction of new policing policies and offers a preliminary assessment of their success together with practical proposals for the future.

At a theoretical level, this title addresses the key problems of criminality and punishment. Is it possible to reconcile the feminist critique of the marginalization of so-called domestic violence with the radical critique of the punitive system as oppressive and counterproductive? Does the protection of women justify infringement of family privacy?

The book should be read in its historical context by students of criminology, law, women's studies and sociology, as well as those concerned with policies and practical measures for dealing with violence in the home.

# Policing 'Domestic' Violence

## Women, the Law and the State

Susan S. M. Edwards

Routledge
Taylor & Francis Group
ROUTLEDGE REVIVALS

First published in 1989
by Sage Publications

This edition first published in 2025 by Routledge
4 Park Square, Milton Park, Abingdon, Oxon, OX14 4RN

and by Routledge
605 Third Avenue, New York, NY 10017

*Routledge is an imprint of the Taylor & Francis Group, an informa business*



**Publisher's Note**
The publisher has gone to great lengths to ensure the quality of this reprint but points out that some imperfections in the original copies may be apparent.

**Disclaimer**
The publisher has made every effort to trace copyright holders and welcomes correspondence from those they have been unable to contact.

A Library of Congress record exists under ISBN: 0803980329

ISBN: 978-1-032-95548-3 (hbk)
ISBN: 978-1-003-58551-0 (ebk)
ISBN: 978-1-032-95566-7 (pbk)

Book DOI 10.4324/9781003585510

# New Preface for Reissue

It has been over four decades since *Policing "Domestic" Violence: Women, the Law and the State* was first published. A title which implicitly contained within it a sense of outrage that male violence against female partners was considered of lesser importance than violence between men on the street. The book attempted to unlock and open up the police, judicial process and the substantive law to scrutiny and account.

I would like to think the call for change that the book demanded made a lasting impact. Of course, some improvements in the protection of women and girls from domestic violence and abuse have been made in the intervening years. Developments in technology and the use of the internet to perpetrate domestic abuse, revenge porn, threatening communications are part of a pattern of control and intimidation in abusive relationships which have necessitated the introduction of 'communications offences' in the Online Safety Act 2023. Judicial training and guidance, CPS prosecutor training and police training have also made an impact. But at the same time in looking at the contemporary landscape there is also a feeling of stagnation and at times of going backwards as the popularist media and especially social media denigrate women at every opportunity and condone violence against them, which in turn impacts on a new generation for whom social media is their primary outlet and information source. Change is not incremental. There is evidence that the sexist attitudes prevalent at the time held by legal personnel, police, prosecutors, counsel and judges are still reflected today in stereotypes about who should be protected, whilst blaming the victim and excusing the perpetrator continues. Misunderstandings are still in evidence, judges remarking that women can go outside or upstairs to escape domestic abuse, prosecutors declining to prosecute where men make countervailing allegations as part of a defense strategy and police pressurising complainants to withdraw charges (See 'Officer "pressured" domestic violence victim to drop complaint months before husband stabbed her,' *The Telegraph* August 27, 2024).

The re issue of *Policing "Domestic" Violence* will introduce a new generation of scholars, activists, practitioners and professionals to the importance of continually holding the state and the justice system to account. Their demands are all the more powerful as in advocating for change they will be able to point to the past and say with chagrin 'this demand was on the agenda 40 years ago'. Intergenerational studies enable learning from the past, recovering important evidence and evaluating how far we have come and how far we need to go. (See 'The Development of Domestic Violence as a Field: Honoring Clare Dalton,' Elizabeth Schneider and Cheryl Hanna, 20 *Journal of Law and Policy* 2011-2012, 343). Working collectively across discipline boundaries is vital, once hermetically sealed and with an entrenched elitism and hierarchy, scholars worked in silos. Socio-Legal studies made a significant inroad into elevating the importance of context, and the impact of feminism within sociology, criminology and the law, engineered change. Those of us working in the area of domestic violence were scrutinised, problematised and marginalised and our work deprecated, but we had one mission to foreground violence against women by men and the complicity of the state who for the most part ignored it. In this objective carving credibility and influence in scholarship and in practice mattered, and my own path unfolded from criminology, sociology and victimology, socio-legal studies and law and then later contesting what seemed a hallowed space, the Bar and pupillage, followed by a period in legal practice and then as now as a Domestic violence/abuse expert witness in effecting change.

*Policing "Domestic" Violence* offered a significant contribution to understanding the legal and policing response to domestic violence, written at a time when violence against partners was 'a domestic' to be written off by police, when constabulary effectiveness was dominated by performance indicators which heralded police success in prosecutions and conviction rates such that the frightened, fearful and reluctant witness was troublesome to this score card. At the time and through firsthand empirical research I set out to document the policing of domestic violence by tracking reporting, recording, and prosecuting, at two London police stations over a six-month period of data collection. The Metropolitan Police at a politically sensitive time for policing granted me full access to police records and 'residency' for long periods in local police stations notwithstanding my use of the word 'police culture' in my application for research approval, a term which had become weaponized. My findings were also politically sensitive, since the number of domestic incidents and crimes I uncovered were at odds with the official statistic for the Metropolitan Police District held by the Home Office Statistics Department, which recorded 384 domestic violence crimes for 1985. I discovered that police were submitting as the official figure for domestic violence crimes only those cases where the victim was willing to support a prosecution, disposing of the rest under the 'no crime' classification. A chance meeting in the lobby of the Home Office in Queen Anne's Gate with the Home Affairs correspondent of *The Times* led to a potentially incendiary news story. I had been warned by a Chief Superintendent outside the Met that reporting on this figure would cause me trouble and was unwise. But silence was not an option. That statistic was political and its impact devastating resulting in refutation of domestic violence and of the need for refuges and funding for victim/ survivors. *The Times* headline of October 6, 1986, reported 'Police statistics fail to show true level of violent crime in the home'. The police responded sympathetically setting up a Working Party appointing me as a consultant and worked towards the better handling of domestic abuse complaints, making a series of recommendations leading to domestic violence units in all but a handful of police stations and changes in recording practices. In the Annual report for 1987, the Commissioner welcomed and acknowledged the research findings. But elsewhere denial of the extent of domestic abuse continued. In 1995, *The Times* ran a full-page article by one of their journalists: 'Knocked for six: the myth of a nation of wife-batterers' which railed into my research and others for, said the journalist, promoting 'one of the central fictions of our age' and accusing me and others wrote: 'the phenomenon of domestic violence had been egregiously misrepresented and ludicrously exaggerated', calling us 'domestic violence racketeers'. Turning the clock forward domestic abuse prevalence for England and Wales year ending March 2022, the police recorded 1,500,369 'domestic abuse-related incidents and crimes' and 1,453,867 year ending March 2023, of which 889,189 were domestic abuse related crimes. (See Domestic abuse prevalence and trends, England and Wales - Office for National Statistics (ons.gov.uk https://www.ons.gov.uk/peoplepopulationandcommunity/crimeandjustice/articles/domesticabuseprevalenceandtrendsenglandandwales/yearendingmarch2023)). Incidentally, my figure for London as a whole in 1985 extrapolated from research in the specific areas studied was 58,000 domestic violence crimes and incidents, given the benefit of hindsight it seems remarkably modest.

As for domestic murder since 1989 approximately 15-18 per cent of all homicide has involved the killing of female partners, though falling in recent years the actual numbers of female deaths have remained relatively comparable over the years. A statistic which is less subject to manipulation by recording practices and yet the obvious inference that proactive policing can reduce this disastrous demise was not then fully appreciated. This death toll continues and year ending March 2020, 46 per cent of all adult female homicide victims were killed by an intimate partner. In 2022, this figure was at 44 per cent. Of all 684 homicides year ending March 2022, female victims were killed by a partner or ex-partner in 59, 10 per cent of cases, falling from 2018 when the percentage was at 14 per cent. (See Homicide in England and Wales Appendix Table 14a https://www.ons.gov.uk/peoplepopulationandcommunity/crimeandjustice/datasets/appendixtableshomicideinenglandandwales).

With regard to the substantive law, following pressure from victim/survivors, front line workers, politicians and academics understanding of domestic violence and abuse began to reflect its reality such that mental abuse, which like physical abuse kept women in a state of fear, frightened, intimidated and silenced, led to challenges to the archaic rigid legal definition of assault under the Victorian Offences Against the Person Act 1861, which contemplated only an episodic physical event. By 2015, domestic abuse was understood as a pattern of abuse and the Serious Crime Act section 76 created a stand-alone offence of 'controlling and coercive conduct'. In her testimony Rosie Duffield, MP, during a House of Commons debate on the Domestic Abuse Bill in 2019, spoke of her partner's coercive control of her. 'Domestic violence has many faces… sometimes there are no bruises...abuse is often all about control and power…they don't threaten… control ...not yet… not at the start…when they think you are sweet and gorgeous' ( See 'MPs moved to tears by Rosie Duffield's domestic abuse story – You-

Tube' https://www.youtube.com/watch?v=XWvYVHiXqS-g&t=25s). Year ending March 2022, 41,626 offences of coercive conduct were recorded and year ending March 2023, 43,774 offences. (See above, Domestic Abuse Prevalence and Trends, Main point 5).

A woman's fear of her abusive and violent partner is now better understood. The Coroners and Justice Act 2009 introduced fear as a trigger for loss of control manslaughter where the victim in defending herself kills the abuser and where there is a history of abuse. However, this partial defence is little attempted as the criteria anomalously remain fixed in the past since fear of 'serious violence' has to be proved. (See Susan Edwards 'Women Who Kill Abusive Partners: Reviewing the Impact of section 55(3) "Fear of Serious Violence" Manslaughter - Some Empirical Findings' Northern Ireland Legal Quarterly 2021 214-239). By 2021, the Domestic Abuse Act 2021 introduced strangulation, a redolent feature of domestic abuse, as a stand-alone offence. (See Susan Edwards, David Malone and Gillian Jones KC *Blackstone's Guide to the Domestic Abuse Act* 2021, OUP 2023).

During the intervening years police and prosecutors, especially from 2000, began to press for better collection of documentary and corroborative evidence where victim/survivors were afraid and reluctant to support a prosecution. Rules of evidence underwent development, and 999 calls made at the time under res gestae rules of evidence were used to support domestic abuse allegations. The seminal contribution in the 1980s of Lenore Walker in the US to an understanding of the response of a battered woman in theorising 'battered woman syndrome' may have fallen out of favor but her understanding of women's fear and reaction to violence and its threat from abusive partners remains sound as does the current need to admit expert testimony of women who kill in self-defense to assist jurors.

Despite advances in policing and support for prosecutions through enhanced evidence there is considerable case attrition. Since 2015 prosecutions as a percentage of reported cases have fallen, and disturbingly there is evidence that a significant proportion of cases are not prosecuted because as Her Majesty's Inspectorate of Constabulary and Fire and Rescue Services (HMICFRS) report either the complainant is 'unwilling to support a prosecution' (outcome 16) or for 'other evidential reasons' (outcome 15).

Public confidence in the police needs to be restored. The murder of Sarah Everard killed by a serving police officer in 2021, the extent of domestic abuse perpetrated by police officers on their partners, the treatment of women at the hands of the police and the treatment of women in custody (see *The Baird Inquiry* 2024, https://www.greatermanchester-ca.gov.uk/media/9861/the-baird-inquiry.pdf) deter women from reporting domestic violence and abuse as does the prosecution prognosis. The National Police Chiefs Council (NPCC) admit police failings (see https://cdn.prgloo.com/media/034ed60aa6564c1fbdcfb03fd8e6a210.pdf national police sdtatement 2024) as do the Association of Police and Crime Commissioners (APCC) in their response to the super complaint brought by the Centre for Women's Justice (see https://static1.squarespace.com/static/5aa98420f2e6b1ba0c874e42/t/5c91f55c9b747a252efe260c/1553069406371/Super-complaint+report.FINAL.pdf.). Whilst the HM Inspectorate of Constabulary, Fire and Rescue Services (HMICFRS) concede that the criminal justice system is not functioning effectively when responding to domestic abuse, and at a time when the Government claims to be addressing abuse as a high priority.

Priorities for the government, the law and the state must now include full implementation of Clare's Law disclosure scheme of those with a history of domestic violence and abuse and attend to the monitoring of Domestic Homicides and Suicides and support local and national delivery of Domestic Abuse Related Death Reviews recommendations mandated in the Prisoners and Victims Act 2024. (See https://hmicfrs.justiceinspectorates.gov.uk/our-work/article/domestic-violence-and-abuse/). Importantly legislation is required to criminalise the conduct of perpetrators where victims of domestic abuse in efforts to escape further violence contemplate suicide as their only avenue of escape. (See Katharine Hoeger and Lis Bates, Executive Summary, Findings and Recommendations: Domestic Homicides and Suspected Victim Suicides Year 3 Report (2020-2023)). The justice system must protect all women and address the exclusion of migrant women from legal aid who have no recourse to public funds leaving them at risk and entrenching discriminatory practices. There is still much to be done.

*Policing "Domestic" Violence* was pivotal in repositioning "domestic" as mainstream, as important if not more so than violence in the streets since women experiencing violence in the home had nowhere to retreat. At the time it was 'just a domestic' even though 47 per cent of all women killed were killed by partners or former partners. The importance of looking back should not be perceived as a mere historical reflection on a bygone era, instead and importantly the teachings of the past can be used as a political tool to press for current change, underscoring that the issues prominent in current debates were had then, the attitudes and tropes held now were held then and the problems of lack of confidence in police, under reporting, under recording, under prosecuting, resistance to expert witnesses were all extant then, as now. We know now that understanding starts, continues and ends with including the survivor's experience. We know now that domestic abuse exists because its condonation is embedded in a society that fails to challenge at every step the habituated denigration of women in public and private spaces and cultural and political and legal institutions. We know now that the wider social and material context needs to be contested at every level of the justice process and especially the media, social media and those who seek a following from promoting misogyny. It is up to every one of us to brace this tide of ignominy and turn it.

Susan S. M. Edwards, 2024

# POLICING 'DOMESTIC' VIOLENCE

## Women, the Law and the State

Susan S.M. Edwards

First published 1989 Reprinted 1991



Sage Publications Ltd
6 Bonhill Street
London EC2A 4PU

SAGE Publications Inc
2455 Teller Road
Newbury Park, California 91320

SAGE Publications India Pvt Ltd
32, M-Block Market
Greater Kailash - I
New Delhi 110 048

**British Library Cataloguing in Publication data**

Edwards, Susan S.M.
Policing 'domestic' violence: Women, the law and the state.
1. Families. Violence
I. Title
306.8'7

ISBN 0-8039-8032-9
ISBN 0-8039-8033-7 Pbk

**Library of Congress catalog card number 89-60526**

Typeset by Colset Private Limited, Singapore
Printed in Great Britain by Billing and Sons Ltd, Worcester

# Contents

# Acknowledgements

I am enormously grateful to many people for their co-operation and assistance in the course of writing this book and conducting the research involved. The police research which forms the basis of chapters 3 and 4 began one morning in November 1983, in a room in the Metropolitan Police headquarters at Scotland Yard in London. In some respects it was not a timely meeting: the Metropolitan Police were still smarting from the criticism and bad press that followed in the wake of the Policy Studies Institute report *Police and Policing in London*. Not surprisingly, researchers were *personae non gratae.* Nevertheless, by June 1984 not only were all research facilities granted, and co-operation and assistance secured, but the Metropolitan Police had also instituted their own Working Party into Domestic Violence.

Chief Superintendent Sheila Ward (QPM), Inspector Annette Payne and Chief Inspector Paul Green were enormously helpful in facilitating access in the initial stages, and research began at Hounslow and Holloway police stations in 1984, where every assistance was offered. Throughout the course of the study, the Metropolitan Police's Community Liaison Division, especially Commander Larry Roach and later Commander W. Boreham, Chief Superintendent Roger Street and Inspector Jayne Stitchbury have maintained interest in the project. Gary Armstrong as Research Assistant collected data on police recording practices and conducted interviews at both locations.

This book, however, considers some wider questions about women, policing and the state, the criminal and civil justice system and the experience of personal violence. Chapter 5 emerged out of many meetings with Women's Aid groups in England and Wales. Manchester Women's Aid was especially helpful in the construction of the questionnaire used to examine women's experience of policing. The women and workers of a refuge in Islington shared their experiences of violence with me, and I am especially grateful to Barbara Street of Welsh Women's Aid and Sandra Horley of Chiswick Family Rescue for assistance and support, and Assistant Chief Constable Alan Bourlet of the South Wales Police and the Wales Regional Training Department. For some of the detailed statistics presented in chapters 2 and 3, I am indebted to the Statistical Divisions of the Lord Chancellor's Department, the Home Office in London and the Royal Ulster Constabulary in Northern Ireland.

The Inner London Education Authority and the Economic and Social Research Council (grant number E00232137) financed the research project entitled 'The Impact of Police Discretion on Domestic Violence in London' upon which chapters 3 and 4 are based. The evaluation study currently in progress and discussed in chapter 6 is being sponsored by the Police Foundation, London.

I am enormously grateful to the Home Office Library for providing me with a visitor's desk, a magnificent book collection and an arresting view of Central London and St James's Park. Most importantly, I am grateful for the sensitive and serious reception that the findings and recommendations of the policing study have had, and to the Metropolitan Police and its Commissioner Sir Kenneth Newman, who had the foresight to change police policy on domestic assault on 24 June 1987. Commissioner Sir Peter Imbert (QPM), as accoucher, has already demonstrated a continued commitment to improving police response to domestic violence by incorporating it in his strategy statement for 1989, announced on 24 January 1989.

Finally, I would like to thank Monica Walker and Sheila Wilyman for reading and commenting on various chapters of this book, Gillian Stern and Stephen Barr of Sage, and the copy-editor, Harriet Barry, for an excellent job.

The views expressed herein may not concur with those of the people who have so kindly assisted me in various ways.

# Abbreviations

AC Appeal cases
ACPO Association of Chief Police Officers
All ER *All England Law Reports*
AQOA All quiet on arrival
ASNT Area searched, no trace
CAD Computer Aided Dispatch
CAR *Criminal Appeal Reports*
CAR(S) *Criminal Appeal Reports, Sentencing*
CCC Central Criminal Court
CL *Current Law*
CLR *Criminal Law Review*
CLRC Criminal Law Revision Committee
CMLR *Common Market Law Reports*
ER *English Reports*
FL *Family Law*
FLR *Family Law Report*
IRLR *Industrial Relations Law Reports*
JP *Justice of the Peace and Local Government Review*
LEXIS Enggen Legal computer database, English General
LEXIS Fedgen Legal computer database, Federal General
LOAP Left on arrival of police
NCPA No call for police action
QBD Queen's Bench Division
SCOLAG Scottish Legal Action Group
SJ *Solicitors' Journal*
SLT *Scottish Law Times*
State Tr State trials
WLR *Weekly Law Reports*

# Introduction
# Domestic Violence and the Law and Order Debate

This book specifically addresses the legal and policing response to violence against women committed by known male 'partners', in the context of wider policing and 'law and order' debates. The responses of the law, policing, the prosecution process, and sentencing to the violent offender have always denied women even the most 'miserable mouse' of protection. At a time when public order situations are being ever more rigorously regulated throughout the western world, the relative non-interference of the law and law-enforcers in spousal disorder of the kind investigated here is increasingly anomalous.

The idea of the 'rule of law' in legal philosophy and political thought is still strong, asserting the value, freedom and neutrality of all laws. Such a claim becomes increasingly untenable as we witness the deepening chasm between the form, content and application of laws designed to regulate public conduct (and especially potential group and public violence) and those designed to regulate private situations. Here we have a clear demonstration of the discrimination and partiality of particular laws, clearly imbued with value-judgements about who and what forms of violence should be regulated. What is the basis of the prevailing view that spousal violence is a family affair, a private matter rarely if ever to be regulated or interfered with by the law, the police or the public? Can law-makers and enforcers and the police in particular justify their traditional complacency, or is this apparent resignation evidence of institutionalized misogyny, since it is undeniably the case that the victims of domestic violence are most often women – cohabitees, girlfriends, wives, daughters and mothers – and the aggressors are men – boyfriends, husbands, fathers and sons. Given this sex divide between aggressors and victims, it would not be illogical to interpret the treatment of both offenders and victims by the criminal justice system as misogynist, too, if too simplistic. But does this complacency arise because the violence happens behind closed doors? And can the state, society, the law and the police continue to dismiss women's appeal to the right to protection merely because the violence occurs beyond the public gaze? Or is such a non-interventionist stance in fact sustained on ideological grounds, given that spouse-to-spouse violence in the street has rarely been regarded as an illegality, unless a threat to public order is created?

While women's right to protection is constantly disavowed in deference to the apparently competing right to individual (male) liberty, what can victims and potential victims facing the threat of assault and death do? Some women simply continue to live with violent men and suffer silently. Some women escape these relationships by leaving. Some women fight back, defend and sometimes kill their father in protection of their mother, their partner in protection of themselves and their children. Here the line between victim and criminal can shift very easily, and it is here, in the defensive reaction, that the battered woman is most decidedly misunderstood. All these matters are addressed in the chapters that follow. It is important to recognize that the concern with spousal violence is an integral part of the broader public concern for improving police response, and should have a major role in the wider law and order debate.

The empirical findings presented in this book are based on two research projects, the first commencing in 1984 and the second starting in 1988. The overall aim of both projects was to examine the legal and policing responses to the problem of 'domestic' or spousal violence. The first project was jointly financed by the Inner London Education Authority and the Economic and Social Research Council. It had several aims. The main objective was to examine serving police officers' attitudes (see chapter 3) and the attitudes of police recruits to the problem of domestic violence, and the impact these attitudes had on subsequent police decision-making, action and recording practices (see chapter 4). The research also sought to examine the victims' perceptions and experiences of the police and the legal system (see chapter 5).

This first study was carried out in 1984–5 in the Metropolitan Police Area in London at two stations, Holloway and Hounslow, chosen because of the different areas they served; Holloway being in the heart of London in the Borough of Islington (inner city), and Hounslow on its boundaries in the Borough of Hounslow. Holloway's area is concentrated in a few square miles, while Hounslow covers a much wider and in part less densely populated area. Holloway had a reputation as a high crime area, and Hounslow slightly less so. The populations served were of similar size: at Holloway the electorate was 192,000, and at Hounslow it was 200,000 at the time of the study. At both these localities 44 interviews were conducted with serving police officers involved in attending domestic violence calls.

Subsequently, an opportunity arose to interview a further sample of 18 officers from a different police force, the Kent Police force (see chapter 3). This opportunity proved to be invaluable, as officers in the Kent force tended on the whole to hold the same views about domestic violence as London officers, thus supporting evidence from other sources which indicates that similar attitudes to domestic violence are generally held throughout police forces in England and Wales, and elsewhere.

The interview study was supplemented by an examination of police records in the London area. And, although police records were not taken in this study to provide an accurate account of police action (for reasons that will become clear), it provided some indications. A further study of police attitudes was conducted using a questionnaire (70 officers were involved) and a follow-up interview in 20 cases.

After the police studies, a study of women victims of domestic violence (as consumers of policing as a service) was conducted via interviews and questionnaires (70) at several refuges in England and Wales. The results of the refuge study are related in chapter 5. Responses were the result of the co-operation of Welsh Women's Aid, Manchester Women's Aid, London Women's Aid and Leeds Women's Aid.

Later, after the introduction of the force order in the Metropolitan Police area a follow-up or replication study of recording practices (only) was conducted, again at Hounslow and Holloway (chapter 6). This study was supported by the Police Foundation. Ideally, officers at both localities would have been interviewed in order that attitudes in 1988 might be assessed and compared with earlier attitudes, but this was not possible owing to lack of resources, and so the follow-up study relied on a examination of record-keeping practice and set out to compare these with 1984–5. The aim of this second study was to assess how far certain aspects of the new force policy had been implemented and whether changes could be identified.

These studies provide evidence about policing in this area that complements studies of police attitudes and women's experiences of policing conducted elsewhere. The empirical findings on police recording practices, however, make a significant contribution to the debate on law and order generally, and to that on domestic violence in particular. The empirical findings are presented alongside discussion of particular court cases and legal analysis, and in the wider context of the political debate around police accountability and attitudes to women in society.

## Accountability, the public/private divide and law and order

Three general questions are of central importance, and provide the broader political and theoretical backcloth to the discussion that follows. First, in recent years political and academic discussions in the

UK, North America and Europe have focused on the problem of police accountability. It has been argued that police accountability becomes increasingly necessary as the police are used as an arm of authoritarian and right-wing regimes, not as crime controllers or crime preventers *per se* but as political buffers between an increasingly alienated and disaffected population and the state. The claim is that the state is becoming increasingly divorced from the needs and interests of many of the people. However, while the discussion of accountability has firmly included a consideration of class and racial perspectives within its mandate, the idea that women may have an interest in what police do, who and what police 'police', is rarely, if ever, seriously considered. How and why, when women constitute over half the population, one-eighth of criminal offenders, are predominantly the victims in rape, sex, murder and spousal violence and equally represented in grass-roots political protest, are their voices ignored? How does this process of edging women's needs and interests out of the debate reinforce traditional victim-blaming attitudes towards women victims held by legal practitioners, police, prosecutors, and sentencers?

The second major consideration guiding this discussion is the clear existence of a public/private divide in law, which organizes and ratifies a different level of response to similar conduct in the two terrains, including a different level of police response and priorities. Both current legislation and policing priorities in public order reflect the view of the present government and the police that the maintenance and regulation of public order are of quintessential importance. By contrast, the law in theory and in practice reflects the relegation of private or domestic 'crime' to that of the lowest priority.

The third dimension to be considered here is the 'law and order' issue, a priority concern for academics and political parties on both Left and Right. Yet to present the interests in this debate as inhabiting two polarized camps would be a mistake, since there are also deep divisions within the two positions. The areas for debate are clear – the causes, prevention, treatment and punishment of disorder, conflict and crime. Broadly, the Right see the route to a more stable society in order, repression and control. Stability is to be achieved by tougher laws controlling crime, industrial conflict and dissent; prevention is increased by criminalizing preludes or perceived preludes to crime or disorder, and this process is completed by the provision of more stringent penalties for rule-breakers. The Left broadly see this package as a recipe for disaster, aggravating and inciting the very public disorder it seeks to avert. For the Left the law is repressive – criminalizing an ever-increasing number and variety of preludes to conduct that may lead to a crime encroaches on civil liberties. Penalties that are keenly motivated by a thirst for retribution are considered to be largely redundant. Yet within these broad responses are real divisions and differences.

The problem of violence against women forces us to confront the intricacies and anomalies of these differences. Yet these contradictions are not peculiar to feminism, but also emerge in victimology and crime prevention issues. Feminists interested in the protection of women from spousal violence, rape and prostitution, while they are pro-victim, do not all seek to restore balance to a criminal justice system that has systematically abrogated the needs of victims and denied them rights, while concentrating on the offender – his perceptions, motivation and problems. Similarly, victimology in its most radical form, in its efforts to promote the interests of victims, has frequently ignored the need to consider the rights of the offender. The problem for victimology in general has been explained by Kirchoff (1988: 10). He illustrates vividly the depth of concern expressed by the American President's Task Force on Victims of Crime (1982), who recommended measures by which the rights of victims are to be achieved at the expense of reverting to a reactionary response to the offender. The Task Force on Victims recommends the negation of bail, the right of the prosecution to expedited appeal, and the abolition of parole, among other measures – in other words an overall tightening-up of the process of law. Feminist victimology also falls into the trap when it claims that all rapists should be locked up, that all men are potentially rapists and that only victims deserve rehabilitation. For example, feminist 'reform' in the field of spousal abuse prevention is calling for more law, mandatory arrest, bail refusal, more police, more prosecution, and more punishment. Yet these feminists are often the very women who have been campaigning for decarceration, fewer police, and less imprisonment for other crimes.

The problem of violence against women evokes diverse socio-political responses. Feminists see legal measures as short-term solutions and look beyond the immediate aim of protecting women to programmes of therapy and treatment as a longer-term solution to the prevention of recidivism in male wife-beaters. But the various feminist positions are by no means clear-cut, and issues of spousal assault, rape, prostitution and pornography pose many penalogical contradictions. Most feminists are however familiar with these contradictions and recognize that the real world of campaign and political action on crime and victimization issues cannot adhere to dogma for the sake of some ideologically fastidious fetish. In campaigns around rape, pornography, prostitution and violence against wives they have traditionally regarded the law as a contradictory and ambivalent mechanism. While regulating certain behaviours oppressively, in its content and application in some instances the law also exonerates particular forms of male conduct against women. As Matza (1964: 61) perceived, the law invites the defendant to neutralize his normative attachment to it by providing a series of legal defences and mitigatory circumstances which in effect deny responsibility and let men off the hook. The rhymes and reasons, excuses and justifications of the rapist and the wife-batterer are well known and documented, both in the annals of case law and in academic research. Some alibis/aliases are more acceptable in law than others. But there is no room here for a dogmatic position that regards the relationship between all laws and groups of individuals as uniform.

The wider debates of police accountability, the application of the public and private dichotomy in law and the law and order debate on crime control, prevention and punishment are discussed in the following chapters through a consideration of the various forms of violence against women, in prostitution, pornography, rape and especially in the assault and killing of women by male partners.

## Approaches to law and order

In recent years criminologists have turned their attention to analyses of crime in relation to the state and responses to law and order. The law and order debate has centered on questions of law, policing, public order and prisons. There is, as De Haan notes, 'a wave of "law and order" ... washing over the western world' (1987: 323). The Right and the Left have been divided (both between and within) in their approaches to an analysis of law, the role of policing and prisons, and in their speculations about the causes of disorder and crime and the various solutions mooted to avert 'crisis' As we have seen, informed by different theoretical and political perspectives on the relationship of law to the state, both positions advocate very different strategies for the achievement of order.

Traditionally, the Left's perspective on law and order has been guided by Marxist theories of law and the state, from Marx and Engels to Pashukanis (1978) (writing in the 1920s), Gramsci (1971) and Althusser (1971). These various theories of the state share a number of axioms fundamental to Marxism and to the Left critique. First, legal relations as well as the forms of state are considered a reflection of the interests of the ruling class. This representation of class interest in law finds various expressions and interpretations throughout the Marxist tradition. Marx and Engels in 1858 opined that 'legal relations as well as forms of state ... are rooted in the material conditions of life . . . The totality of these relations of production constitutes the economic structure on which legal and political superstructures arise' (Fine 1984: 86). Althusser, in developing the materialist conception of the state and of law, defined not only the repressive nature of the state and its functioning in the interests of the ruling class, but the form which it takes.

> The State is thus first of all what the Marxist classics have called the State apparatus. This term means: not only the specialized apparatus (in the narrow sense) whose existence and necessity I have recognized in relation to the requirements of legal practice, i.e. the police, the courts, the prisons; but also the army, which (the proletariat has paid for this experience with its blood) intervenes directly as a supplementary repressive force in the last instance, when the police and its specialized auxiliary crops are 'outrun by events'; and above this ensemble, the head of State, the government and the administration. (1971: 137)

The state within the various formulations of orthodox Marxism is regarded as a class weapon. This view is particularly held and is most demonstrably sustained by those writers engaged in an examination of property laws and laws relating to labour, industry, ownership and control. In accord with a Marxist conception of law, all laws institutionalize repression and control in both form and content. Within this, any laws that may appear to be reformist or liberal cannot be. Instead, reformist laws are merely 'juridic illusions', their purpose and function being to defeat class antagonisms and circumvent the revolution by a massive and orchestrated con trick, through the dialectic which turns on its head the true relation of law to the state and makes fools of us all.

Marxists argue that it is through the apparent impartiality and neutrality of the mechanisms of the law, i.e. the police and the army, that the state is able to defend bourgeois interests. Yet the law is neither neutral nor 'value-free', and this claim is no more than political trickery. Pashukanis, in reply to those theorists and politicians who argued that the law is a 'pure form of thought' ( e.g. Stammler, discussed below), used a parody:

> If the law is 'a pure form of thought' then it is possible to avoid the ugly fact that the capitalist law of private property means the misery of unemployment, poverty, and hunger for the proletarian and his family, and that in defence of this law stands police armed to the teeth, fascist bands, hangmen and prison guards: and that this law signifies a whole system of coercion, humiliation and oppression. (1978: 283)

These various shades of Marxist perspective translate into particular political practices that lead to resistance to and challenge of expressions of law, forms of policing and kinds of punishment. Traditionally, the struggles of the Left have been characterized by demands for less oppressive laws and policing, greater accountability and the abolition of repressive punishment.

By contrast, the wave of 'law and order' to which De Haan refers is represented in and by a right-wing and reactionary response which demands more control, through the creation of more laws, the massive extension of police powers both on the street and in the police station and the institutionalization of more punishment. This political position is guided by an adherence to the idea that the rule of law is a necessary and unqualified human good, a perspective that derives unwittingly or consciously from Hegel's view of the rational state, where the 'rule of law' represents the most vital stand against despotism. And, clearly, right-wing rhetoric in defence of certain law-and-order practices which the Left regard as unconscionable echoes the view that almost any kind of repression and oppression is justified if the ultimate aim is the prevention of despotism.

The 'rule of law' theory is founded on two major claims, currently central to right-wing Conservative and Republican thinking on law and order. First the 'rule of law' is argued to represent the general will of the people and express the interests of the communality. Second, the law is considered neutral, since it is universal in its application. As Stammler argues within this perspective, 'The concept of law is a pure form of thought' (quoted in Fine 1984). This view is reflected in the current Conservative and Republican reformist movement, which is characterized by its efforts towards the codification and generation of more substantive law regulating public order and the expression of certain forms of ideological commitment such as the promotion of homosexuality. It is represented in UK law in the Criminal Attempts Act 1981, the Public Order Act 1986 and the Local Government Bill 1986. Such laws and proposals widen the range of criminalized conduct and extend the groups of persons legitimately under surveillance, charged, detained and prosecuted. This regulationist movement has provided the main impetus and ratification for the extension of police powers, both on the streets in terms of surveillance and stop and search and in police stations in terms of detention. The Police and Criminal Evidence Act 1984 especially facilitates the widening of police discretion and the use and application of 'reasonable belief' in a *post facto* justification of police conduct. A similar reformist zeal is found in recent legal expressions and attempts to reorganize the prosecution process, aspects of the trial process and the penal system, where jury challenges prove too costly, the right to trial for certain offences too expensive, the right to police complaints procedure investigations too cumbersome.

In England and Wales, the Criminal Justice Act 1988 introduced some major changes in legal procedure. While some provisions are to be welcomed, particularly those relating to the evidence of children in sexual abuse cases (including the opportunity for children to give evidence through video link, s. 32(1)), and the abolition of the corroboration requirement in the unsworn evidence of children (s. 34(1)), other provisions reflect a radical move towards curtailing defendants' rights. The Act has abolished the right to opt for jury trial in certain offences (ss. 37–42), and has abolished peremptory challenge (s. 118).

The Criminal Justice Act 1988 will also have some specific consequences for the processing of spousal assault cases, in which, for example, the court will now be required to give its reasons for granting bail to a person accused of a serious offence (s. 153). This could lead to greater protection of women from abusive spouses, since only in exceptional circumstances will bail be granted. Bail refusal, while often seen as a serious infringement of a defendant's rights and traditional freedom, should be the subject of special consideration in the case of spouse abusers, where the granting of bail is likely further to threaten the safety of the spouse. (At the time of writing a homicide of a wife has already been committed precisely because magistrates had allowed bail to a wife abuser while the police had made an application objecting to bail.) In addition, the relegation of common assault and battery to summary offences will only serve to reinforce the traditional view that such offences are inconsequential. And while this relegation may not be a dangerous one for one-off cases of assault and battery, cases of common assault and battery that are repetitive and committed within the domestic context should not be so relegated.

Left-wing idealism and right-wing reformism or regulation may be the two polarized positions at the opposite ends of the 'law and order' spectrum, but within these perspectives are contradictions and differences. Within the Left over recent years significant differences have emerged, most markedly about the nature of the political response to the problem of law and order. The orthodox view that law is simply an instrument of class oppression has become stagnant, redundant and facile. From within the Left new critiques have emerged from two different sources. Indeed this critical element has always been present – the difference is that now it is more organized, united and vocal, and determined not to be ridiculed or nullified by Left idealists as informed by right-wing opinion.

Within the Left, while none would favour a total abandonment of Marxist theory of law and the state, to cling blindly to ideological orthodoxy would be to ignore the real conditions of life for many and to ignore the need for law to protect as well as to punish. The path towards the resolution of these contradictions is not self-evident.

Hence the emergence of diverse and sometimes countervailing political positions, recognizing variously that crime is a serious business and that crime and the impact of the criminal justice system differentially affect the poor, impoverished and powerless. The Left critique on law and order has several different and quite separate branches. E. P. Thompson, in his critique of both classical jurisprudence and traditional doctrinal Marxism argues that the law also functions as a 'form of mediator between and within the classes and not only as an instrument of class domination'.

This is a view that unites both left-wing realism and some strands of feminist criminology. Left-wing realism represents a newly emergent strain within mainstream criminology, rejecting the position of idealists. Realism argues for a recognition of the need for laws on policing and incarceration, yet it denies any allegiance to right-wing emphasis on order and control. Left idealists who continue to cling to the rhetoric of orthodox Marxism consider the entry of realists into the political arena as a betrayal. But the realists' arguments are too concrete and practical on class and law issues to be rejected. Taylor (1981) and Lea and Young (1984) maintain that all laws and all police cannot simply be abandoned altogether; instead the best of law and policing must be rescued. The fundamental question is not simply about retention of present laws or their abolition, but about how law and police powers can be harnessed for a democracy that takes account of poor, working-class and black people. Greater accountability and a democratically controlled police force serving the interests of the people and not the state have been key preoccupations of left-wing realists in recent years. Hence, if law can harness the powers of the state and its police, the engagement with law and legal reform is not a class betrayal. Such an engagement can actually serve to prevent and subvert the very excesses feared. 'What if the Church and the State are the mob that howls at the door!' (Thompson 1980: 189). So far so good, but Stan Cohen is not impressed. He feels the left-wing realists, 'by their overall commitment to "order through law" ... have retreated too far from the theoretical gains of twenty years ago. Their regression into the assumptions of the standard criminal law model of social control – criminalization and punishment – is premature' (1986: 131). But this objection overstates their position; they are not arguing for the recognition of an implacable relation of all laws, but simply that all laws cannot be abandoned.

Left-wing realists and disenchanted left-wing feminists have been among the first to challenge the banal idealism of the Marxist orthodoxy on law and the state. It is not possible to abandon all laws. Traditional Marxist analyses have never seriously addressed the question of sexual divisions in society and power divisions within the family. Nor have such analyses considered the implications of the public/private dichotomy in law which defines what is public, what is a priority, what is important, and at the same time what is private and what is inconsequential. Consequently, political practice, or as some would prefer 'praxis', has rarely if ever considered either the question of 'crimes' against women, or the exploitation and appropriation of women, as part of the overall agenda. Left-wing feminists' demands for more legal intervention, more policing and more punishment for particular classes of offenders (for example rapists and violent offenders who offend against women) are demands that have been seriously misunderstood. Their demands cannot simply be reduced to and equated with right-wing Conservative regulation, since feminists' demands for protection through law and policing and right-wing homogenized efforts towards control derive from very different theoretical conceptualization of the relation of law to the state, and very divergent political standpoints. In the apparent demand for more law and policing in the area of violence against women, feminists are simply urging the same consideration for women victims in the home as has already been given to non-spousal and non-partner victims in the street. Feminist criminology would urge a similar consideration of females as victims of crime. Indeed feminist criminology has been for over two decades focusing on crime and the criminal justice system and its differential impact on women and children, who find themselves victims in their own homes of crimes committed by family members.

Feminist criminology has not only been critical of Marxist approaches to law but also of left-wing realism, and of radical and mainstream criminology. Mainstream criminology has developed without any acquaintance with gender and criminal justice issues. From Steven Box's *Deviance, Reality and Society* (1971) and Rock's *Deviant Behaviour* (1973) to Cohen's *Visions of Social Control* (1985) and Rock's *A History of British Criminology* (1988) (excepting the contribution of Gelsthorpe and Morris), gender and its impact on law, crime and criminal justice issues have been largely absent from their analyses (see Heidensohn 1985; Rock 1986; Morris 1987; Gelsthorpe and Morris 1988). The centrality of gender in some studies on crime, law and order, victimization and criminal justice has resulted not in the development of a gender perspective within mainstream criminology, but in a feminist criminology without. Radical criminology has been similarly guilty of omitting women's issues and gender from the agenda while making grandiose claims to radicalism (Young 1988). Left-wing realist criminology, while taking on law and order issues as part of an analysis of crime, again marginalizes the question of gender. Despite Cohen's proposals for a cognitive remapping' (1985: 1), no such remapping has taken gender on board.

**Feminist scholarship**

Within the law and order debate, traditional Marxist analyses of law, left-wing realism, left-wing idealism and the regulationist response of the Right have all in their various ways eclipsed, marginalized or negated the problem of sexual division within the law, its application, and policing priorities and response. As many feminists concede, the law mediates and regulates sex/gender largely irrespective of the class struggle, although the women who fare the worst are more likely to be poor (Smart 1986: 110). Feminists engaged in the study of crimes against women, and of the further victimization of women in and by the criminal justice process (see Schwendinger and Schwendinger 1974; Klein 1981; Scutt 1986), have also articulated the disproportionate victimization not only of the poor and black women but also of particular groups such as female family members (Hanmer and Stanko 1985), while some feminists have gone further and argued that all women are potentially at risk from all men (Schechter 1982).

While looking to law reform and policing to protect women, feminists have also focused on the differential treatment of women both as offenders and as victims, as it is mediated by class, race, gender role and sexuality. In the pursuit of an understanding of women's position under the law and in relation to policing, feminist scholars have turned their attention to a variety of considerations within the general topography of violence against women, and women's location within family, reproductive, health, citizenship, employment, social security and welfare laws. They have repeatedly focused on the issue of patriarchy in the form, content and application of law. And in political practice feminists have repeatedly engaged with the law precisely in order that excesses of public or state power in the private and family sphere may be controlled and that excesses of patriarchal power, manifest in individual expressions of violence against women (among other forms) may be regulated. Feminist scholarship is about a particular way of seeing the world as mediated by sex/gender considerations. It involves an ideological commitment of the kind Becker understood in his seminal paper on crime, 'Whose Side Are We On?' (1967). Some feminists argue that it also involves a particular methodological perspective (see Cain 1986).

The commitment to an analysis of patriarchy and gender have characterized both the feminist 'critical studies' perspective and the focus of political struggle by feminists working in and around the crime/law and order debate. Feminists working in the area of critical legal studies have sought to reveal the gender-specific nature of law in its concepts and in its application as a function of patriarchy and in maintenance of the wider division between public ('real') and private ('inconsequential') issues. As Brown points out in her review of some recent contributions to the debate (1986: 433), such analyses can either be grouped around the idea of patriarchy: 'Law as men versus women'; or else grouped around an analysis of law via the familialist model, which focuses on the dichotomy of law and gender into and along men (public) and women (private) lines.

A consideration of patriarchy has been central to an understanding of sex/gender division within the law (Smart 1976; Klein and Kress 1981; Edwards 1984), the criminal justice process (Worrall 1981; Carlen 1983; Farrington and Morris 1983; Edwards 1981; Edwards 1984; Eaton 1986) and policing (Cain 1986), and to an appreciation of the under-representation of women's everyday experiences, exploitation and appropriation, and sexual and physical violence against them, in the public debate. It has long been recognized from a variety of perspectives that the law unequally represents and embodies class interests (Dicey 1969; Pashukanis 1978; Hirst 1980). But it is the precise juncture of bourgeois and male interest which constitutes the corner-stone of women's experience and corresponding oppression. In everyday experience women's need for protection, women's voice as victims of crime, as criminal offenders and as victims of the law has been totally eclipsed. Klein and Kress (1981) identify this male syndrome as amnesia.

Within the criminal justice process women have received differential treatment. Part of this differential treatment stems from informal mechanisms of male control. Male constructions of appropriate femininity have ordered women's lives. Women have been silenced through the insistence on female conformity and the denial of political participation. This insistence on conformity (see Heidensohn 1985; Green, Hebron and Woodward 1987: 75) has also resulted in the restriction of opportunity for illegality, together with punishing stringently those women who violate cultural demands for conformity. Edwards (1984, 1985d, 1986a) has indicated the ways in which female offenders, for example, are sentenced more punitively where their crimes are considered untypical of women, and where their private lives depart from conventional profiles of domesticity, motherhood and wifehood. Likewise, Chambers and Millar (1983, 1986), Stanko (1985) and Adler (1987) have graphically portrayed the way in which protection for victims of sexual assault is predicated on conformity to models of appropriate female behaviour, where a whole literature continues to impute blame (see Amir 1971; Pizzey and Shapiro 1982).

Women's dependence on men, rather than patriarchy and male domination *per se*, has also been considered an essential pillar in any analysis of women's powerlessness and subordination. Scutt (1981), Smart (1984) and others have examined dependence within the family and discussed the way in which women's engagement with law has been located and defined primarily through men. Scutt (1981: 2) focuses her analysis on laws that have subsumed women as dependants. She examines the doctrine of coverture, which assumes that husband and wife are one person in law, for example, 'where a wife committed a crime in the presence of her husband, she was presumed to have committed it under coercion.' Smart (1984) has more recently examined women's economic dependence on men within the family, and the ways in which family law has structured and perpetuated this.

Significantly, gender divisions in law also correlate with the dichotomy between the public and private domains. O'Donovan writes: 'It is not enough for legislation to be passed, regulating the public sphere, if the private sphere remains unaffected' . . . (1985: 1). This distinction between public and private is maintained in politics and everyday life, and is also reflected in law. The writings of feminist political theorists similarly reflect on the public/private dichotomy. Meehan, writing on political theory, has this to say: 'This . . . has led to an emphasis on state institutions as the proper units of analysis in political science, defining the private as personal and non-political' (1986: 128). This marginalization of the private sphere, and by extension of the interests of women who occupy this domain, has led many feminists to argue for the recognition of the personal as of equal importance, with the slogan 'The personal is the political!'

The importance of this distinction to an understanding of women's experience under the law has become increasingly prominent in research on violence against women, within the family in particular. Hanmer and Maynard (1987) and Pahl (1985) argue that the inadequate protection afforded women victims of violence in the home can in part be explained by perceptions of public/private distinctions. And it is this dichotomy that masks the seriousness of the problem of private violence. The recent focus on public order and the growing awareness and fear of public disorder minimizes by detraction the significance for women of violence in private. Feminist writers who explain women's position in law in terms of patriarchal power, and those who cite the dichotomy of public and private, both concede that women's relationship to law is not an immutable one. As O'Donovan argues, it is particularly in the private relationship of marriage that 'Privacy . . . has been given a stipulated meaning of non-regulation by law' (1985: 107).

Feminist scholarship has been characterized by a broad concern with issues of patriarchy, public and private divisions in law and the ongoing absence of these issues from the wider academic and political debate. But the struggle to place women on the police accountability and law and order agenda has rallied around several specific issues.

**Feminist realist campaigns around law**

The theoretical perspectives on women and the law have not been characterized by the contradictions posed by left-wing realism and left-wing idealism. But these two positions, with their respective views on law, control and punishment have been influential in shaping feminist struggles around particular campaigns. Largely ignored by criminology's left-wing realism notwithstanding Young's perfunctory acknowledgement that 'crimes like mugging, wife battery and child abuse are actions which cannot be absolved in the flux of determinancy' (1985: 49), feminists have continued to develop their own interpretations and politics. As we have seen, feminist idealists have argued that the state and the law, the legal mechanism and the police, are part of a patriarchal structure, under which attempts at legal reform are only tinkerings within the overall system of control and regulation - so legal change serves only to perpetuate the basic conditions of patriarchy. Here violence against women by individual men and the portrayal of these violent acts are seen as products of a wider cultural climate and iconography. Caputi, in her book on sex murder, embodies this position when she provides a 'political analysis of the most extreme form of patriarchal violence' (1987: 19). By contrast, left-wing feminists who turn to an improved police response, better laws and a more sympathetically trained police force, judiciary and magistracy as part of a wider set of demands for reform, may loosely be seen to identify with 'Left realism'. Feminist scholarship has always agreed that not all laws work to oppress women (see Cousins 1980). And in campaigns around pornography, prostitution, spousal abuse and rape, feminists have been deeply ambivalent about engaging with the law to bring about broader social reform relating to gender role and the treatment of women.

Feminist *campaigners* have however always seen some laws as capable of improving the position of women in society. It is certain that nineteenth-century feminist reformers regarded the law as the major lever in their campaigns and struggles for greater participation of women in public life and social reform. It is true that the various property, guardianship and franchise reforms of the Victorian period acted as the great equalizer in women's improved economic and political status. But it is also true that the Vagrancy Acts and Contagious Diseases Acts of the nineteenth century subverted the possibility of equality, and represented the crassest form of patriarchal privilege and divisiveness. The tension between either engaging with the law to change society or not engaging, and so perpetuating inequality, characterizes the response of feminist idealists and realists to the problems of rape, domestic violence, prostitution and pornography. For many Marxist feminists the possibility of changing through the law either the position of women, or the way in which men habitually regard them, is often rejected. The English Collective of Prostitutes (ECP) in the UK opposed the Sexual Offences Act 1985 which sought to criminalize the male client seeking the services of a prostitute on the streets, and vociferously contended that any further criminalization of prostitution would serve only to penalize the prostitute further. The Act, designed to penalize the kerb-crawler, for some represented an equalizing force in law in a society loth to surrender to any system of non-interference. Collins labours this difficulty when he writes: 'In effect each piece of reformed legislation re-affirms the ideology of the rule of law and this adds to the stability of the system of power found in capitalist society' (1984: 138).

Feminist realists by contrast have traditionally engaged with the law and campaigned politically through trade unions, and political parties over the question of what is to be done about spousal violence, child abuse (physical and sexual), and the exploitation of women and children in pornography. While it is true that some feminists have systematically called for more laws, more policing and more criminalization of conduct in these particular areas, it would be a grave error to regard this apparent 'law and order' response as similar to right-wing law-and-order thinking. Nevertheless, this move towards protecting victims of violence treads a precarious path which almost inevitably dictates harsher measures for the offender. Nelken recognizes this dilemma: 'critical writers, including those writing from a feminist perspective, now seem to be arguing for more rather than less use of the criminal law . . .' (1987: 108). The champions of the 'more law and order for the protection of women in the pursuit of justice' stance have straddled a variety of feminist issues. Andrea Dworkin (1981) and Susan Griffin (1981) have argued for more policing, more law and more punishment in protecting women from the excesses of pornography. But, as Rosalind Coward points out, violence against women in film and representation is not amenable simply to legal regulation. Indeed, pornography *per se* may be the wrong object of attack, since the representation of women as masochistic, depersonalized, and as commodities exists not only within pornography but outside it too, in what are considered legitimate portrayals of women (Coward 1982: 19). A similar resistance to penal sanctions is strongly put by Brants and Kok 'penal law must always be ultimum remedium: a last resort' (1986: 269). And Smart reminds us of '. . . the paucity of gains for women arising out of the pursuit of law reform' (1986: 109).

Feminists have been concerned with the *application* of laws, as well as with their form and content. Here one of the major points of focus has shifted from a concern with judicial and magisterial discretion in sentencing rapists, child-abusers, pimps, and spouse-abusers to a consideration of police use and abuse of their powers in dealing with these cases. Women's engagement with policing issues has been examined both by academic researchers and by political activists, focusing on spousal violence (see Dobash and Dobash 1980; Binney, Harkell and Nixon 1981; Pahl 1982) and prostitution (McLeod 1982; Jeffreys and Radford 1984; Edwards and Armstrong 1988; Dunhill 1989). In the early 1980s left-wing Labour councils also set up police monitoring groups. Issues relating to women and policing (street safety, self-defence, rape, prostitution, violence, strip-searching) were taken up in their research, campaigns and publicity. Significantly, London Labour councils began to fund political research into questions of policing and resources. The Islington Crime Survey (MacLean, Jones and Young 1986) and the Hammersmith and Fulham Survey (1986) were funded by the local councils. In 1982, the Greater London Council (abolished on 31 March 1986 by the Thatcher Government) Police Committee Support Unit launched the monthly publication *Policing London*. Its emergence marked a crisis of policing particularly evident in the capital. The Metropolitan Police Force and the City of London Police Force, unlike other police forces in England and Wales, are accountable to the Home Secretary alone, rather than to the community. The police response to the Brixton disturbances of April 1981, together with the generally increasing use of force, led to increasing concern among the Left. In addition, a study conducted by the Opinion Research Centre for London Weekend Television showed that Londoners generally lacked confidence in the police. Less than 20 per cent of those interviewed felt that the police were doing a good job. *Policing London* became an important vehicle for publicizing the issues of policing by coercion, the extension of police powers and the need for democratic control. The publication drew attention to the class, gender and race bias of the police and to the victimization of working-class and black people.

By 1985, *Policing London* had begun to focus on questions of gender, class and race in a consideration of women's engagement with the police as victims, offenders and activists. The treatment of women (particularly black and Asian women) suspects and offenders, victims of spousal violence and of sexual assault became focal concerns, together with the specific implications for women of the new police legislation and public order proposals.

## Feminism, Left realism and criminology

The problem, notwithstanding Left realism or radical criminology's claim to have made a radical shift towards a consideration of law and differential victimization, is that the difficulties of women within this have been marginalized and the critical contributions of feminist research have simply been left out. Radical criminology's claims remain hollow. It has failed to consider crimes by women, crimes against women and the way law and the criminal justice system defines women. The academic and theoretical separation of the issues of women and crime from those of victimization has been largely forced upon us by the intransigence of orthodox and radical criminology, the class obsession and gender-blindness of realists, and the hegemony and zealousness of some personalities within criminology. Male Left realists have not integrated the needs and interests of women or the conceptual and ideological orientations of feminism into their wider concerns, and this failure reinforces their adherence to the paramountcy of male class analysis. Feminism has been relegated to the margins, occasionally invited into the inner zones when, for example, the issue of spousal violence becomes one of the several interests of large-scale victimization surveys.

Even the more recent claims for a radical victimology are ridiculous in their omission of the victimization of women and children from the mainstream. In an edited collection from the Left realist camp, Phipps magnanimously acknowledges: 'However, the most important contributions to a radical consideration of victims have come from feminist writers about rape and sexual assault, and violence against women and children (Brownmiller 1975, Smart 1976, Pizzey 1974)' (1985: 110). Anyone with any understanding of the politics of female victimization would not and could not mention Brownmiller, Smart and Pizzey in the same context (see discussion on Pizzey in Chapter 5). By so doing Phipps reveals his lack of understanding of these contributions and at the same time homogenizes what are essentially very divergent views on particular feminist concerns. Notably, these 'most important contributions' are never mentioned again, and the focus of debate is around the class question and totally gender-blind.

The recent establishment obsession with large-scale victimization surveys, although making no claim to radicalism (and conservative in their methodology) continues to mask the uniqueness of being a victim of particular crimes by reducing the experience and its sequel to a numerical exercise. No specific issues concerning women's victimization are addressed in governments' victimization studies (conducted in the US by Wes Skogan and M. Maxfield among others, and in the UK by Mike Hough and Pat Mayhew). Interestingly, however, women have been working on the question for a very long time - since long before Left realism was born. Left realism, as far as the issues relating to violence against women are concerned, is no more or less radical than any other newly emergent systematic critique. So far it has failed to learn from feminist scholarship and campaigns, or else deliberately ignored this considerable body of thought and action. If Left realist criminology is to be saved from the inevitable redundancy of its classical position it must take women's issues and campaigns and the writings of radical women academics on women's issues seriously.

# 1
# The State and Policing: The Under-representation of Women's Interests

## Government reaction to public disorder

In recent years the concern of the state and the police has been with the problem of public order. The increasing control of street behaviour, argues the Left, has been excessive, particularly in the control of blacks and youths. It is no accident that black suspects are more likely to be remanded in custody. Twelve per cent of all black suspects are remanded in custody, compared to 6 per cent of white offenders. Furthermore, those West Indians and Africans in custody have far fewer previous convictions for previous offences (NACRO 1988). Feminists have, however, seen this trend towards imposing public order as disastrous for two reasons. First, there is the more obvious problem of infringement of personal liberty. Second, the focus on street crime creates an exaggerated fear of the streets which in turn deflects attention away from other crimes and fears, especially violence behind closed doors inflicted by male partners.

The widening of state powers through the law, particularly in the Police and Criminal Evidence Act 1984 and the Public Order Act 1986 provides clear instances of law becoming an increasing threat to civil liberties and democratic rights. E.P. Thompson predicted this enlargement of police powers and the threat to democracy, citing among others the 'clipping of the coinage of civil liberties, the enlargement of police power, the dissemination of calumny against dissenters . . . the surveillance and intimidation of radicals . . . the orchestration through the media of a 'law and order' *grande peur* and the cry of "national interest"' (Thompson 1980, cited in Fine 1984: 169).

In recent years the increasing control by the police of public order as opposed to private family order situations is self-evident, both in the powers provided to the police by the Police and Criminal Evidence Act 1984 and the Public Order Act 1986. Turning to the first Act, the extension of police powers or rather ratification of conventional police practice regarding suspects and offenders focuses on street conduct. Section 1(1) provides for the 'stop and search' of persons or vehicles if an officer has 'reasonable grounds for suspecting that he will find stolen or prohibited articles' (discussed further in chapter 3). The Act gives the police the power to 'police' conduct and suspects in the home by allowing them to enter and search premises without a warrant for the purpose of arrest. This power of entry is also extended to 'saving life or limb or preventing serious damage to property' (s. 17(c) ). While a substantial amount of police time and resources have been poured into stop and search and entering premises for the purpose of arrest, especially in connection with burglary, robbery and drug offences, it seems unlikely that the police have used this power so often to enter premises where the life or limb of a female partner has been in jeopardy.

The general arrest conditions in section 25(3)(a, b, c, d) of the Act give police the authority to arrest those whom they think have not given their real name and address (a, b, c); or to prevent the person causing physical injury to himself or others (d(i)); causing damage to property (d(iii)); committing an offence against public decency (d(iv)); or those simply standing on the spot causing an unlawful obstruction of the highway (d(v)). The arrest conditions also allow for arrest of a person where it is necessary to protect a child or other vulnerable persons (s. 25(3)(e)). The police have been criticized for the over-enforcement of law with regard to conditions a to e (Brogden 1985: 91), yet few arrests have been made in the name of protecting a child and probably none at all for the protection of vulnerable women (see chapter 6), although it is widely agreed (Thomas 1988: 259) that 'the "other vulnerable person" could be a partner subject to domestic violence.'

The Public Order Act 1986 provides another example of substantive law increases to police powers to deal with street disturbances and crime. But again it seems unlikely that this increase of police powers will result in the greater protection of women. The Act creates public order offences where there is 'threatening behaviour'. The definition of 'threatening behaviour' is a highly subjective one. Women describe sexual harassment as 'threatening behaviour', but to include this in any legal definition was considered tantamount to launching a woman's charter, and legally impossible to prove and thereby enforce, so it was dropped from the Sexual Offences Act 1985. It remains to be seen whether sexual harassment will be recognized as 'threatening' now that the Public Order Act is in force. All marches and processions are required to give notice, and some marches can be banned while others will be subject to conditions, such as being given a route out in the country where the marchers can make their voices heard to a few sheep or cows. Recent amendments include the power to single out 'hippies' for control and punishment by making their behaviour criminal through trespass. At the end of the day, will prostitute organizations, peace women and women campaigners find their voices muffled under this Act? In the name of 'law and order' 'power to direct trespassers to leave the road' was an added clause to address the mischief of the 'peace convoy'. Section 39(1) of the Act states that 'if the senior police officer reasonably believes that two or more persons have entered land as trespassers and are present there with the common purpose of residing there for any period, that reasonable steps have been taken by or on behalf of the occupier to ask them to leave . . . he may direct those persons, or any of them, to leave the land.'

With widening social inequalities, public order becomes increasingly hegemonized and central. The increasing polarization of social classes has manifested itself through rising social and political discontent, voiced in industrial and civil protest. Economic inequalities have given rise to the heightening of racial tensions, as black British and ethnic minorities face the certainty of an unemployed future. In some areas prospects of any kind of work are negligible, and the country itself has become divided; particular regions and inner cities have been the victims of economic policies that impoverish them and in some cases rob them of a heritage and way of life. Wide regional variations in unemployment reflect the differing impact of economic and regional policy. In March 1987, and March 1988, in the North the unemployment figures were 16.2 and 13.5 per cent, compared with the North West at 13.8 and 12.0 per cent; York and Humberside at 13.2 and 10.9 per cent; West Midlands, 13.1 and 10.1 per cent; East Midlands, 11.0 and 8.4 per cent; the South West, 9.6 and 7.6 per cent; East Anglia, 8.8 and 6.0 per cent; and the South East at 8.1 and 6.1 per cent, while Greater London (included in the South East) had figures of 9.0 and 7.5 per cent (*Employment Gazette*, May 1987, table 2.3, p. S21; May 1988, table 2.3, p. S21).

After the experience of inner city disturbances in 1981 in Southall, Brixton, Liverpool (Toxteth), Manchester (Moss Side) and in the West Midlands (discussed in some detail in Cowell, Jones and Young 1982), and later events at Brixton and Broadwater Farm (Gifford 1985), police concern has focused on preventing these situations and controlling them when they arise. Likewise, in the scene of industrial conflict, in the long miners' strike (March 1984–5), at Wapping (January 1986, see Commissioner of Police of the Metropolis 1986: 137), and at Orgreave (Bunyan 1985), the police have played a pivotal role in the control of these essentially employer–employee disputes (Lewis and Wiles 1984). Indeed, as Wallington (1987) observes, during the miners' strike alone 4317 out of 10,272 charges in England and Wales were for section 5 'breach of the peace'. And this stance, use and interpretation of the law was ratified in legal precedent in the appeal courts. In *Moss and Others* v. *Charles McLachlan* (*Times* Law Report, 29 November 1984; 1985 IRLR 76), it was decided on appeal that the 'police had reasonable grounds for apprehending an imminent breach of the peace when they arrested four defendants after stopping a convoy of striking miners on the M1 in Nottinghamshire, preventing them from continuing to collieries nearby.' (For further discussion see Wallington 1987). And in *Thomas and Others* v. *National Union of Mineworkers (South Wales Area) and Others (Times* Law Report, 1 February 1985), where it was decided that mass picketing was a common law nuisance and an offence under section 7 of the Conspiracy and Protection of Property Act 1875.

In response to all these public order problems, no attempts have been made to address some of the grievances which precipitate them; rather, the Conservative government has given the police even more power to regulate and control. Public order, picketing and industrial legislation, together with the police and criminal evidence legislation, give police greater powers to deal with outbreaks of civil disorder and street crime, often direct reactions to state policy. The question of individual violence within the home, against wives and female partners, with its low visibility, becomes further marginalized and subordinated to the overriding concern with public as opposed to private order, and with the apparent public challenge to state power.

During the last few years, governmental and public inquiries have reflected this preoccupation with public order, a preoccupation reflected in the peaks and troughs in prosecutions for public order offences since 1981 (see table 1.1). Both Lord Scarman in the Brixton Inquiry (1981) and Lord Gifford in the Broadwater Farm Inquiry (1985) concluded that the breakdown in public order arose not merely as a response to social and economic problems, but, more importantly, as the consequence of failed initiatives in police/community relations. The main shortcomings of the police identified by Scarman focused on:

> the unwillingness to consult on police operations, and 'hard policing' [saturating an area with police for some general or specific anti-crime drive] . . . [and] . . . other factors that have helped to build up the image of an unimaginative and inflexible police presence . . . in Lambeth: notably the conduct of some officers in their dealings with black people, and the formal and complicated system for handling complaints against the police. (1981: 66, para. 4.71)

And in the Gifford Report, the committee of inquiry urged the need for ' "co-operative policing", by which we mean a policing strategy by which the police at all levels co-operate (on a basis of mutual

Table 1.1 *Public order offences, 1980–1985*

| | Riot | Unlawful assembly | Against state or public order | Public Order Act | Disorder |
|---|---|---|---|---|---|
| *1980* | | | | | |
| Males | 42 | 104 | 1,468 | [a] | 12,610 |
| Females | 2 | nil | 59 | [a] | 992 |
| *1981* | | | | | |
| Males | 66 | 104 | 1,333 | 32,530 | 10,163 |
| Females | 4 | nil | 85 | 1,702 | 837 |
| *1982* | | | | | |
| Males | 21 | 55 | 1,534 | 30,651 | 10,054 |
| Females | nil | nil | 65 | 1,566 | 779 |
| *1983* | | | | | |
| Males | 27 | 91 | 1,471 | 20,089 | 10,151 |
| Females | nil | nil | 67 | 1,496 | 837 |
| *1984* | | | | | |
| Males | 190 | 403 | 1,831 | 20,163 | 8,999 |
| Females | nil | 6 | 43 | 1,500 | 678 |
| *1985* | | | | | |
| Males | 31 | 274 | 1,676 | 26,654 | 7,845 |
| Females | nil | nil | 64 | 1,369 | 466 |

[a]Public order offence not separately recorded.

*Source*: *Criminal Statistics, England and Wales*, vol. 1, *Supplementary Tables*, 1980–5.

respect and equality) with those various agencies which represent the community, in order to deter and detect those crimes which the community believe to be priority evils' (1985: 194).

Not only male suspects but women suspects too have fallen foul of the law in respect of this recent focus on street crime. The Police and Criminal Evidence Act 1984, part iv, s. 38(1), (2)(i) and (iii), allows the police to remand a man or a woman in police cells overnight because 'his name or address cannot be ascertained or the custody officer has reasonable grounds for doubting whether a name or address furnished by him as his name or address is his real name and address'; or because 'the custody officer has reasonable grounds for believing that the person arrested will fail to appear in court to answer to bail.' These sections particularly affect prostitute women working in London and other major cities.

In the Paddington/Sussex Gardens area of London it is the policy (in July 1988) of Paddington Green Police Station to detain women arrested for prostitution offences overnight, pending a court appearance the following morning. This practice is by no means peculiar to this area of London. Other areas and other police stations have also been observed to detain women on charges of prostitution until the following morning. Women arrested in connection with prostitution offences have also often been prosecuted for carrying weapons for self-defence. So prostitute women face the choice of risking prosecution for possession of an offensive weapon or else exposing themselves to considerable danger by not adequately defending themselves.

While addressing the problems of the extension of police powers on the street, Left realism has tended to get itself exclusively tied up with the concern over street crime and the differential impact of victimization on the working class, rather than arguing simultaneously for the recognition of the differential impact on women of sex crimes, rape, assault, murder and crimes of violence, spousal violence and spousal homicide. At the same time feminists focusing exclusively on women's victimization have not been taken seriously as they have not attempted to challenge the conventional left-wing orthodoxy. That to many would be seen as a compromise. On the streets, the new powers vested in the public order legislation reflect the state's growing concern to control and contain what it sees as 'the enemy within', i.e. those who oppose government policies. On many occasions demonstration has been the only means available to publicize grievances. Women's pressure groups such as Women against Rape, Women's Aid, Women against Violence against Women, Women against Pornography, Women and Peace and many others have relied on the right of free assembly. That right is currently under seige. Women have also come into close contact with the police as peace protesters; many have faced criminal charges for breach of the peace and offensive behaviour. As Benn observes: 'There have been a huge number of arrests for trivial offences (1,775 between September 1981 and March 1984) (1985: 131). The Ministry of Defence's public order role has expanded in recent years, after peace protests at military bases at Greenham and Hartlepool. In 1979–80, the Ministry of Defence police force dealt with two demonstrations, compared with 900 in 1983–4 (Ministry of Defence figures).

## Patriarchy and male interest in the police force

The 'rule of law' and the administration and application of law is variously experienced. In the process of applying law, individuals bring to it particular perceptions and attitudes, so that its application becomes selective and inconsistent. The police are among a number of agencies involved in the mediation, translation and negotiation of law. Laws are variously translated, depending on the predilections of individual police officers and the police organization, within the possibilities and ambit of procedural rules. The selective application of law is not only affected by class ideologies, as Marxists would argue, but also by perceptions of race, sex and gender roles. In this section the patriarchal attitudes of both police officers and the overall police organization are discussed, as such attitudes inevitably influence the exercise of discretion and shape what police 'police' and how. It is worth noting that the recruitment of men and women in the criminal justice system is far from balanced, and the attitudes and perceptions of an overwhelmingly male personnel, and thus character of the organizations involved, are highly relevant.

Within the police organization, as within other key social and political institutions in society, patriarchal attitudes and patriarchal structures of power in employment and promotion opportunities perpetuate women's subordination through sexist stereotyping. The police organization is imbued and saturated with ideologies that have worked against the recruitment and promotion of police women (Gelsthorpe 1986; Jones 1986: 20). The same divisive attitudes have also significantly influenced the police response to crime and victims, priorities, policies, operations and police accountability. Consequently, incidents within the private domain, for example violence against women and sexual misconduct, have been considered less serious than incidents involving violence and sexual abuse occurring in public. The policing of women, whether in public or private matters, whether as victims or offenders, protesters or campaigners, has been influenced by police stereotypes of appropriate female behaviour. These stereotypes often form the basis of police judgement of likely guilt or innocence, blame and responsibility. As Reiner argues, 'the cop culture . . . both reflects and perpetuates the power differences within the social structure it polices. The police officer is a microcosmic mediator for the relations of power in a society' (1985: 87).

One of the main problems within the police force is the extent and pervasiveness of sexist attitudes which influence both policing involving women and recruitment and the promotion prospects of women officers. The low number of women officers generally, and in high-ranking positions in particular, translates back into police culture, ensuring that patriarchal attitudes go unchallenged. Patriarchy is not simply perpetuated by individual male attitudes, but by the organization itself, through its informal rules and its rather more formalized structure of internal procedures and regulations.

'The dominant values of the Force are still in many ways those of an all male institution such as a rugby club or boys' school', write D.J. Smith and J. Gray (1983: iv. 91) of the Metropolitan Police in London. This ethos has no boundaries, and is true of police forces in England and Wales, America, Europe and elsewhere. Research in America, notably the work of S. Martin (1978), found evidence of a 'male club' in the American police force, and Lee Potts found that 'police work has generally, both in America and abroad, been considered men's work' (1981: 9). Within this broad pro-male attitude there are wide variations, from edging women out to misogyny, but the glorification of maleness is consistent. Smith and Gray found the 'cult of masculinity' in the Metropolitan Police in London characterized by drinking as a test of manliness and physical courage. Smith and Gray (1983) and Stith (1986), among others, found that this 'cult of masculinity' had a significant influence on police officers' behaviour towards women, and particularly towards women offenders and women victims of sexual and violent assault.

The male club has persisted, not simply because 'male' values of courage, strength and toughness have been demanded, nor because the police organization may have attracted men with sexist attitudes, but also because of its more formalized rules and requirements. Historically, recruitment in the police organization has been characterized by the exclusion of women. Until the turn of the century there were no women officers, and at first they were only allowed to take second place. They were accepted only as long as they did 'women's work'. And so, in both Britain and America, opportunities for women in police work were available only in the 'police woman's department', where there were no promotion prospects.

In the US, in 1903, the first patrol woman was appointed. Her job consisted of assisting detectives in cases involving women and children. By 1910, Los Angeles had appointed its first regularly paid policewoman, and by 1916 twenty-five cities in twenty states had woman police officers (Mishkin 1981: 22). In Britain the first woman 'police aide' was appointed in 1907. She took statements from female victims of assault, but had no arrest powers. In 1918, the Division of Woman Police Patrol became the first official body of policewomen, with special responsibility for sex offenders, prostitution, female offenders and juveniles. But, as Lock (1979) and Bland (1985) argue, the woman police officer in these years had a key role, not in the protection of women, but paradoxically in their surveillance and control (1985: 33). In 1922 the pendulum swung back; after the Police Act of 1919 the Home Secretary was empowered to regulate police pay and conditions of service. After the recommendations of the Desborough Committee (1920) women officers in the Metropolitan Police were cut from 112 to 24, and many forces outside London dispensed with women officers altogether. Indeed, it was not until the early 1970s that women began to be recruited in every force in America and Britain. As Milton writes: 'of the 1,330 law enforcement agencies surveyed by the International Association of

Chiefs of Police (IACP) in 1969, only 34 per cent had any full time sworn officers, and in those departments, women made up less than 2 per cent of the total force' (1972: 16). In the United States in 1973, women comprised 12 per cent of the police workforce, but were not evenly distributed throughout all departments. In fact 88 per cent of women employees occupied non-sworn positions, and of the sworn officers, they were predominantly in the lowest ranks. Horne (1979: 345), from observations of FBI statistics for 1977, found that only 2.7 per cent of the total US police force were sworn-in female officers, while in the UK, in 1977, 78,432 officers were male and 6,371 were female. Similarly, in the Metropolitan Police in London, 9 per cent of police officers (up to the rank of inspector) are women (Smith and Gray 1983: iv. 91). In 1982, the Metropolitan Police Force received 3,693 applications from women, 24 per cent of all applications, compared to 11,582 applications from males, yet 17 per cent of the men were recommended for acceptance, and only 7 per cent of the women. Smith and Gray (1983: iv. 246) were told that it is unofficial force policy deliberately to keep the proportion of women down to 10 per cent. And although the Report of the Commissioner of the Police of the Metropolis (1986: 92–3) shows the proportion of women recruits as increasing, from 150 in 1984 to 207 in 1985 and 292 by 1986, women officers still represented under 10 per cent of force strength. Yet the Metropolitan Police claims in the Commissioner's Report to be committed to equal opportunities policies (p. 102). Jones (1986: 136) interviewed male and female police officers to find that most men (80 per cent) and women (61 per cent) felt that women should form no more than 20 per cent of the force, while 50 per cent of men and 36 per cent of women felt the figure should be 10 per cent.

One woman police constable interviewed by Smith and Gray (1983: iv. 94) said 'I hate the place.' She said she had gone back to the Hendon police training college recently for a course, and had been shouted down whenever she opened her mouth by male colleagues, with jeers like 'Yah, what do you know, you're just plonk' (plonk is a derisory slang word for women in the force). Women recruits in 1986 said that things were changing, but that at Hendon women were still not allowed to participate in certain sports and felt they were not equal. L.K. Lord accedes: 'Because the barriers to female police officers have been built into the formal and informal structures of the work organization and into the culturally prescribed descriptions of male–female interaction(s), only significant changes within the occupational setting and within the greater community will eliminate them' (1986: 91). Jones found similarly, that women's promotion prospects were frustrated by 'the unwritten criteria' of recommendation and promotion, in which the 'mark of affinity' was paramount: jobs go to 'people like us' (1986: 131).

Resistance from male officers towards women in the force is being contested, but the fact remains that the presence of policewomen is still largely resisted by male officers. In the interviews I conducted with male police officers in London, reported in detail in chapters 3 and 4, few policemen wished to be paired up with women officers for patrol duties. Male officers justified this attitude by claiming that women lacked the necessary strength to do the job. Similarly, in America and Canada this question of physical strength has presented a major obstacle to women's occupational progress. Research studies both here and in the US echo the overriding prejudice. Hindman, in a survey of California Police officers (1975), found that 91.2 per cent of male police officers believed that women lack the physical strength required to do the job. In addition, 57 per cent of male officers stated that women officers would be totally unable to cope with family disturbances. Later work conducted by Vega and Silverman (1982: 31) found similar negative attitudes to women officers expressed by male policemen in Florida. Few male police officers considered a woman officer to be equally effective, while 75 per cent of policemen considered women to be totally incapable of handling violent situations. These attitudes were not restricted to serving police officers, but mirror attitudes of men generally, as Golden (1981) found. In her study of 134 male students enrolled in a university-level programme in law enforcement administration at a mid-western university in the USA, 69 per cent of students felt that women lacked both the physical strength and the skill required to do the job. Bloch and Anderson (1974) found that male officers expressed an overwhelming preference for male over female partners. As little as 48 per cent felt it important to incorporate women into the police force. Even the more recent research findings of Lord reflect the persistence of these attitudes. He writes 'the traditional police attitude about the "inherently" masculine nature of law enforcement makes the prospect of having a female partner or co-worker particularly offensive to some male officers' (1986: 83).

In the United States the Equal Employment Opportunity Commission has attempted to contest police efforts to 'edge women out'. Since 1972, separate tasks for women in the force have ended, but promotion prospects are still bleak. In *Wood* v. *City of West Miami* (1980), the Mayor of the City of West Miami had told a female applicant for a police officer position that selection preference was given to 20-year-old war veterans and, at a second interview, flatly told her he did not want to appoint a woman. In another blatantly discriminatory case (*Meith* v. *Dothard*, 1976), in the Alabama Police

Department, women were excluded from being state troopers because they did not meet the height requirement: 5 feet 9 inches. Other examples of less blatant discrimination have consisted of excluding women from certain aspects of police work. The Pittsburgh Police Department, for example, had a policy of assigning women to the Missing Persons Section of the Detective Branch, though only at the level of patrol(man) (Potts 1981: 16).

One of the most blatant cases of discrimination to be taken to the UK Court of Appeal is the policy of limiting police women to duty in the Crime Prevention Bureau juvenile section. In the UK women still face both direct and indirect discrimination and harassment. While equal opportunities cases have gone some way towards challenging entrenched institutional practices, individual police forces need to address this issue of equality of opportunity on a daily basis and not only in response to a particular case decision. In *Johnston* v. *Chief Constable of the Royal Ulster Constabulary* (Case 222/84; [1986] 3 CMLR 240) a complaint was brought by a woman officer in the full-time reserve of the RUC against the practice of not allowing female officers to carry firearms. The effect of this was to hinder career prospects. The court, in deciding in Johnston's favour, pointed out that women should not be excluded from particular employment 'on the ground that public opinion demands that women be given greater protection than men against risks which affect women and men in the same way and which are distinct from women's specific needs of protection' (see O'Donovan and Szyszczak 1988: 199). Women officers in the Metropolitan Police were similarly prevented from carrying firearms until 1986 (only 21 of its 2,622 authorized firearms officers are women). And, turning to detective inspector rank, only 4 of the 367 detective inspectors are women, while at February 1986 only one woman was at commander level (see chapter 6 for recent developments).

Some have argued that the integration of women police officers into the force will change the masculine ethos of the organization and, in certain instances, provide a much improved, more sympathetic service to the public, especially to women and child victims of crime. Others are more sceptical and less certain that an injection of women into the force can really change anything. Research has shown that the advent of women in the force so far has played only a marginal role in affecting that masculine ethos. Instead, most women survive by becoming like men (see Martin 1978). The growing presence of women in the force has not necessarily been a direct challenge to the police patriarchy either in the UK or in America, although in Britain the influence of policewomen like Thelma Wagstaff (Commander) has led to substantial changes from within in the investigation of rape and other offences. Wagstaff, in her address to the Police Superintendents' Association Conference in September 1986, nevertheless claimed that there are still many categories of rape which police, courts and society tend to regard with scepticism (*The Times*, 1 October 1986).

Promotion and recruitment remain difficult for women. It is still the case that the police force, as an organization, is a bastion of male authority and masculine interest. It is precisely this profile of male interest and privilege that determines, to a large extent, what is policed, and who are protected.

## Policing: the under-representation of women's interests

Chief Superintendent Roger Street of Streatham Police Station in south London, in a paper presented to the 1988 Annual Conference of the Howard League for Penal Reform on the subject of 'Women and Policing', recognized the under-representation of women's interests in policing issues. He said:

> So far as domestic violence was concerned, women who participated in the determination of eventual policy, indicated dominantly that they felt that it was not treated seriously in the Criminal Justice System. Police practice had always been based on the assumption that, other than in extreme circumstances, what happened in a male–female relationship was essentially a private matter between the parties concerned. What clearly emerged from the exercise was that women had a right to expect the protection of the law, whether or not they had a close relationship with the offender. The new policy therefore was based on this fundamental tenet and included a number of strategies which sought to achieve this. (p. 4)

Despite the endeavours of senior police officers, it remains the case that women's interests are under-represented in policing, as in the public and political arena. The all-pervasiveness of patriarchal attitudes in society, in law and in policing has had certain fundamental consequences for what is policed and who are protected. As has already been argued, violence in the home is accorded a low priority because it happens behind closed doors, has a low visibility, occurs within a sphere traditionally considered private and is perpetrated against women by male partners. It is also the case that the police treatment of rape victims and prostitute women and their response to the sale and distribution of pornography, all of which involve violence against or exploitation of women, are matters accorded a low priority and sometimes insensitively handled. Much of the criticism of policing by left-wing women's pressure groups is concerned with precisely these issues, where rape victims are treated unsympathetically and charges dropped, prostitutes are subject to constant surveillance and arrested while ponces, pimps and punters are rarely prosecuted, and women are exploited in pornography while sellers and distributors are rarely prosecuted and even more rarely convicted. Police priorities depend on the visibility of the illegality, and the pressure from public opinion. For 'public opinion' read, as Dicey (1969: 72) acknowledged, 'those citizens who have at a given time taken an effective part in public life . . . and made legislation in accordance with their interests'.

It is no accident that the man who beats his wife on the street is more likely to be prosecuted than the man who behaves in exactly the same way in his own home. The visibility of their behaviour is one of the reasons police regularly arrest and prosecute prostitutes for street soliciting, whilst the organizer, producer and controller of prostitution, who organizes behind closed doors in saunas, clubs and massage parlours goes unseen and relatively untouched. Again, in the pornography trade it is the visibility that creates the 'offence'. In these as in other cases, such as the policing of domestic violence, rape, prostitution and pornography, the police response has been antipathetical to women's interests. But to blame the police for the legal and evidential requirements in a rape trial which put the victim on trial, to blame the police for the drafting of a law relating to prostitution that penalizes women only and not their clients, and to blame the police for unworkable obscene publications legislation which leads to an apparent under-enforcement of law relating to the seizure of pornographic material would be to miss the point raised at the outset. The law in its form and content, and in its application, mirrors particular interests. In a society which is organized around the control of women by men, the laws, as well as the application of those laws, reflect patriarchal interests.

Any consideration of the application of law and the question of police accountability must recognize that the law is the basis for much of what police do. These laws affect women, often denying their interests. One barometer of the implementation of law is provided by examining official statistics on the incidence of certain crimes and on their prosecution and conviction. While we have no reliable criminal statistics on the extent of violence against wives, figures for prostitution and allied offences, and obscene publications, indicate a disproportionate number of prosecutions of men for offences of violence against women, pornography and controlling prostitution, compared with the number of women prosecuted for offences relating to prostitution, considering what is involved in each offence. Do these variations in prosecution reflect differences in crimes committed, or do they reflect instead the amount of police time and effort spent in the control of women prostitutes on the streets, and the amount of police time spent in the control of men who manage prostitutes, and men who sell and distribute pornography? In 1982, for example, there were 308 prosecutions for obscene publications (including possession and distribution). In 1983, this figure had risen to 523; by 1984 it had risen still further to 623; by 1985 it had fallen dramatically to 320; and in 1986 there were only 161 prosecutions. The setting up of the Crown Prosecution Service in 1986 (see chapter 6) can account for the fall in prosecutions for obscene publications, because of the overwhelmingly high acquittal rate in previous years (47 per cent). Yet there seems to have been no similar moratorium for prostitute women.

### *Policing prostitution*

As Melissa Benn has written:

> prostitution is controlled through the control of women. Women are still deemed responsible for the act of sex with men, and its aftermath. Harassment, linked to a kind of understanding between police and prostitutes about the operation of an inoperable law, characterizes police behaviour to prostitute women. (1985: 129)

The control of women in prostitution has a long history, and it is evidently continuing in the current repressive climate, particularly influenced by the growing fear of AIDS. Because of the high visibility of prostitution in certain areas, much police time and effort is spent in controlling it through prosecution (with the effect, rather 'like a water bed', of displacing it elsewhere). Yet the women at the receiving end of this arm of the law are usually the most vulnerable of all. The UK Criminal Law Revision Committee, in its Seventeenth Report, conceded that 'All too often those who practise prostitution are likely to become the victims of exploitation or to contact venereal disease' (1985: 2, para 1.5), a sentiment absent from the earlier sixteenth (1984b) and fifteenth (1984a) reports. Yet these voices have so far gone unheard, and no action has been taken.

The Contagious Diseases Acts of 1864 and 1866 stand as testaments in British history to the extraordinary powers of the police in the control and surveillance of working-class and largely poor and powerless women. Under these Acts, any woman on the street was compulsorily screened for venereal disease, investigated, segregated, isolated, violated and detained. The police were vested with the necessary powers to arrest, detain and forcibly examine women. The system of control was operated by the 'plain clothes' or 'morals' police. Some were *agents provocateurs*, as Pearson observed: 'sometimes, the keener officers would even try to pick up girls in the street and, if their advances were welcomed, took this as proof that they were for sale' (1983: 61). And, as the campaigners for the repeal of the Act found, the police were often over-zealous in the control of such women. One superintendent was known to have explained to women on numerous occasions that 'a new law had come into operation, and if she did not submit to forcible examination she would be imprisoned three or four months with hard labour' (McHugh 1980: 149).

Today, police engagement in surveillance, arrest and prosecution of prostitute women is as committed as ever. In 1983, the Metropolitan Police Force waged a concerted drive against prostitution in the King's Cross area of London. This drive was reflected in an increase in prosecutions for prostitution in the 1983 figures, which reached an all-time high of 10,674. In 1982 there had been 6,062, and the 1985, 1986 and 1987 figures were 9,406, 9,402 and 8,486 respectively (see table 1.2). No similar war was waged against procurers, pimps and ponces, or against male violence to women. Clearly, the regulation and control of prostitution has been a major policing preoccupation (McLeod 1982; Edwards 1987b, 1987c).

In 1959, with the introduction of the Street Offences Act in England and Wales, it became the responsibility of police when cautioning women to put them in contact with a social service agency. A government circular was issued to that effect, but it is not clear whether officers ever obeyed this instruction. While the police have arrested prostitute women partly in response to the law, the pressures from right-wing moralists and from middle-class residents have made a significant mark on the history of control. It is clear that some officers have not been altogether convinced of the necessity of this repressive zeal. By 1979, even the Police Federation, in submission of evidence to the Home Affairs Sub-Committee on Women, recognized the redundancy of prison sentences for prostitutes. Many officers have been understandably frustrated with the police role in regulating an essentially 'nuisance' or 'morals' offence. Contrary to popular Left feminist ideas about the policing of prostitute women, many police prosecute prostitutes because their activity is a nuisance, because the law is easily enforced and convictions automatically secured, and not because of any stance against prostitute women *per se*. Officers arresting prostitutes in London revealed in their conversations with Edwards and Armstrong (1988) a genuine concern that prostitute women are decidedly not criminals, just a nuisance in the same vein as drunks and vagrants. And patrol officers in Wolverhampton clearly demonstrated a concern for both prostitute women and their children, by warning women of perverse punters and warning them that they would be 'nicked' later if they persisted in loitering and soliciting.

Table 1.2 *Prosecutions for loitering and soliciting for the purpose of prostitution in England and Wales, 1980–1987*

| | 1980 | 1981 | 1982 | 1983 | 1984 | 1985 | 1986 | 1987 |
|---|---|---|---|---|---|---|---|---|
| Total proceeded against | 3,482 | 4,324 | 6,062 | 10,674 | 8,836 | 9,406 | 9,402 | 8,486 |
| Discontinued | 6 | 15 | 11 | 17 | 20 | 48 | 26 | 40 |
| Withdrawn | 140 | 182 | 247 | 215 | 211 | 197 | 278 | 263 |
| Total found guilty | 3,336 | 4,127 | 5,804 | 10,442 | 8,605 | 9,161 | 9,098 | 8,183 |
| Total for sentence | n.g. | n.g. | n.g. | 10,440 | 8,605 | 9,161 | 9,096 | 8,182 |
| Absolute discharge | 25 | 39 | 30 | 62 | 114 | 134 | 129 | 267 |
| Condit. discharge | 513 | 686 | 746 | 800 | 706 | 694 | 795 | 755 |
| Fine | 1,880 | 2,389 | 3,983 | 9,294 | 7,588 | 8,149 | 8,047 | 7,018 |
| Probation | 324 | 379 | 448 | 251 | 184 | 174 | 112 | 138 |
| Supervision | 4 | 11 | 3 | 3 | 6 | 6 | 7 | 1 |
| Community service | 116 | 115 | 96[a] | 5 | nil | nil | nil | nil |
| Otherwise dealt with | 8 | 7 | nil | 5 | 6 | 4 | 5 | 3 |
| Suspended prison sentence | 254 | 228 | 298[a] | 13 | nil | nil | 1 | nil |
| Unsuspended prison sentence | 205 | 204 | 187 | 6 | 1 | nil | nil | nil |

[a] After the Criminal Justice Act (1982), s. 71, prison was abolished for this offence, as was the community service option as an alternative to imprisonment. Note that in 1980, 1 recognizance was given and 6 dealt with in accordance with the Magistrates' Courts Act (1952), s. 28; in 1981, 1 offender was dealt with by way of recognizances, 1 was given a hospital order under s. 60 of the Mental Health Act (1959) and 7 dealt with under the Magistrates' Courts Act (1980), s. 37. In 1982, 1 hospital order and 1 'section 37' were given.

n.g. = not given.

*Source*: *Criminal Statistics, England and Wales*, vol. 1, *Supplementary Tables*, 1980–7.

Nevertheless, some police officers and forces have been more zealous in their prosecution and moral condemnation than others. For example, during the height of the Yorkshire Ripper inquiry in the North of England, Detective Chief Superintendent Hobson told the BBC: 'this year we have arrested and cautioned many prostitutes. There is still a hard core in existence here. No, there will be no amnesty for them. We have taken steps to stamp out prostitution' (Kinsley and Smyth 1980: 19).

Attitudes, however, are changing. Generally, police officers are now much more aware of the violence frequently inflicted on prostitute women than ever before – and they blame the victim less than before. In London the murder of a prostitute in Paddington turned out, as police suspected, to have been committed by her ponce. Police increasingly recognize that women prostitutes are at risk from violent ponces and violent punters. Nevertheless the law and policing strategies undoubtedly place women at greater risk, by forcing them to work in isolation and with the continual harassment of police surveillance.

With the introduction of the Sexual Offences Act 1985, the law provided in spirit for the prosecution of the kerb-crawler. Yet the small number of prosecutions and convictions so far reflects a reluctance on the part of police, the Crown Prosecution Service and the courts to tackle the problem seriously, if at all. Yet the police claim that the problem lies not with an uneven and selective enforcement policy, but with totally unworkable and poorly drafted legislation. Criminal statistics for 1986 showed that a total of 220 men were prosecuted, resulting in 189 convictions. Set against the thousands of women prosecuted in 1986 for prostitution, it seems at the very least unfair; at the most a problem of under-enforcement. The police do not need poorly drafted legislation to bring their reputation for selective enforcement further into disrepute. By 1987, after much criticism, the situation had changed quite significantly: a total of 307 men were prosecuted and 275 convicted. Even so, if the demand for prostitution well outstrips the supply (at about eight to one; my estimate), mathematically *ceteris paribus* it should be possible to have eight times as many prosecutions for kerb-crawlers as for prostitute women. Clearly, then, the number of prosecutions for kerb-crawlers is still very low indeed.

This under-enforcement of the law arises largely from evidential difficulties, as proof of persistent soliciting of women is required. At the end of the day police practicality rules, and prostitutes continue to be prosecuted in large numbers because of their visibility and accessibility, while the kerb-crawler, though not exempt from scrutiny, is largely exempt from prosecution. There are wide variations *between* forces in respect of the use of caution, and in prosecutions, however. In 1987 Greater Manchester police prosecuted 65 men, West Midlands 57, the Metropolitan Police 39, West Yorkshire 31 and Devon and Cornwall 22.

Feminists are divided over the role of the penal law in prostitution and allied offences. The English Collective of Prostitutes and The National Association of Probation Officers are in favour of the total decriminalization of all prostitution laws. The ECP and Prostitutes for the Reform of the Laws on Soliciting (PROS) were vehemently opposed to the Sexual Offences Bill which sought to penalize the kerb-crawler. Left feminist realists have instead argued that some regulation is necessary to protect women from the organizers and controllers, and to protect poorer neighbourhoods and residents living in 'red light districts' from the offence of the 'pick-up'. As Eileen Fairweather writes:

> I am sick of those socialists and sociologists, mostly male or living in the safety of surburbia, who dismiss the 'law and order' debate as just another Tory vote catcher . . . the far left continues to push its lunatic line: that all criminals no matter how vicious are in some way rebelling against capitalism . . . several women on Hillview were sexually attacked. Over the years you get used to being kerb crawled every night, every day asked if you do fellatio when you just pop out to the shops. (1982: 375–7)

Where there is money there is control by men. And so a degree of legal control is required to prevent the worst excesses of exploitation, violence, intimidation and enforcement by pimps. But the present system of law and policing which attempts to deal with the excesses and evils of prostitution by controlling the weakest element – women who loiter and solicit on street corners – is manifestly illogical or else misogynist.

### *Policing pornography*

Pornography is another of the several concerns dividing the Left and the feminist movements in America, the UK and Europe. Some feminists regard pornography as insufficiently penalized by legal sanctions, and the laws controlling porn as under-enforced by the police, thus bolstering by compliance a social fabric which allows the representation of violence against women as a form of entertainment (see Lederer 1980; Dworkin 1981; Griffin 1981). In the US, MacKinnon and Dworkin have defined pornography as a civil rights violation, and as an instance of sex discrimination and breach of the first amendment. For MacKinnon obscenity law provides a very different analysis and conception of the problem (1985: 20) where obscenity is the moral idea, 'pornography, by contrast, is a political practice, a practice of power and powerlessness'. It is another issue about which radical male criminology has had nothing to say, and left-wing realism has been silent, indicating further the total impotence of left-wing realism and radical criminology for women's issues and feminism. Andrea Dworkin exposes the contradictions pornography poses for the male Left:

> The intellectual defences of pornography have leftist origins. They are not quite accurately characterized as 'defences' either – because with rare exceptions the intellectual left has advocated pornography as crucial to liberation. Leftist writers from Abbie Hoffman to Gore Vidal to leftwing investigative journalists publish in pornography magazines and the actual producers of pornography are men, not exclusively but in shocking numbers, who were active in the anti-war movement, who are roughly my age, who were my political comrades. (Dworkin 1982: 28)

The issue of the debasement of women within and outside pornography has never been central to the male Left, since it would force them to radically rethink their own perceptions of women and their own sexuality. Consequently, the male criminologist, from both Left and Right, cannot consider these issues until he 'comes out', admits and confesses his own affinity with pornography, male power and violence. That is not to say that all men automatically conform to the male stereotype, but without doubt men have yet to discuss the problem male violence against women poses in their lives. Central to some of the demands of left-wing feminists has been the call for more accountable laws and a more accountable police force. The law and its enforcement has been considered vital to the condemnation of presentations of violence against women. The Criminal Law Revision Committee's *Working Paper on Sexual Offences* (1980a), following Wolfenden (1957: para 13), stated that the role of the criminal law is:

> to preserve public order and decency, to protect the citizen from what is offensive or injurious and to provide sufficient safeguards against exploitation and corruption of others, particularly of those who are especially vulnerable because they are young, weak in body or mind, inexperienced or in a state of special physical, emotional or economic dependence.

Yet it has to be said, even though it is less readily explained, that both the law and the police have singled out homosexuality as the prime target in the preservation of moral decency and family life rather than the issue of pornography. For many police forces, preservation of heterosexual behaviour in public places is the decency to be maintained. Chief Officers of Police have variously guarded 'public order and decency', and to that end have under-enforced and over-enforced the law in these matters. But they have inadequately protected society from the abuse of women in pornography.

In contrast to the complacency and absence of public debate in the UK on the subject, pornography and the protection of women was the focus of major government reports – in the USA and in Canada (Attorney General of Canada 1985). In the United States, 1986 saw the publication of the Attorney General's *Report on Pornography and Prostitution* (the Meese Report). It reflects the current protectionist zeal of the Left and the repressive and censorious zeal of the Right over what is morally harmful and what and who should be protected. It took America by some storm, and in the UK (where such things do not happen) the anti-sex and pro-purity campaigner Mrs Mary Whitehouse demonstrated a keen interest. (She was reported to have personally carried a draft of the report to Britain.) The published version of the Meese Report, in two hefty tomes, numbers some two thousand pages. Meese's message is that a direct link exists between pornography of the violent sort and rape (p. 323), and it is this message that wins the support of both left-wing feminists and right-wing evangelists.

The Meese Report comes down on the side of Brownmiller (1975), stating that pornography 'promotes a climate in which the ideology of rape is not only tolerated but encouraged'. It also concludes definitively that there is an interrelationship between pornography, prostitution and organized crime. The report includes evidence from Aladena Fratianno of La Cosa Nostra (American mafia) fame, in which Fratianno described the relationship between porn and crime in the 1970s:

> *Interviewer*: Is it possible for any person to become a major distributor of pornography in the United States without becoming involved in organized crime?
>
> *Fratianno*: I doubt it . . . because there's so much involved and I don't think they would let them . . . somebody would report 'em . . . you know, they would do something. They might go so far as killing them. (pp. 1041–2)

The Meese Report goes further: 'Physical violence, injury, prostitution and other forms of sexual abuse are so interlinked in many cases as to be almost inseparable except according to statutory definitions' (p. 1055). The report links murder, damage to property, prostitution, narcotics and tax violations to pornography, and as evidence of the link between organized crime and pornography many of those involved in pornography have gone missing or been silenced. Robert DeSalvo, a prominent figure in the distribution of the film *Deep Throat*, who gave evidence on behalf of the United States in the Peraino trial (arising from its distribution) has disappeared, and is very probably dead (p. 1056).

The Meese Commission solicited the views of government officials, right-wing reformists and left-wing feminist campaigners and activists, including Andrea Dworkin. She made an impassioned plea to the Commission, urging them to recognize the link between pornography and violent crime against women.

> I am a citizen of the United States and in this country where I live, every year millions of pictures are being made of women with our legs spread. We are called beaver . . . our genitals are tied up . . . real rapes are on film and are being sold in the market place, women are penetrated by animals and objects for public entertainment . . . urinated on and defecated on, women are made to look like five-year-old children for anal penetration . . . there is amputee pornography . . . there is a trade in racism as a form of sexual pleasure . . . there is a concentration camp pornography . . . and this material exists because it is fun, because it is entertainment, because it is a form of pleasure and there are those who say it is a form of freedom. The women in the pornography, sixty-five to seventy per cent of them, we believe, are victims of incest and child sexual abuse. They are poor women

> . . . frequently picked up by pimps and exploited. Pornography is used in rape . . . to plan it, to execute it. We see increasing use of all elements of pornography in battery . . . including the rape of women by animals, including maiming, including heavy bondage, including outright torture. I live in a country where if you film any act of humiliation or torture, and if the victim is a woman, the film is both entertainment and it is protected speech . . .' (pp. 769–72)

Dworkin called for more laws, more policing and more control. In view of Dworkin's evidence, how can anyone dare to argue that to decide for or against censorship is to take a private moral position, not a fit subject for legal action. No one has yet said that the motiveless killing of a man on the street is a matter of private, not public, morality. Pornography of the kind outlined by Dworkin involves harm.

Meese concluded that 'obscenity impacts on society in a number of ways which defy scientific standards of assessment' (p. 29). His findings reinforce what some feminists have been arguing for a long time, but his report is concerned with the promotion of a 'wholesome community', rather than the protection of women *per se*. Its censorious stand creates a dilemma, especially for the Left. It drew up 92 recommendations for the justice system and for law-enforcement agencies in the direction of more punishment and control (p. 459), including prosecuting more vigorously those engaged in the production, distribution and sale of the material and procuring or 'pimping' individuals to take part in pornographic sessions for the production of this material. It called for a massive effort to eliminate child pornography.

The feminist response to the Meese Report has been divided. As *Time* magazine reported: 'According to various feminists, the Meese Commission Report was good for the movement (Law Professor Catharine MacKinnon), bad for the movement (ACLU Attorney Nan Hunter) or basically irrelevant to feminist interests (movement pioneer Betty Friedan)' (*Time*, 21 July 1986: 18).

Ros Coward remains sceptical about whether legal regulation of pornography is the most appropriate way of tackling the problem:

> I don't think that feminism can afford to get caught up in the major political positions which have hegemonized our thinking about pornography; that is the liberal, 'anything goes so long as its private, without offence to "reasonable" people' or the pro-familial right-wing anti-sex position. Neither of these political positions has anything in common with feminism. (1982: 20)

Betty Friedan similarly argues that 'As repulsive as pornography can be, the obsession with it is a dangerous diversion for the women's movement' (*Time* magazine, 21 July 1986: 18). (See also Eckersley 1987.)

Pornographers have been quick to defend their freedom to publish. Americans watching 'Meet the Press' on 13 July 1986 heard Christie Hefner tell viewers that *Playboy* magazines were 'liberating . . . they provide women with an important opportunity of exploring their own sexuality'. Despite Christie's assurances of the liberating impact of her lucrative estate in 1986, the *New York Times* (4 February 1985) reported on the potential harm of such empires.

> The December 1984 issue of *Penthouse* carried this eroticized torture into the 'men's entertainment' forum with a series of photographs of Asian women bound with heavy rope, hung from trees, and sectioned into parts. It is not known whether this pictorial incited a crime that occurred two months later, where an eight-year-old Chinese girl living in Chapel Hill, North Carolina, was kidnapped, raped, murdered and left hanging from a tree limb. (Attorney General 1986: 793–4)

Many stores have in fact removed *Playboy* and *Penthouse* from their shelves after receiving a letter from the Meese Commission. It is not only people like Christie Hefner who argue that porn liberates. In criminal trials, the defence often manage to call medical experts who attest to the therapeutic value of such literature and images. In the UK Ben's Books trials in 1975 Dr Richards, witness for the defence, was shown several pictures in the magazine 'on trial'.

> *Counsel*: This is a picture of a female in chains, tied up, and a naked man pointing a sword at the woman's genitals . . .
> *Dr Richards*: This is for the public good because it produces a masturbatory situation. I would certainly prescribe it for a patient.
> *Counsel*: Picture of a naked man with a cat of ninetails striking a woman on her genitals.
> *Dr Richards*: This can stimulate a man. It has great therapeutic value.
> *Counsel*: Girl, with distress in her face, arms manacled, and has cuts. She is tied up. A man with a bayonet is inflicting cuts.
> *Dr Richards*: I have known patients who could benefit by masturbating on this. (quoted in Whitehouse 1982: 128)

Even where reform is accepted as necessary, the effect of legislation depends on the enforcement of the law by police, the courts and the judiciary. Inevitably, whatever laws might be introduced, the police role is pivotal. The Meese Report made a series of law-reforming proposals, but no proposals about law enforcement or policing, although the report was critical of the police who, it argued, had in the past adopted a policy of conscious oversight in policing pornography. Instead the report opted out:

> Initially, the decision to adapt or enforce obscenity laws should reside, within constitutional limits, with the citizens of each community. While

> prioritization of resources, like other obscenity law enforcement policy, is a matter within the prerogative of each individual jurisdiction. (Attorney General 1986: 31)

The question of pornography in Meese is treated as inhabiting the domain of obscenity, a matter to be regulated by the community, rather than the domain advocated as the approriate forum by MacKinnon, that of civil rights.

In the UK too feminists and the Left are divided about the use of the law in response to the excesses of sexual violence and exploitation of women in pornography, although all agree that some pornography exploits and degrades women.

No public debate on the scale of the American one has taken place in the UK. Pornography continues to be seen as a minor matter, often provoking amusement rather than concern. The Williams Committee Report on Obscenity and Film Censorship (1979), a much meeker, more modest offering than the Meese Report, drew similar though far less committed conclusions (p. 61). For the Williams Committee, pornography constituted primarily a public nuisance problem. The Report's final discussion on the proposals stated that it was crucial that the recommendations could be translated into legislation which was rational and workable. It concluded that the present law should be scrapped and totally revised, and that the law should rest not on 'obscenity' or 'indecency' but partly on the basis of moral harms caused. The principal objective should be to prevent offence, and to prevent offensive material being made available to young people. And it specified restriction of material which portrays, deals with or relates to violence, cruelty or horror, or sexual, faecal or urinary functions or genital organs' (Williams 1981: 160).

In any debate over pornography the police come in for most of the criticism - for under-enforcement of the laws relating to obscene publications, including the Obscene Publications Act 1959, s. 2, and 1964, the Protection of Children Act 1978 and the Indecent Displays (Control) Act 1981. But the abuse of women is endemic within society, and not purely a matter for regulation by the law or control by the police. The lack of protection of women, and their exploitation, are perpetuated in the wider social and political climate which continues to seriously underestimate the extent of the problem. For instance, Clare Short's Indecent Displays (Newspapers) Bill, which would have outlawed the pictures of bare-breasted women on page 3 of the *Sun* newspaper, was met in the Commons in 1987 with guffaws and, as one feature-writer put it, the pointing of two unmannerly fingers from male MPs who thought page 3 was good fun and an institution to be preserved. Clare Short, like many other feminist campaigners, has found that on such issues even the more serious press descends to the lowest level of news reporting. Andrew Rawnsley, the *Guardian* feature-writer, has described Clare Short as the 'luscious lefty', 'gorgeous pouting Clare Short, Labour's Ladywood Lovely' (14 April 1988). There have been few public discussions at governmental level about the problem of pornography.

Campaigners and supporters of her Bill, and a similarly spirited Private Member's Bill presented by Clement Freud MP in 1986, reflect concern not only over explicit sex but also about the constant portrayal of women as sexual commodities outside pornography. This portrayal is part of the large-scale representation of women as sex objects for male gratification and violence in the media, particularly in advertising, where marketing strategies designed to sell everything from the most innocuous bar of soap to sensual lingerie denigrate women. This iconography is also sustained in the language and images used in academic as well as lay explanations for victimization in rape, spousal violence and prostitution. Central to these representations is an attempt to turn reality on its head, to transpose cause and effect, and create an image of women which is consistent with the way in which men wish to see them, not as they would wish to be depicted.

Given that these representations of women exist both within and outside pornography, we must challenge not only certain images within hard and soft pornography, but also the institutionalization of violence against women through the mass media (particularly in advertising), in images which debase female sexuality, repeatedly portraying women as objects for male use and pleasure or male hatred and sadism – all wrapped up in a deceptive veil of female seduction and longing. Kathleen Barry has referred to this as 'cultural sadism', a 'distinct social form that consists of practices that encourage and support sexual violence, defining it as normal behaviour' (1984: 26). Women Against Violence Against Women, and Women Against Rape and Pornography, are groups in both America and Europe that unite in this endeavour to challenge and eradicate through law and social reform these forms of violence against women.

Anti-porn moves along the lines of those in the USA have taken place in the so-called 'liberal' European and Scandinavian countries where pornography has been decriminalized for some while. Feminist groups have been protesting over the very same issue – arguing that pornography is not freedom, and that restriction of its production, sale and distribution is not a violation of the tenets of 'freedom'. Brants and Kok (1986), in a study of law in the Netherlands, and Soetenhorst (1989), in a study of pornography reform in Holland, Denmark and Sweden, argue for finding 'humanistic and democratic ways of dealing with undesired life events like sexual violence'. Their writings raise once again the dilemma regarding the appropriateness of the penal law and police and criminal justice involvement in limiting the excesses of sexual violence in pornography, when the law in itself is seen as repressive and patriarchal, and when the modes of representation of women that are offensive (slavery, bondage, masochism, and death) are also found outside pornography.

UK law is unsatisfactory, and has proved its inability to halt the production, sale and distribution of pornography. The law is at present a nonsense founded on two unrelated tests. On the one hand there is the test provided for by section 1 (1) of the Obscene Publications Act 1959, which rests on the capacity or potential of material to 'deprave and corrupt'. Such material is deemed 'obscene' under the Act. Here, juries are called upon to assess the effect of the material under consideration on others - so subjective a task that juries tend to acquit; given the high acquittal rate the number of prosecutions for obscene publications has fallen significantly since the introduction of the Crown Prosecution Service (see chapter 6). The second test involves deciding whether material is 'indecent or obscene', and is provided for in the Customs Consolidation Act 1876, s. 42, the Post Office Act 1953, s. 11, and other Acts relating to public and indecent displays. This test is much broader in scope than that provided for by the 1959 Act, but can only be applied to items imported or sent through the post. Ludicrous contradictions have followed from these two tests, since it has been shown that it is illegal and unlawful to import an item because of its 'indecency' under the 1876 Act, while perfectly legal to buy and sell the same item over the counter, without a contravention of the obscenity criteria contained in the 1959 Act.

This difficulty has already been amply demonstrated in the continuing legal wrangle between Gay's the Word Books (Noncyp Limited) and HM Customs and Excise Commissioners over the present situation in law which allows for the purchase of items in Britain but makes illegal their import from countries outside the EEC. After a five-year saga Gay's the Word Books intend to take their case to the House of Lords and the European Court, since their alleged breach of customs law demonstrates not only the inconsistency in present obscenity laws but also and perhaps more importantly the fact that heterosexual material of a similar nature would not be in breach of customs regulations.

Gay's the Word Books had for some time been aware that consignments of books for which they were billed were not arriving in their full complement. In 1984 officers from Customs and Excise raided the flat of one of the directors looking for visual pornography, which they did not find. Officials took away some 90 titles, which they kept for over a year on the grounds that they were, in the opinion of customs officials, 'indecent and obscene'. During the months that followed the bulk of these books were returned (including *Witches Heal*, a book on homeopathy for women), customs officers having decided that only a handful were 'obscene'. Most of the books designated as obscene were of a similar nature to books about heterosexual sex sold in British Rail station bookshops, at British airports and through Sunday newspaper bookclubs. The 'gay' element led books on gay sex to a harsher scrutiny and a more stringent and narrow application of the 'indecent and obscene' test. Gay's the Word Books asked leading newspapers to cover the story. One year later the *Guardian* finally reported in a small feature (26 June 1985). On 11 July 1986, after eleven months of investigation, charges against Gay's the Word (Noncyp Ltd) were withdrawn. This move followed a decision on another case in the European Court, whose ruling declared that 'it was unlawful to ban imports of items that could be manufactured and traded at home.' Indeed, one of the books which formed part of the original seizure, *Aphrodisiac*, was also published in England.

This ruling followed Article 36 of the EEC Treaty, which exempts the movement of goods between member states and had been followed in the case of *Conegate Ltd* v. *HM Customs and Excise* (1987 QBD 254), in which it was decided that 'indecent' or 'obscene' goods which can be lawfully made or sold in the UK can also be imported provided they are of EEC origin. In the Conegate case the haul consisted of inflatable dolls with pubic hair and oral, vaginal and anal orifices imported from Germany. However, while such a consignment could be imported in accordance with the 1876 Act, such items could not be posted, as this would breach the Indecent Displays (Control) Act 1981.

The decision in *Conegate* affected the Gay's the Word case, at least tangentially, since the books at issue by Gay's the Word were imported from America and not from the EEC, although the same titles would not have been declared illegal if imported from the EEC. Gay's the Word in their defence said that the confiscated books did not contravene the Obscene Publications Act, applying the section 4 (1) test which allows for an acquittal under section 2 of the Act if 'the article in question is justified as being for the public good on the ground that it is in the interests of science, literature, art or learning.'

In December 1988 the appeal court rejected a section 4 defence (*R.* v. *Bow Street Magistrates' Court and Another ex parte Noncyp Ltd*, Court of Appeal (Civil Division), 14 December 1988 LEXIS Enggen). Gay's the Word are taking the case further in defence of books which, if about heterosexual sex, they believe would not have fallen foul of the Customs and Excise restrictions. The law relating to obscene publications has done little to protect women, although the Criminal Justice Act 1977 makes the possession of pornographic material which includes children a criminal offence. The Williams Committee had said in 1979 that 'The law in short is a mess', but the words seemed to have fallen on deaf ears. The mess was not apparently confined to the state of the law. The Metropolitan Police's 'Dirty Squad' was, as Simpson puts it, 'engaged in actually running the pornography business . . . further discredited the system' (1983: 21). Cox, Shirley and Short (1977), in their study of the 'Dirty Squad', found that police officers collaborated with those in the pornography business. Officers would warn shopkeepers of impending raids on their premises, and shopkeepers would hand over money 'bribes' in order that they be left alone. This selective enforcement was to cease after the trial of several officers in the seventies in which Commander Wallace Virgo was implicated (see *The Times*, 22 September 1973), and a case brought by Blackburn for the non-enforcement of the law (*Blackburn* v. *Metropolitan Police Commissioner*) (see Doig 1984: 239–42).

There is, as yet, no educated awareness about what pornography is. The definitions shift, and 'pornography' in fact covers a wide range of images. Image 1: scenes of men and women in couples or in groups having sex, orally and vaginally. Image 2: scenes of men urinating in women's mouths, ejaculating over women. Image 3: scenes of women bound and gagged, while knives are being plunged through them or having objects forced into their vaginas while their breasts are tied up and cut, or being beaten and raped by men. Image 4: scenes of men and women defecating in jars while having oral sex. Image 5: scenes involving men, women and children in concentration camps, mutilation and death. Representations (Image 1) of nudity, intercourse and oral sex do not necessarily contain images of violence or coercion, nor do they always degrade either men or women. Yet these images are classified alongside images that depict violence against women. Here lies the contradiction raised earlier by Dworkin: so long as no distinction is made between explicit sex and images of violence and degradation we will not progress with our definition of pornography or our attempts to deal with the problems it causes. Whatever position is taken, it remains the case that some representations within pornography are of mutually pleasurable activity, 'sexual expression between two people, who have enough power to be there by positive choice', while other representations involve the 'lethal confusion of sex with violence' (Steinem 1980: 23) where power relationships are unequal. Few, except perhaps the police, recognize that pornography is linked with other forms of vice – drugs, violence, prostitution and child abuse. But in the

UK new enforcement drives are nevertheless being called for. Superintendent Iain Donaldson of the Metropolitan Police's Obscene Publications Squad outlines the dilemma for the police who, he argues (1987), tread a narrow path between those who argue that pornography is freedom and those who argue that it can do untold damage, arguments reflected in the difficulty of gaining convictions. Although the seizure of publications by the Metropolitan Police has increased, prosecutions are often unsuccessful, or nor brought, because pornographic material is not necessarily 'obscene' within the legal meaning. It is time for a public review of the law and policing in this area.

It is clear that violence against women involves not only the direct individual experience of violence, as in rape and assault, sex-murder and other forms of homicide, but also acceptance of representations of violence against them both in pornography and in the media. This iconography sets the scene for the marginalization of women's needs and interests in dealing with rape, spousal violence, and prostitution, as well as in everyday life. The cultural representations of women are part of the atmosphere in which women are habitually viewed. The law and the police have a place in eradicating the viler forms of such sexism. Similar continual vilification and misrepresentation of black people, for example, would be regarded as racism of the worst form. The depiction of women as enjoying domination and masochism, and as commodities and sex objects for the gratification of male lust and perversion is horrible misogyny. What is needed is first a heightening of awareness, and second a revision of the law and its application.

For S. Atkins and B. Hoggett the marginalization of women's interests, at least in so far as prostitution and pornography are concerned, begins with the law. 'While the Street Offences Act was increasing the censorship of women who exploited their own bodies for profit, the Obscene Publications Act 1964 and the repeal of the Theatres Act were reducing almost to vanishing point the censorship of others who sought to do so' (1984: 80). Of course it is not only a question of police under-enforcing or over-enforcing - the law regulating prostitution and obscene publications itself allows for over-enforcement and under-enforcement according to its practical workability. While police attitudes and styles (Wilson 1968; Cain 1973; Reiner 1985) affect policing, it is both situational demands and the prosecutability of cases that guide police action. And with the introduction of the Crown Prosecution Service in the UK the successful prosecution of offences seems to have become the prime consideration.

# 2

# The Law and its Operation

## Introduction

There is no such thing as abstract equality before the law. Instead, the law in its form, content and application institutionalizes inequalities and differential treatment. This is nowhere more apparent than in the law dealing with male violence against female partners. This chapter addresses the question of how far the form and content of the law institutionalizes differential treatment in respect of partner violence as compared with violence against strangers on the street. And it asks: how does the law ratify the marginalization and eclipsing of violence against women, providing almost a cultural acceptance and condonement of male violence against women?

An analysis of the substantive law has always been integral to feminist scholarship. Indeed a study of the legal form has provided the starting-point for a close examination of rape and related issues. Feminist writers studying substantive law have revealed the way in which the legal form and legal content of laws, and, procedural and evidential rules, are neither neutral nor abstract. They argue that the simple 'rule of law' claim cannot be defended. Close examination of the law relating to rape has demonstrated most forcibly the value-laden assumptions behind it (Edwards 1981; Adler 1987; Temkin 1987).

Analysis of substantive law has also provided the starting-point for feminist and legal scholars in their critique of the lack of protection afforded victims of partner assault and partner/spousal homicide. Freeman (1980) states clearly that the law itself constitutes the problem. While that is in part true, the law would not be sustainable if it were not the case that a wider social and cultural fabric of images and ideas similarly present women as responsible for their own demise and men as possessed of a natural entitlement to correct, chastise and sometimes batter justifiably. Dobash and Dobash (1980), McCann (1985), Parker (1985), Faragher (1985), Montgomery and Bell (1986) and Edwards and Halpern (1988) variously focus on problems within the civil and criminal law, concluding that the law subverts rather than facilitates protection for women.

How does the law then constitute the problem and subvert women's protection? First, by the division of available remedies into civil (via injunctions) and criminal (via criming). This division within the law carries with it clear symbolic functions. The public/private dichotomy translates back into police perceptions that reinforce the conventional opinion that violence against wives or female partners is in certain ways distinct from violence towards non-family-members in the street. Second, even within criminal jurisdiction, the form and content of the law and the regulation of violent conduct has made a clear distinction between behaviour on the streets and behaviour in the home. This distinction is formalized not only by a difference in police attitudes to the two situations, but by the very legal rules and procedures that govern the police response and the gathering of evidence from strangers and from spouses. Proof of violence or threatening or suspicious behaviour on the streets depends largely on police evidence; in many cases the police are the chief prosecution witnesses. Private order in the home is not similarly monitored (and one would not wish it to be, but still the difference is there). The fact remains too that even where there is considerable evidence of criminal behaviour the police rarely intervene. Instead the *victim* must make a complaint and press charges.

Third, until 1984 the law created significant differences between criminal assault of a legal wife and that of a female partner/cohabitee or a stranger, so far as the rules of evidence are concerned. In stranger violence, and in violence between persons acquainted or known well to one another, the complainant/victim can be compelled to give evidence against the aggressor. The wife, by contrast, until 1984 was not legally compellable. This marital exemption was explained by a concern to preserve the sanctity of marriage, which no amount of violence by husband against the wife was seen to vitiate. Fourth, with regard to the prosecutability of domestic violence (as indeed in all cases), the police are called on to anticipate the views of prosecutors (the Crown Prosecution Service) on the strength of the evidence, the likelihood of a conviction, the credibility of the witness and whether such a prosecution would be in the public interest. The prosecutors' interpretation of these considerations and their decision to proceed in such cases will undoubtedly influence the nature of cases the police report to them. Broadly speaking, then, the law in itself, together with its application by legal personnel (including the police and Crown Prosecutors) constitutes part of the problem of the lack of protection for wives, cohabitees, girlfriends, ex-wives, ex-cohabitees and ex-girlfriends. If this is so, one possible solution to the legal and procedural problems is to embark on a reform of present law.

Indeed, it is over the precise nature of this 'reform' that feminists are so deeply divided. The refuge movement, the campaign for battered women and feminist researchers hold very different views regarding the causes of male violence, and the most appropriate form of legal intervention and subsequent punishment. Traditional and radical criminology and left-wing realism has been totally absent from the debate. The first step sought by most feminists (and there does seem to be agreement here) is the criminalization of all cases involving evidence of physical injury. In all such events the police should bring a prosecution, regardless of the wishes of the victim, and regardless of the later decision of the Crown Prosecution Service. I would argue that the (civil) non-molestation injunction should be replaced by a criminal charge and prosecution.

Throughout recent history, violent assault committed against a wife, cohabitee or sexual intimate has been systematically diverted away from the criminal justice process and dealt with as a civil matter, or a minor misdemeanour – or victims have been told to cope with it on their own. The decision to divert cases out of the criminal justice process or to 'down-crime' and reduce the charge is taken at the discretion of the charge officer. Nevertheless, discretion could not be exercised in this way unless the substantive law made such decisions legally permissible. Violence between family members not bound in marriage or common law relations, as for example between brother and sister or father and son, have also been treated differently from street violence, or violence between non-family-members in private. The problem of domestic violence between spouses and cohabitees is made even more acute by the substantive law, which defines the relationship between man and woman in marriage as uniquely different in terms of evidence, and by the prevailing family ideology that permeates these procedures. Women as a 'sex class' have historically been denied legal status in their own right. The problem for married women has been more acute, as they have been regarded in substantive law primarily as economic dependants, a status reflected in laws governing taxation, income, maintenance, welfare benefits, financial provision and divorce. Matrimonial law has placed women under certain obligations reflected in a husband's right to 'consortium', loosely defined as his right to her sexual, domestic and other services. By contrast, men have been accorded the power to chastise as of right. Personal violence has been dealt with in two different ways, largely dependent on the relationship of victim to suspect and whether the offence is committed in public or in private. Spousal violence against a legal wife or partner has been treated as a minor criminal infraction or else as common assault since the nineteenth century.

This trivialization is paralleled in the USA, Canada and Australia. Yet, over the last two decades in the USA, Canada and Australia the substantive law has been extensively amended in the direction of providing more remedies (usually of a civil nature) to the battered wife or female partner. The result has been double-edged, in that the wife/cohabitee/partner's right to protection under the criminal law has further been weakened, with the result that she has been edged out of the criminal justice system in all but the most serious of cases. During the last few years fears have been growing that moves in the USA and the UK towards using the Family Court to deal with family matters would be disastrous for spousal violence cases.

It is the contention of this chapter that the present two-tiered system of justice in the civil and criminal courts in England and Wales, Europe, North America, Canada and Australia presents a major obstacle to the protection of women from male violence in the home. This proliferation of legal provisions creates an illusion of choice and equality. Yet this *is* only an illusion, since civil and legal remedies deal out a different order of justice. The existence of these two levels perpetuates the public/private dichotomy in substantive law, distinguishing between violence against wives (private) and other violence (public), and reinforces the survival of the public/private divide in case law and in policing and in everyday culture.

## The historical legacy

The substantive law regulating violence against wives in the home is constructed of matrimonial, civil and criminal statutes. A woman's position in law has traditionally become considerably weaker if she is a legal wife rather than a cohabitee or partner. A wife upon marriage forfeited her right to protection from assault by her husband, and could not be compelled to give evidence against him. Case law promulgated the view that the chastisement of a wife was the prerogative of her husband. Consider, for example, Brady's *The Lawes Resolution of Women's Rights* (1632), which states: 'A man may beat an outlaw, a traitor, a pagan, his villein or his wife . . .', a sentiment later voiced in Blackstone's *Commentaries*, where a husband is empowered to correct his wife. 'For as he is to answer for her misbehaviour, the law thought it reasonable to entrust him with this power of restraining her, by domestic chastisement . . .' (1857: 470). Yet the only restraint placed on a husband's extent or degree of 'chastisement' was that 'he did so in a moderate manner.' The law thereby legitimized a certain degree of violence against wives without interference or comment. When a wife appealed to the law for protection from a husband's violence, he was very rarely restrained and seldom, if ever, reprimanded. The courts resolutely refused to intervene, unless, as in the case of *Bradley* v. *Wife* (1663;

cited in Cleveland 1896: 222), it could be proved that her life was in absolute danger.

During the nineteenth century, feminists looked to a reform in substantive law to bring about the changes so desperately needed to protect women. They also regarded the continuation of spousal violence as a problem rooted in the economic dependence of women on men, which forced women to stay on with violent husbands, and looked to reform in matrimonial law that might free women from such economic dependence. In 1853 the Aggravated Assault Act was introduced. It was an Act devised for the better prevention and punishment of aggravated assaults upon women and children, and for preventing delay and expense in the administration of certain parts of the criminal law. It provided, upon conviction, for the imprisonment of the offender for a period not exceeding six months, or a fine of up to £20, and was immediately hailed as an important watershed. Eight years later it was consolidated in the Offences Against the Person Act 1861, s. 43. This section states:

> When any person shall be charged before Two Justices of the Peace with an Assault or Battery . . . upon any female, either upon the Complaint of the Party aggrieved or otherwise, the said Justices, if the Assault or Battery is of such aggravated Nature that it cannot in their Opinion be sufficiently punished under the Provisions herein-before contained as to Common Assaults and Batteries, may proceed to hear and determine the same in a summary way . . .

It soon became clear that the new law was a gravely retrogressive step. First, all cases of assault, whether of a partner, cohabitee, stranger or spouse, committed on a woman by a man – however serious, however life-threatening – were to be dealt with in accordance with this section. This included cases of attempted murder or grievous bodily harm. Second, the historical legacy of section 43, which originated in the 1853 Act, permitted serious cases, as well as the less serious, to be diverted away from the Assizes and Quarter Sessions (the more appropriate legal forum, where if differently charged they would have been heard on indictment) to be considered instead summarily before a magistrate. In a Report to the Secretary of State, for the Home Department, on the State of Law relating to Brutal Assaults (1875), many justices expressed their grave reservations about the appropriateness of the use of section 43 'aggravated assaults' for wife assault. They considered that such cases were too grave to be heard before magistrates, and should be triable only at Assizes and Quarter Sessions. Yet from 1853 onwards assaults against women have been systematically relegated to the lower courts, while assaults against men by men have been heard as section 18, section 20, or in the less serious cases section 47 assaults (under the

Offences Against the Person Act 1861), before a judge and jury, and attracted much heavier sentences upon conviction.

Tomes (1978), in her analysis of the criminal statistics for aggravated assault in England and Wales in the nineteenth century, notes a decreasing use of the 1853 Act and its later consolidation in section 43 of the Offences Against the Person Act from the middle to the end of the century. She interprets the dramatic fall in prosecutions as evidence of the deterrent impact of the substantive law. It is difficult to find one's way through the intricacies of nineteenth-century law and criminal statistics, yet without a shadow of doubt Tomes's interpretation is wrong. Was there in fact a decline in prosecutions? Yes, there was a decline in *section 43* prosecutions, as this section of the 1861 Act fell into disrepute. It was increasingly recognized that serious cases should not be tried before magistrates with such trivial remedies available, such that men who had nearly murdered their wives were being fined £20. The reported cases did not drop out of the system altogether; rather, cases of assault against women by men were increasingly heard in the Assizes and Quarter Sessions, in accordance with sections 18, 20 and 47 of the Act. Assaults against women were, by the end of the nineteenth century, heard in the same courts as assaults against men by men. In addition, cases of wife assault were prosecuted in increasing numbers in the magistrates' courts, under section 47 'assault occasioning actual bodily harm'. Tomes's conclusions are erroneous because the decline in the number of section 43 prosecutions was a result of choices about which section to use; the wider view gives the correct picture.

During the nineteenth century not only was violence against women seen as less deserving of justice than violence against men, but women were also deterred from reporting incidents to the police by their economic vulnerability and dependence on their aggressors, and the fear of retaliation. Legislators sought to address this problem, recognizing that it was impossible for the battered wife to leave a husband if she had no income or capital and no alternative accommodation, and was denied the right to property in her own name. In 1878 the Matrimonial Causes Act was introduced, which allowed for the granting of a separation order to a wife who could prove a husband's cruelty. In addition the Act provided for a wife's financial provision in the form of a maintenance order, so long as no adultery could be proved against her. Clearly this was not an automatic right, but one wives had to earn.

> If a husband shall be convicted summarily or otherwise of an aggravated assault upon his wife the court or the magistrate may, if satisfied that the future safety of the wife is in peril, order that the wife shall be no longer bound to cohabit with the husband; and such order shall have the force

> and effect in all respects of a decree of judicial separation on the ground of cruelty ... No order for payment of money by the husband, or for the custody of the children by the wife, shall be made in favour of a wife who shall be proved to have committed adultery ... and that any order for payment of money or for the custody of children may be discharged by the court or magistrate by whom such order was made upon proof that the wife has since the making thereof been guilty of adultery ... (ss. 4(1), 4(2))

In practice, however, as case law reflects, women were not likely to reap the benefits of the new law, as cruelty had to be seen to be serious and persistent. In addition, their own characters had to be seen to be impeccable. Women had to earn the right to financial support; it was neither an automatic right nor a propitious gift. Violence against women in the home, coupled with economic dependence on men meant that then, as now, most women were able to do very little more than suffer in silence.

## Private matters: private remedies – civil law

### *The substantive law*

During the twentieth century substantive law has continued to offer only a 'miserable mouse' (Sir George Baker in *Davis* v. *Johnson* [1978] CA 1 All ER 860) of protection to the battered wife, common law wife or cohabitee, by relegating violence against her to a different and lesser consideration within law. In criminal law one of the main problems has been that of obtaining satisfactory evidence. Traditionally, wives and cohabitees have been reluctant to prosecute spouses, and the matter has been left to them. In the face of no evidence in the case of a wife complainant, or a 'hostile witness' in the case of a cohabitee complainant, charges of common assault are sometimes brought by prosecutors, as being most likely to result in conviction. Section 42, 'common assault', states that 'upon complaint by or on behalf of the Party aggrieved' the accused 'shall upon conviction ... be committed to gaol ... for any term not exceeding two months or shall pay a fine not exceeding five Pounds ...'

By the 1970s the introduction of new civil laws in the UK, USA, Canada, Europe and Australia provided further legal remedies for the wife, this time within the civil law. The public/private dichotomy in law was firmly set, although advocates of the new laws stressed the widening of choice and the extension of protection, rather than differential or disparate treatment. The extension of the law reinforced popular family ideology, reaffirming the belief that marital violence was indeed different from other violent crime.

In the UK, the USA, Canada and Australia the battered spouse may seek some measure of legal protection through several non-criminal remedies. When the legislation was introduced it received an enthusiastic reception from legal reformists and from left-wing feminists, who argued that where a spouse is reluctant to press charges under criminal jurisdiction, the civil law can at least provide some measure of protection. In recent years many left-wing feminists who were the first to welcome the civil provisions have criticized the law on two well-argued grounds. First, as experience has shown, the availability of civil provisions has resulted in the diversion of serious assault cases to the civil courts. Here again we see the errors of nineteenth-century down-criming reflected today. Secondly, the civil law, as it is presently framed, allows for very wide judicial discretion in the interpretation of its ambiguous wording, which means that few orders are made by the court or can be properly enforced. The Domestic Violence and Matrimonial Proceedings Act 1976 has enabled the aggrieved party of a marriage to make an application for one of four types of injunction, restraining the aggressor from molesting the applicant or any child living with the applicant. Section 2(1)(c) empowered the courts to make an order excluding the aggressor from the home, or the vicinity, or else required him to permit her to enter and remain in part of the house. In grave cases of violence or molestation a power of arrest could be attached to the injunction, giving the police the power to arrest if they so chose in cases where an injunction had been breached.

Yet the precise interpretation of what kind of behaviour constitutes 'molestation' within the act has been a matter largely for the courts, and, as we shall see in the discussion on case law, the precise meaning of 'molestation' has changed within judicial decision-making over the years, sometimes departing from the spirit of the original legislation. Again, when and for how long an ouster injunction is appropriate has been a matter of great disagreement. The 1976 Act was originally intended to provide protection for the battered wife and common law wife. But the common law wife or cohabitee remained unprotected, in civil law, until the House of Lords ruling in *Davis* v. *Johnson* ( [1978] 1 All ER HL 1132). In the House of Lords decision, given on 9 March 1978, Lord Diplock, Viscount Dilhorne, Lord Kilbrandon, Lord Salmon and Lord Scarman upheld the original ouster injunction against Nehemiah Johnson, which had earlier been restored by the Court of Appeal decision in *Davis* v. *Johnson* by Lord Denning, Master of the Rolls, Sir George Baker, Lord Justice Shaw (Lord Justices Goff and Cumming-Bruce dissenting) ( [1978] 1 All ER 841).

In this case Jennifer Davis and Nehemiah Johnson were joint tenants of a council flat and they lived together as man and wife. In the words of the Court of Appeal report, 'The appellant was frequently beaten by the respondent and subjected in at least two instances to extreme violence of a horrifying nature.' Two days after the imposition of the injunction the Court of Appeal overruled an ouster injunction in another case where the parties involved also lived together as man and wife and were also joint tenants. Here, in *Cantliff* v. *Jenkins* ( [1978] 1 All ER 836) Lord Justices Stamp, Orr and Ormrod overruled an ouster order made by Mr Recorder Stewart Oakes at Bolton County Court on 19 September 1977. It was on this basis that Nehemiah Johnson successfully appealed at a lower court hearing on October 26. These two Court of Appeal decisions left considerable ambiguity in the minds of many as to whether a battered woman could ever oust a man unless she had sole proprietary interest and he none at all. Davis appealed to the House of Lords, where the decision in *Cantliff* v. *Jenkins*, was overruled.

A further problem with the 1976 Act was that applications could only be heard in the county court, where procedures were long, cumbersome and complicated.

In response to some of the criticisms of the 1976 Act, in 1978 a further civil provision was introduced, which although limited to wives, was more accessible. The Domestic Proceedings and Magistrates' Courts Act gave magistrates in the lower courts the power to make an order for the protection of a party to a marriage (s.16 (2)), or to a child of the family (s.16 (10)). In addition, magistrates were granted the power to evict the violent spouse under an exclusion order (s. 13 (3)). And in serious cases a power of arrest could be attached (s. 18 (1)). This legislation, and the magistrates' court as a forum, provided for a speedier hearing, as cases could be heard without delay by adding such applications to the criminal list. In addition, magistrates could also make expedited orders in ex-parte proceedings. In 1983 the Matrimonial Homes Act was introduced, regulating the rights to occupancy and ownership of the matrimonial home. The Act is restricted to married couples only, and provides for the exclusion of spouses under certain circumstances (ss. 1 and 9), including violence, and after a case law decision in *Richards* v. *Richards* ([1983] 1 All ER 1017), discussed more fully later, it was decided that an application for an ouster will normally be considered under this Act.

Within case law considerable confusion and difference has arisen about the appropriateness of the provisions where violence is alleged and not substantiated (in the court's view), and the application is for ouster exclusion. Traditionally, applications for ouster exclusion have been far less successful than non-molestation injunctions/personal protection orders. The rules governing discretion on ouster applications allow for a wider interpretation, and case law has resisted the removal of a man from his home, always considered a 'Draconian' measure (see Edmund-Davies in *Phillips* v. *Phillips* [1973] 2 All ER 423).

In the USA there has been a similar proliferation of civil remedies during the last decade. In New York City and Washington DC, together with many other major cities, a 'civil protection order' has been available to the battered wife or cohabitee for some time. The Family Court Act 1962, amended in 1977, provided 'for dealing with such instances of disorderly conduct and assaults'. On the filing of a petition the court can issue a summons or an arrest warrant in cases where 'the safety of the petitioner is endangered' (s. 827), or can 'dismiss the petition, suspend judgement for six months, or grant a civil protection order' (s. 841). A protection order can be granted in accordance with one or several of seven conditions implicating the aggressor or the applicant:

> to stay away from the home, the other spouse or the child;
> to permit a parent to visit the child at stated periods;
> to abstain from offensive conduct against the child or against the other parent or against any person to whom custody of the child is awarded;
> to give proper attention to the care of the home;
> to refrain from acts of commission or omission that tend to make the home not a proper place for the child;
> to notify the court or probation service immediately of any change of residence or employment;
> to co-operate in seeking and accepting medical and/or psychiatric diagnosis and treatment, including family casework or child guidance for himself, his family or child.

In 1979 the Protection From Abuse Act was passed in Kansas, allowing family members to seek injunctive relief from abuse. This move came about as a result of local and state-wide reform efforts, including the Governor's Committee on Domestic Violence. The Act is closely in line with civil remedies available in virtually all other states, following the lead of Pennsylvania. To obtain protection the victim must first file a petition. Within ten days the victim is required to prove the allegation. Meanwhile, a temporary ex-parte order may be granted, ordering the offender to 'refrain from abuse', granting exclusive possession of the house to the victim, or evicting one of the parties. Since 1979 other states have implemented similar legislation (e.g. the Family Violence Protection Act 1982 in Wyoming and in Utah the Spouse Abuse Act 1981).

In Canada, by the Family Law Reform Act 1980 (Ont.), s. 45, the Matrimonial Property Act 1980, s. 12, and the Family Law Reform Act 1978 (PEI), s. 45, the law provides for the possession of the matrimonial home to be granted to a woman where refuge accommodation is inadequate or when the court feels that it is in the best interests of the child. In Ontario and Prince Edward Island, injunctive orders in accordance with the Family Law Reform Act of 1980 (Ont.) and 1978 (PEI) are available to restrain men from molesting women. As in the UK and the USA the Canadian legislation has its limitations. For example, as Pibus (1980: 48) points out, exclusion orders are available to married woman only, and non-molestation injunctions, while available to unmarried couples, can be made only to couples who have been living together for five years or else have a child. In practice exclusion or non-molestation orders are difficult to obtain, and in Ontario and Prince Edward Island there is no provision for the attachment of a power of arrest (see Commonwealth Secretariat 1987: 29).

### *The granting of civil orders in England and Wales: the county court*

Statistics on the number of non-molestation and ouster orders applied for and granted, while not giving any indication of the extent of the problem of wife and partner abuse, do provide information on the administration of justice in the civil courts and the success or failure of legal efforts to protect women. Civil law, like criminal law, is fettered and shaped by case law decisions, and the subjective responses of judges and magistrates to the problem of marital violence. For those who thought that civil law provisions rather than criminal law remedies would contain fewer practical difficulties and evidential requirements for women trying to achieve some measure of relief, the available evidence is highly discouraging.

Of applications for injunctions filed between 1983 and 1987, very small percentages were refused. In theory the criteria for refusal have been insufficiency of evidence of violence or molestation or threat of violence. Despite the general upward trend in the number of applications made over these years, which might indicate more violence and/or a greater sympathy on the part of the courts with the plight of the battered wife, evidence from women victims and their advocates suggests that in fact injunctions are proving much more difficult to secure, and as a result many women are actually deterred from making applications. Evidence submitted to the Police Monitoring and Research Group in London in 1986 disclosed that courts varied enormously in the kind of evidence they required before granting either non-molestation or an ouster order or attaching a power of arrest. It was revealed that at Bromley, Edmonton and Woolwich county courts in the London area a medical report was required before an injunction could be granted. A power of arrest required even more stringent evidence of physical assault (see London Strategic Policy Unit 1986: 23). This requirement of medical evidence from a GP or casualty officer suggests that the degree of evidence needed in civil cases is as stringent as in criminal cases, where a witness's statement, a police officer's statement, and medical evidence are all required. Yet despite the undoubted difficulties, figures on refusals over the last few years reveal a small and steady increase to a peak in 1985, followed by decline, and the numbers of applications continue to rise. It must also be acceded that many women, aware of the degree of evidence required to satisfy a court before an order is granted, may prefer not to make an application at all, so doubtless much domestic violence goes unreported.

Of applications granted during these five years, 1983–7, a small proportion of non-molestation or ouster orders were made with a power of arrest attached (average around 24 per cent). Yet if we compare these figures for powers of arrest with the actual numbers of exclusion orders granted, it can be seen that there are fewer instances in which powers of arrest are attached than there are orders for exclusion. (In the Principal Registry (London), not covered in table 2.1, in 1986 only 463 applications were made, 18 were refused, and all orders granted were for non-molestation. None were granted for exclusion (*Judicial Statistics* 1987: Table 5.17, p. 51). This must mean that in some cases, even where an exclusion order has been granted this is not backed up with a power of arrest. It must also mean that very few, if any, non-molestation injunctions carry a power of arrest.

The low number of powers of arrest granted with non-molestation and exclusion injunctions is a cause for great concern. The traditional assumption has been that where an injunction has been granted there will be little need for the attachment of a power of arrest except in exceptional circumstances. In addition, where an ouster injunction is granted, it is often argued that there is little need for a power of arrest since the offending party has already been removed and that removal is protection enough. These sentiments are both reflected in case law on non-molestation and ouster injunctions, and are considered the correct interpretation of section 2(2) of the 1976 Act. At present the view is that the court has no jurisdiction to grant a power of arrest where parties are not living 'in the same household as husband and wife', and an ouster effectively removes that 'same household' criterion. For example, in *Harrison* v. *Lewis*: Re S ( [1988] 18 FL 477–8), the Court of Appeal emphasized that attaching a power of arrest to an injunction was a serious matter and that courts should be cautious about doing this. In *Tuck* v. *Nicholls* (Court of Appeal, Civil Division, 27 October 1988, LEXIS Enggen) the 'living together'

Table 2.1 *Non-molestation and exclusion orders sought in county courts in England and Wales, 1983–1987*

| | Applications made | Total refused | | Total granted | Non-molestation | | Others (exclusions) | | With power of arrest | |
|---|---|---|---|---|---|---|---|---|---|---|
| | | No. | % | | No. | % | No. | % | No. | % |
| 1983 | 10,820 | 367 | 3.0 | 10,453 | n.g. | n.g. | n.g. | n.g. | 2,501 | 22 |
| 1984 | 14,510 | 380 | 2.6 | 14,130 | n.g. | n.g. | n.g. | n.g. | 3,568 | 25 |
| 1985 | 13,531 | 511 | 4.0 | 13,020 | 9,202 | 71 | 3,818 | 29 | 3,314 | 25 |
| 1986[a] | 15,526 | 441 | 3.0 | 15,085 | 10,360 | 69 | 4,725 | 31 | 3,647 | 19 |
| 1987[a] | 16,011 | 472 | 2.9 | 15,539 | 10,636 | 68 | 4,903 | 32 | 4,264 | 28 |

[a]Excluding Principal Registry in London, which is included in *Judicial Statistics* from 1986.

n.g. = not given.

*Source*: *Judicial Statistics, England and Wales*, 1983–7.

test was reaffirmed as a precondition for granting ousters, non-molestations injunctions and the power of arrest. In an appeal against a non-molestation order, an ouster order and a power of arrest Mrs Lord Justice Butler-Sloss reiterated the viewed so often expressed in these cases that the ouster was a 'draconian measure'. The ouster order and power of arrest were discharged.

On the first count, I believe that without a power of arrest all injunctions, whether they be for non-molestation or for ouster, are rendered redundant. To give an abuser a warning without imposing any penalty at all should that warning be flaunted is to give no warning at all. As to the second count, the assumption that having removed the abuser from the premises is of itself sufficient to protect the victim is not borne out in evidence. As I detail in chapter 3, one third of all spousal homicides are committed upon women by men when the parties are no longer residing together. Simply, an ouster or non-molestation injunction without a power of arrest is no deterrent.

Women's Aid groups, women victims and legal advocates also see the main weakness and uselessness of injunctions in this reluctance to grant a power of arrest, which in effect renders the order impotent. The main problem is that the courts, notwithstanding evidence of violence, prefer to get a verbal undertaking from the aggressor that he will not harm the applicant again, rather than legally safeguarding that violence does not recur by attaching a power of arrest to the order. Yet injunctions without a power of arrest are not worth the paper they are written on. This view has been reflected since 1976 by police officers and legal practitioners alike (see Report of the Select Committee on Violence in Marriage, 1975, vol. 1, para. 45). One solicitor in 1987 summed up the difficulty in this way:

> If I am beaten up by my husband and come to see my solicitor and I shoot off to the court and I get an order restraining him from molesting (which is an injunction), there is a return date a week later, where he can say his piece, and contest it especially if he has been kicked out. Instead of hearing all the evidence and ordering him not to molest you, not to stay in the house, not to nick the children from school . . . the judge will say 'well, I won't order you to, if you don't want me to, Mr Bloggs, because if you are saying you don't beat up your wife, you won't mind giving me an undertaking', but what they very rarely do is attach a power of arrest.

Understandably, Woman's Aid feel that legal changes should be towards prioritizing a woman's future protection by making the power of arrest mandatory. Instead, the courts take his promise not to molest as sufficient security of her future protection.

An examination of powers of arrest granted by region shows that some circuits are even more reluctant than others to grant a power of arrest (see table 2.2). In 1985 all other circuits except London and the

Table 2.2 *Regional variations among county courts in England and Wales in the granting of powers of arrest with injunctions, 1985–1986*

| | 1985 | | 1986 | | 1987 | |
|---|---|---|---|---|---|---|
| | Orders granted | Power of arrest as % of all orders | Orders granted | Power of arrest as % of all orders | Orders granted | Power of arrest as % of all orders |
| Midland and Oxford | 2,468 | 18 | 2,731 | 19 | 2,745 | 20 |
| North Eastern | 1,571 | 9 | 1,871 | 10 | 1,891 | 12 |
| Northern | 1,410 | 18 | 1,497 | 20 | 1,914 | 26 |
| London | 2,153 | 45 | 2,803 | 35 | 2,800 | 37 |
| Provinces | 1,823 | 60 | 3,620 | 31 | 3,608 | 36 |
| Wales and Chester | 848 | 17 | 907 | 22 | 867 | 29 |
| Western | 1,747 | 16 | 1,656 | 19 | 1,714 | 24 |
| England and Wales | 13,020 | 25 | 15,085 | 24 | 15,539 | 28 |

*Source*: *Judicial Statistics, England and Wales*, 1985, table 4.14; 1986, table 4.14; 1987, table 5.17.

Provinces (South of England) fell below the England and Wales mean (at 25 per cent) for attaching a power of arrest. Contrary to popular belief, London granted powers of arrest in 45 per cent of all applications before them, and this was the case for 60 per cent of all applications made in the Provinces. In 1986 there was a levelling out between the regions, although chances of getting a power of arrest attached to any injunction still remained slightly higher in London and the Provinces than elsewhere. For both 1985 and 1986 the chances of getting a power of arrest attached to an injunction for non-molestation or ouster in the North Eastern Circuit were quite frankly remote. By 1987 all previously below-average circuits showed a slight 'thaw' in their earlier reluctance to grant a power of arrest, with the North Eastern Circuit continuing its demonstration of a mean application of the law.

These differences between circuits immediately suggest that there is protection by geography or region! The extent of women's protection from violence in fact depends on differences between particular courts and the approaches they adopt. Looking at the figures on a court-by-court basis, while for example those in London and the Provinces when examined as a whole are more likely to attach a power of arrest, not every court in these circuits follows this pattern.

A woman who is a victim of violent abuse often needs to have the violent aggressor removed in order that her protection may be ensured, yet the courts have been reluctant to grant such applications. Lord Salmon, in *Davis* v. *Johnson* ( [1978] 1 All ER 1132 at 1152), said 'I find it difficult to believe that it could ever be fair, save in the most exceptional circumstances, to keep a man out of his own house for more than a few months.'

Of all orders granted in accordance with the 1976 Act only a small proportion are made for exclusion (see table 2.3). In 1985 13,020 orders were made, of which 29 per cent were exclusion orders. In 1986 15,085 orders were made, 31 per cent of which were exclusions. Figures which distinguish between exclusion and non-molestation orders were not available before 1985, but by 1987 a total of 15,539 orders were granted, 4,903 of these being exclusion orders, a total of 32 per cent of all orders made (excluding the Principal Registry).

The regional profile shows wide variations in the propensity to grant exclusion orders. Variations between circuits seem to be the result of individual differences between judges and recorders, rather than of real differences in the degree and nature of the molestation and violence in cases brought before them. In 1985, the Northern Circuit granted the largest proportion of exclusion orders and London the lowest. By 1986 London and Midland and Oxford granted the largest proportion of exclusion orders, the London area in particular demonstrating a radical change since 1985. While the number of non-molestation orders granted remained roughly the same, the number of exclusion orders more than doubled. In 1987, London and Midland and Oxford continued to grant the largest proportion of exclusion orders.

In investigating the behaviour of individual courts in granting (or not granting) non-molestation or ouster orders, 24 county courts (out of 187) were randomly selected from the 53 counties, on the basis of high, middle and low numbers of non-molestation orders granted for the first quarter in 1985. This figure was then compared to the number of exclusion orders granted in the same court, and these two figures were compared with any change from 1985 to 1986. The selected sample is presented in table 2.4. It can be observed that although some courts granted a high number of orders for non-molestation, this was not always reflected by a similar proportionate figure for exclusion (see Bow, Willesden and Lincoln, for example, for 1985 and 1986). Some other courts tended to grant exclusion orders roughly for every two non-molestation injunctions granted (see Bristol, Reading and Leicester). Yet other courts tended to grant more exclusion orders than non-molestation orders (see Portsmouth for 1985 and Birmingham for both 1985 and 1986). While most courts tended to maintain similar levels of non-molestation orders in both years, Coventry showed a dramatic decline and Birmingham a dramatic increase. Several courts show a distinct change in the relationship of non-molestation to exclusion orders from 1985 to 1986. All the London courts show a greater preparedness to grant

Table 2.3 *Regional variations in non-molestation and exclusion orders granted in county courts, 1985–1986*

| | 1985 | | | | | 1986[a] | | | | |
|---|---|---|---|---|---|---|---|---|---|---|
| | Ref. | Non-molestation orders | Exclusion orders | Exclusion orders as % of orders granted[a] | Power of arrest as % of orders granted | Ref. | Non-molestation orders | Exclusion orders | Exclusion orders as % of orders granted | Power of arrest as % of orders granted |
| Midland and Oxford | 106 | 1,657 | 811 | 33 | 18 | 71 | 1,687 | 1,044 | 38 | 19 |
| North Eastern | 53 | 1,147 | 424 | 27 | 9 | 38 | 1,280 | 591 | 32 | 10 |
| Northern | 61 | 932 | 478 | 34 | 18 | 42 | 1,053 | 444 | 30 | 20 |
| London | 120 | 1,672 | 481 | 22 | 45 | 105 | 1,761 | 1,042 | 37 | 35 |
| Provinces | 86 | 1,931 | 892 | 32 | 60 | 110 | 2,696 | 924 | 26 | 31 |
| Wales and Chester | 31 | 593 | 255 | 30 | 17 | 35 | 638 | 269 | 30 | 22 |
| Western | 54 | 1,270 | 477 | 27 | 16 | 40 | 1,245 | 411 | 25 | 19 |
| England and Wales | 511 | 9,202 | 3,818 | 29 | 25 | 441 | 10,360 | 4,725 | 31 | 24 |

| | 1987[a] | | | | |
|---|---|---|---|---|---|
| | Ref. | Non-molestation orders | Exclusion orders | Exclusion orders as % of orders granted | Power of arrest as % of orders granted |
| Midland and Oxford | 69 | 1,847 | 898 | 33 | 20 |
| North Eastern | 42 | 1,365 | 526 | 28 | 12 |
| Northern | 37 | 1,352 | 562 | 29 | 26 |
| London | 106 | 1,747 | 1,053 | 38 | 37 |
| Provinces | 125 | 2,504 | 1,104 | 31 | 36 |
| Wales and Chester | 47 | 611 | 256 | 30 | 29 |
| Western | 46 | 1,210 | 504 | 29 | 24 |
| England and Wales | 490 | 10,636 | 4,903 | 32 | 28 |

Percentages rounded to nearest figure.
[a]Excludes Principal Registry figure which is included in the England and Wales total in *Judicial Statistics* from 1986.
*Source*: *Judicial Statistics, England and Wales*, 1985, table 4.14; 1986, table 4.14; 1987, table 5.17.

Table 2.4 *Variations in non-molestation and exclusion orders between individual county courts, 1985 and 1986*

| | First quarter 1985 | | First quarter 1986 | |
|---|---|---|---|---|
| | Non-molestation orders | Exclusion orders | Non-molestation orders | Exclusion orders |
| Birmingham | 10 | 36 | 69 | 81 |
| Blackwood | 35 | 2 | 20 | 4 |
| Bow | 75 | nil | 30 | 41 |
| Bristol | 53 | 35 | 48 | 37 |
| Bromley | 30 | nil | 10 | 3 |
| Cardiff | 34 | 4 | 19 | 23 |
| Coventry | 72 | 6 | 28 | 12 |
| Edmonton | 49 | 8 | 64 | 15 |
| Huddersfield | 12 | 3 | 12 | 3 |
| Leeds | 37 | 7 | 137 | 22 |
| Leicester | 40 | 21 | 21 | 31 |
| Lincoln | 41 | nil | 15 | 2 |
| Liverpool | 43 | 45 | 42 | 4 |
| Manchester | 31 | 17 | 14 | 14 |
| Newport | 30 | 6 | 25 | 18 |
| North Shields | 16 | 4 | 9 | 3 |
| Plymouth | 46 | nil | 36 | nil |
| Portsmouth | 40 | 52 | 32 | 1 |
| Reading | 37 | 20 | 46 | 28 |
| Scunthorpe | 26 | 28 | 46 | 5 |
| Swindon | 16 | 11 | 6 | 1 |
| Wandsworth | 65 | 5 | 92 | 11 |
| Willesden | 76 | nil | 66 | 83 |
| Wolverhampton | 15 | 9 | 13 | 1 |

*Source:* Figures supplied by kind permission of the Lord Chancellor's Department (Statistics Division).

exclusion orders, and Willesden seems to have changed its 1985 style altogether – from granting no exclusion orders for the first quarter in 1985 to granting 83 exclusion orders for the same period in 1986. Birmingham's profile changed in a similar dramatic way. Either molestation and violence against women is variable geographically and over time, or there is little consistency in the application of the law from court area to court area and over time.

That judges are reluctant to grant exclusion orders in accordance with the 1976 Act, unless violence is severe and 'plain as a pikestaff', is borne out not only in the case law, but also by the low numbers of ouster orders made in the months immediately after the 1983 Richards decision where the House of Lords overturned an exclusion order (discussed below) compared with orders for 1986. Looking at the ouster figures by individual court, it seems that variations in the

Table 2.5 *Non-molestation and exclusion orders in London county courts, 1985 and 1986*

| | First quarter 1985 | | First quarter 1986 | |
|---|---|---|---|---|
| | No. | %[a] | No. | %[a] |
| Applications made | 630 | 100 | 881 | 100 |
| Total refused | 39 | 6 | 35 | 4 |
| Total granted | 591 | 94 | 846 | 96 |
| Non-molestation orders | 503 | 85 | 587 | 69 |
| Exclusion orders | 88 | 15 | 259 | 30 |
| With power of arrest | 278 | 47 | 282 | 33 |

[a]Percentage of applications granted.

*Source*: Figures supplied by kind permission of the Lord Chancellor's Department (Statistics Division).

number granted may be explained more readily by the attitudes and ideologies of local judges to domestic violence than by regional factors, as was suggested above. Comparing figures for the first four months of 1985 with the first four months of 1986 (see table 2.5 for the London area) suggests that the decision in *Richards* v. *Richards* might have had an immediate impact on the decisions made in the London courts during the months that followed. However, the impact seems not to have continued into 1986, when more ousters were granted.

In accordance with section 2(5) of the 1976 Act, a county court injunction may be enforced by the applicant/plaintiff making an application to the court for an order that the party in breach of the injunction (non-molestation or ouster) may be committed to prison. The onus is on the applicant to seek enforcement. Judges for their part possess a very wide discretion as to whether or not they consider a committal order to commit a man to prison where there has been a breach of an appropriate measure. Committals to prison are made for varying periods when there is evidence of persistent breaching of an injunction. The course frequently taken is to attach a power of arrest to an existing order if no power of arrest is currently in force, and where a power of arrest is in force to make a suspended committal order. In 1987, following applications to the court in connection with a breach of an existing injunction, 274 men were committed to prison, constituting 1.7 per cent of all orders initially made. This was a decrease over 1986, where 2.4 per cent of all orders resulted in a committal. Where committals are deemed appropriate and sentences upheld the degree of violence is usually extraordinary or the offender has been seen to be in persistent breach of the conditions of the injunction. In the case of *Mulligan* v. *Lake* (Court of Appeal, Civil Division, 16 November 1988, LEXIS Enggen), the defendant appealed against an order of imprisonment committing him to prison for 12 months for contempt. An injunction with a power of arrest had been ordered against him, and he had consented to that order being made. Yet:

> on 23rd July at about 2.30 in the morning the defendant forced his way into the plaintiff's premises and he there committed a very serious assault upon her. He jabbed her, although not seriously, with a knife; he threw her to the ground and knelt upon her; he attempted to stuff a coat in her mouth; put her undoubtedly in fear of her life, and threatened to kill her.

The police arrested him for breaching the injunction and the defendant was sentenced to 12 months. He appealed on the basis that the power of arrest originally attached was misdirected, since at the time the parties were not living together. The court accepted this, thereby reaffirming the limitation and scope of the interpretation of the 1976 Act, although the appeal against sentence was dismissed.

Similarly, in *Mesham* v. *Clarke* (Court of Appeal, Civil Division, 14 November 1988, LEXIS Enggen), a two-year appeal against sentence was dismissed. Here the appellant was in contempt for further assaulting the victim by striking her with a frying pan and kicking her in the legs. In this case the man had repeatedly flouted the order of the court over a period of two years. In addition, there were wide variations in committal from region to region. Figures for 1987 show that in the Midland and Oxford region 1.8 per cent of all orders granted resulted in a committal, compared to 2.9 per cent in the North Eastern region, 2.2 in the Northern region, 1.4 in London (no committal for the Principal Registry), 1.9 in the Provinces, 2.5 in the Wales and Chester region, and 0.9 in the Western region. These variations suggest that enforcement of injunctions is as inconsistent as the granting of a power of arrest.

### *Civil orders in England and Wales: the magistrates' courts*

In the magistrates' courts 'the public and private divide' is maintained and reflected in an even greater unwillingness to grant a power of arrest in unexpedited orders, and a similar disinclination to oust a man from his home. The Domestic Proceedings and Magistrates' Courts Act 1978, while it provided for an immediate hearing for the abused party in the magistrates' court is restrictive in its scope, applicable only where there is evidence of cohabitation and violence. The fate of applications made under this Act provides further evidence of women's often thwarted efforts to obtain any real protection within the home. The figures for 1984 in table 2.6 clearly suggest that a power of arrest is a remote possibility unless the order is expedited. Figures for 1985 reflect a decrease in applications granted overall, a decline that continued in 1986. The proportion of exclusion orders with powers of arrest seems to have been rising slowly, but the

Table 2.6 *Protection and exclusion order applications decided at magistrates' courts in England and Wales, in accordance with the 1978 Act*[a]

| | 1982 | | 1983 | | 1984 | | 1985 | | 1986 | | 1987 | |
|---|---|---|---|---|---|---|---|---|---|---|---|---|
| Type of application | No. | % | No. | % | No. | % | No. | % | No. | % | No. | % |
| s. 16(2) or 16(3), family protection or exclusion order | 5,740 | | 5,180 | | 5,800 | 68[b] | 4,420 | 65[b] | 4,160 | 65[b] | 3,720 | 65[b] |
| s. 16(6), expedited order | 2,940 | | 2,560 | | 2,680 | 31[b] | 2,350 | 35[b] | 2,190 | 35[b] | 2,040 | 35[b] |
| s. 18, power of arrest | | | | | | | | | | | | |
| (i) with protection or exclus. order | 960 | | 830 | | 860 | 15[c] | 820 | 18[c] | 840 | 20[c] | 670 | 18[c] |
| (ii) with expedited order | 1,320 | | 1,190 | | 1,230 | 46[c] | 1,150 | 49[c] | 1,190 | 54[c] | 1,110 | 54[c] |
| Total power of arrest | 2,280 | 26[b] | 2,020 | 26[b] | 2,090 | 27[b] | 1,970 | 29[b] | 2,030 | 32[b] | 1,780 | 31[b] |
| Total granted | 8,680 | | 7,740 | | 8,480 | | 6,770 | | 6,350 | | 5,760 | |

[a]Domestic Proceedings and Magistrates' Courts Act (1978).
[b]percentage of total applications granted.
[c]percentage of type of order granted.
*Source*: *Home Office Statistical Bulletin*, Statistics of Domestic Proceedings in Magistrates' Courts – England and Wales 1982–7, table 1, p. 6; Issue no. 36/86; Issue no. 17/87; Issue no. 20/88.

decline in applications granted suggests a reduction in the use of the magistrates' courts as a forum for resolving family violence.

The role of the magistracy in domestic violence cases is pivotal both in civil proceedings under the 1978 Act and in criminal proceedings under the criminal legislation. In considering the appropriateness of granting an application for personal protection, exclusion and/or power of arrest, the magistrate must apply his or her discretion in considering whether violence has occurred, whether there has been a threat of violence and whether an injunction is necessary for the future protection of the applicant. In granting a power of arrest the view is that the magistrates must be satisfied that an assault is likely to happen again.

Again, it seems to me that the wrong considerations are being taken into account. No one can crystal-ball-gaze and predict whether a man will reoffend. Men with previous records have proved that reoffending is a possibility and a likely outcome. Men with no previous record of violence are considered less likely to reoffend, but then every reoffender has been a first-time abuser. Such logic, which relies on magistrates' assumptions about the likelihood of reoffence, places women in great danger. The role of the courts should be what they claim it to be, namely to ensure the protection of the wife. The only way to protect women is legally to safeguard, as far as is possible, against an assault happening again, by attaching a power of arrest. At the moment the courts' line seems to be that we won't act to prevent a future occurrence, but we will come in after it has happened.

The statistics reveal on a national and year-by-year basis a dip in all civil applications in 1985. Such trends must be seen in the light of legal and non-legal influences, which inevitably have a bearing on the use of discretion in these cases. During 1985 case law decisions seemed to have a greater impact than the growing social and political concern about family violence and spousal assault. Substantive law has also been shaped by case law decisions in the Court of Appeal and in the House of Lords.

### *The case law in the Court of Appeal and House of Lords*

On the whole the courts have erred on the side of a cautious and mean application of the laws on domestic violence, reflected in the difficulty of obtaining ouster/exclusion orders and non-molestation injunctions and personal protection orders with a power of arrest. Case law trends since the 1976 and 1978 Acts reflect a continuing preoccupation with two quite different and irreconcilable concerns. While it has been the wife or female cohabitee who has turned to the law for protection from a violent cohabitee or spouse, the courts have been concerned with (a) whether it can ever be appropriate to exclude a man from his home and (b) whether the interests of children have been considered sufficiently or too much. The judgement in *Richards* v. *Richards* ( [1983] 1 All ER 1017 CA; 2 All ER 807 HL), rather than leading to a clarification of this difficult and ambigious area, cast it into further obscurity. In this case the wife petitioned for a divorce on the ground of her husband's unreasonable behaviour. Meanwhile, she vacated the matrimonial home and applied to the court for an order excluding him, so that she might return. Lords Justice Cumming-Bruce and Dillon in the Court of appeal considered her allegations of 'unreasonable behaviour' to be unfounded and trivial. Nevertheless, in spite of these findings, an exclusion order was indeed granted on the basis that the persistence of such a warring atmosphere was considered detrimental to the children's interests (see 1 All ER 1017 CA). The husband appealed against this decision to the House of Lords, where the ouster judgment was overturned. The Lords' reasoning had in the past produced a different judgment. Lords Hailsham, Diplock, Bridge and Brandon all voiced considerable concern over what they considered to be the potentially serious effect of the exclusion order upon the husband. They felt the order unjust, and argued that the Appeal Court judges had been wrong in reaching their judgment by prioritizing the interests of the children above the interests of the father. In making paramount the children's interests they were wrong in principle, and on this basis the order was overturned. Lord Scarman agreed that the order should be overturned, not because of the serious effect on the father of exclusion, but because of the effect on the children of losing a good and affectionate father (see 2 All ER 807 HL, at 817). In other words Lord Scarman in the House of Lords and Lords Justice Cumming-Bruce and Dillon in the Court of Appeal all put first the interests of the children, but reached different judgments, while Lord Scarman and the other Lordships reached the same decision via completely different routes. Hamilton has said (quite rightly) that 'it seems there are almost as many interpretations of Richards as there are courts' (1984: 25).

Both the decisions in *Richards* v. *Richards* and the introduction of the Matrimonial Homes Act 1983 (ss. 1 and 9) have had an impact on county court practice. Some courts in the wake of *Richards* seemed to return to a more rigid requirement of evidence of violence, paying scant regard to the original intention of the legislation which offered protection to women alleging 'molestation'. If the drop in applications for both non-molestation and exclusion orders observed for 1985 is a result of the immediate impact of *Richards* in some courts, then clearly it can be seen how the sentiment in *Richards* and later cases is at variance with the earlier precedent established in *Davis* v. *Johnson* ( [1978] 1 All ER 1132). In this case, Lord Salmon articulated the meaning of section 1 of the 1976 Act when he said that a paramour should not be excluded from the home or vicinity unless guilty of serious molestation (p. 1151). Lord Scarman took a wider and more robust view when he stressed that the aim and intention of the Act was to protect a wife or cohabitee from physical violence or the threat of it (p. 1156).

Case law decisions on exclusion orders reflect the sentiment expressed in *Richards* about women attempting to exclude men in order to acquire property rights, rather than the concern expressed in *Davis* v. *Johnson* for their protection from molestation. The decision in *Freeman* v. *Collins* ( [1983] 4 FL 649/13; FL 113) is an example. In this case the common law wife moved into the appellant's council house. He had used violence against her, and had been convicted and fined £80 in the Criminal Court. He was violent again, and the judge made an exclusion order, but the appeal against this order was allowed. Lords Justice Eveleigh and Dunn limited the exclusion order to one month, so that the housing authority would have time to deal with the woman's application. (It is well known that housing authorities considering an application arising from violence against a party take considerably longer than a month to decide on the case.) However, it is highly debatable whether the applicant was trying to acquire property rights; it seemed more likely that she was trying to get some form of protection. In *Wooton* v. *Wooton* ( [1984] 5 FLR 871; 15 FL 31) the female cohabitee applied for an exclusion order. Judge Slack refused on the grounds that the respondent's violence was involuntary as it occurred during epileptic fits. In the judge's assessment, immediate protection was not called for, since the last act of violence had taken place over a year before the hearing. The Court of Appeal upheld the judge's decision and dismissed the appeal. However, they did not agree with Judge Slack that the involuntariness of the violence constituted a sufficient reason to dismiss the applicant for exclusion. Instead they dismissed the appeal on the basis that the matter was a housing concern and the applicant did not in their view require urgent protection.

In the case of *Thurley* v. *Smith* ( [1984] 15 FLR 875; 15 FL 31–2) the woman left the joint tenancy after violence, and was living in refuge accommodation when she applied under the 1976 Act for an exclusion order excluding him from the joint tenancy so that she could reoccupy, or at least be rendered 'unintentionally homeless' in order that she might apply to be rehoused. She was refused, and on appeal, it was decided that the court should exercise its power on the principles stated in the 1983 Act and

Sir John Arnold granted a three-month ouster against the man. As the discussions in these cases tend to confirm, where the matrimonial home is a council tenancy, women frequently find themselves on a 'see-saw' between housing authorities who are reluctant to recognize them as genuinely homeless and judges who are reluctant to exclude a man from 'his' home. As Pearl expresses it:

> Emphasis on the housing situation, and on the declared position of the local authority, will invariably result in an ouster injunction either for a period of time or until further order. In contrast, emphasis on the interrelationship of the parties, and their behaviour toward each other, and the children, may well result in a refusal to grant the ouster order. So far as the woman is concerned, this result enables her to be treated by the local authority as unintentionally homeless. (1986: 29)

In the case of *Ryan* v. *Warne* (Court of Appeal, Civil Division, 12 May 1986, LEXIS Enggen) a non-molestation order and an exclusion order were made out against the respondent. In this case the judge made no finding of violence, but granted the orders on the basis that it was not in the child's interests to be subjected to the perpetual atmosphere of conflict which prevailed between the adult parties. The respondent took the case to the Court of Appeal, where the order was overturned on the basis that the child's interests had been prioritized, while the misconduct of the wife and the exemplary conduct of the father had not been sufficiently taken into account. But in fact it is very difficult to tell whether the judge in making the original order had ignored the conduct issue. He may well have endeavoured to consider all these facts equally.

In 1985, 1986 and 1987, in accordance with sections 1 and 9 of the Matrimonial Homes Act 1983, 1,602, 1,405 and 1,071 applications were made in matrimonial proceedings, and for these same years 504, 410 and 226 applications were made in non-matrimonial cases. The decline in applications from 1985 to 1987 suggests that the *Richards* case may have made an initial impact that declined over the years.

There is no explicit reference to violence in this Act, save a reference to conduct (s. 1.3), under which 'the court may make such an order as it thinks just and reasonable having regard to the conduct of the spouses in relation to each other.' The Act is primarily concerned with protecting the rights to occupation of husband and wife. The battered wife receives little protection, since her need for protection, and the subsequent exclusion of the violent or threatening party, may be incorrectly interpreted as a device used to secure a property advantage. The need for protection from a violent spouse or cohabitee is unavoidably connected with securing a property advantage. Unfortunately, case law has constructed applications for protection and exclusion as devious attempts to deny the other party property rights. Battered women need protection; protection requires separation; and separation must on occasion lead to exclusion. Even with the introduction of civil remedies offering protection from a violent partner, non-molestation injunctions and personal protection orders and orders for exclusion are difficult to obtain. The existence of civil remedies has served to divert cases of violence between family members, especially a husband's violence towards a wife, away from the criminal arena. Moreover, with the introduction of the Crown Prosecution Service (discussed in detail in chapter 6), together with the higher standards of evidence and proof now required in criminal hearings, a dramatic increase in the number of applications for protection in the civil courts might be expected. But if civil courts are also more stringent and cautious in their application of the law, it may well be that women will lose out on protection altogether.

The approach adopted in certain areas, circuits and courts to granting domestic violence orders reflects not only wide variability in judicial discretion but informal guidelines. For example, in July 1987 the North Eastern Circuit issued guidelines for interpretation of the 1976 Act in terms of orders for non-molestation and exclusion. 'It is submitted that the procedural vehicle afforded by the DVMPA 1976, by way of originating applications, is still appropriate for emergency protection including an exclusion order notwithstanding *Richards* v. *Richards* ( [1983] 2 All ER 807).' But it is not known to what extent other areas develop their own guidelines and hence 'styles' of legality in these matters.

The role of solicitors is crucial to an understanding of the regional variations in applications made for non-molestation injunctions and ousters. As the police feed cases into the criminal prosecution system, solicitors feed applications for remedy into the civil courts. So solicitors have a pivotal role in this process of civil justice, and are its translators and mediators (Smart 1984).

### Public remedies for public wrongs: criminal remedies

Violence committed against wives, cohabitees, girlfriends or lovers in the privacy of the home, unlike violence against strangers or acquaintances committed in private or in public, is rarely dealt with in the criminal courts. When made the subject of a criminal charge, violence against women intimates is frequently 'down-crimed', defined as an assault when attempted murder pertains, as common assault when assault pertains, or differently assigned as a crime of criminal damage or breach of the peace. There is still a tremendous resistance to treating such crimes in the same way as others, and many legal practitioners, including police, magistrates and the judiciary consider that the criminal court is not the appropriate place to resolve such essentially 'private' matters. In Britain the criminal remedies available for protection against a violent aggressor are to be found in the Homicide Act 1957, the Offences Against the Person Act 1861, the Sexual Offences Act 1956, and the Sexual Offences (Amendment) Act 1976.

*Homicide and violence*

Cases of spousal murder are provided for, as with murder generally, in accordance with the Homicide Act 1957. Under this Act the defendant, if he admits the offence, has three options. He can be convicted on a murder charge (s. 1), or of manslaughter (provocation) (s. 3) or of manslaughter (diminished responsibility) (s. 2). Most men convicted of wife-killing find a partial defence of provocation successful. However, where a woman killed her violent husband this defence was not successful. In *R.* v. *Duffy* ( [1949] 1 All ER 932) the court heard that a long course of violent conduct and the infliction of mental suffering did not amount to provocation, when she retaliated by killing him. The judge advised the jury: 'You are not concerned with blame here - the blame attaching to the dead man.' Interestingly, this very aspect becomes crucial when a husband kills a wife. In *Taylor* ( [1987] CA 9 CAR(S) 175) Chief Justice Lord Lane said at the appeal of Taylor against sentence for the manslaughter of his common law wife: 'More importantly and more immediately, Margaret Little had been in the habit of staying out late and she was not in the habit of disabusing him of the idea that perhaps there was another man in the background.'

While prosecutions for murder cannot, for obvious reasons, be avoided, prosecutions for assault and grievous bodily harm against wives, cohabitees or intimate female friends can (see chapter 4 for a further discussion).

In England and Wales figures for 1982 indicate that 458 men were homicide suspects, compared with 52 women. In 1983 there were 381 male suspects compared to 57 females, and in 1984 428 male suspects and 65 females. When males killed, they killed sons or daughters in 8 per cent of cases, parents in 5 per cent of cases, spouses in 23 per cent, other family members in 4 per cent, lovers in a further 4 per cent, friends in 32 per cent, others known to them in 3 per cent and strangers in 20 per cent of cases. By contrast, when women killed, in 48 per cent of cases they killed sons or daughters, parents in 5 per cent, spouses in 23 per cent, other family in 3 per cent, lovers in 2 per cent, friends in 14 per cent, others known to them in 3 per cent and strangers in 2 per cent of cases.

In 1985, 445 males, compared to 73 females, killed. Males killed sons and daughters in 7 per cent of cases, parents 3 per cent, spouses 22 per cent, other family members 3 per cent, lovers 4 per cent, friends 33 per cent, others known to them 3 per cent and total strangers 22 per cent. Females killed sons and daughters in 50 per cent of cases, parents 4 per cent, spouses 20 per cent, other family members 4 per cent, lovers 1 per cent and friends 15 per cent, others known to them 1 per cent, and strangers in only 2 per cent of cases.

From these homicide figures it can be concluded that violence against wives is a very common occurrence. It can also be seen that females are more likely to be victims of family violence, whereas males are three times more likely to be murdered by a stranger or unknown suspect. Yet, notwithstanding these facts, women continue to be denied adequate protection in the home because insufficient emphasis is placed on the importance of crime prevention there.

*Threats to kill*

Women also experience violence in the form of threats of violence and threats to kill. Such threats have been reported in several victimization surveys (Hanmer and Saunders 1983) and have also been a not untypical experience reported by women in refuges (Binney, Harkell and Nixon 1981; Montgomery and Bell 1986) and women in self-defence actions (Schechter 1982; Walker 1984). The courts have rarely recognized women's fear of threats of violence, or the imminent danger they may indicate. Proof of actual violence is required before such threats are recognized as real. In *O'Callaghan* ( [1987] 9 CAR(S) 1 187), where the offender had already proved his intentions by committing some damage, he was convicted of threat to kill a girlfriend, and a sentence of eighteen months' imprisonment was upheld. The appellant had a long history of convictions for violence. In the appeal of *Munroe* ( [1987] 9 CAR(S) 3 408) the appellant's sentence of three years' imprisonment was reduced to two years. Munroe had a history of violence against his ex-cohabitee (who left him because of his violent behaviour), and persisted in pursuing her with abuse and threats. On two occasions he threatened to kill her. 'On the first occasion he made verbal threats when he met her in the street with the children, on the second occasion he went to her home, made further threats and broke the glass in the front door of the house' (p. 409). The court held that 'the threats to kill, although frightening, were no more than words . . .' (p. 409). Yet those words were: 'I will never leave you alone, you know you can't get away from me . . . wherever you are I will find you . . . I will have you all . . . I will kill you all' (p. 409).

In most instances when such threats are made in a domestic context they are not taken seriously enough by the police or by the civil or criminal courts. I have already shown that the civil courts are extremely reluctant to grant a spouse any kind of order unless there is evidence of violence and in addition in their view that violence is likely to recur. And although *Criminal Statistics* for 1987 indicate that 671 men were proceeded against for threats or conspiracy to murder, most of these cases were outside the domestic context. However, it may be of some significance that since 1984 proceedings have increased significantly. There were 276 in 1984, and 442 in 1986.

*Assault*

The 1861 Offences Against the Person Act provides for the action of common assault under section 42, outlined earlier in this chapter. Section 47, an assault occasioning actual bodily harm, is triable, either way (either in the magistrates' court, or in the crown court), and is punishable on indictment with a maximum of five years' imprisonment. The government, in its White Paper on Criminal Justice (1986), proposed to replace the provisions of section 42 and the 'either way' offence of common assault (s. 47) with a new provision, allowing only summary trial of common assault with a maximum of 6 months' imprisonment and/or £2,000 fine. The Criminal Justice Act (1988) which followed may well result in the trivialization of domestic incidents even further. Interestingly, in a case in 1985 (*R*. v. *Harrow Justices ex parte Osaseri*, 81 CAR 306) the court explained the reason for limiting cases brought 'upon complaint by or on behalf of the party aggrieved' to summary trial. Section 42, the court explained, 'was intended to be reserved for cases of minor assault of the kind which commonly arises from disputes between neighbours'. Under the 1861 Act section 20 (grievous bodily harm) is punishable with a sentence of imprisonment for five years, while section 18 of the Act (grievous bodily harm with intent) carries with it a maximum sentence of life imprisonment. Prosecutions under any of the assault sections for spousal or partner assault are very few indeed. Even where there are such prosecutions, it is only occasionally that sentences are in any way comparable with sentences meted out to non-domestic violent offenders. And in cases that do come to court a history of violence is evident, almost without exception.

For example, in the case of *R*. v. *Dunning* ( [1984] 6 CAR(S) 337) a sentence of three years in prison was upheld for a man who stabbed his wife. She had left him, and was granted an order under the Domestic Violence and Matrimonial Proceedings Act (1976). In the case of *R*. v. *Buchanan* ( [1980] 2 CAR(S) 13) the court decided that where the wounding was with intent 'the courts must impose sentences appropriate to the gravity of the offence despite the domestic background', and a sentence of two years' imprisonment was upheld. Despite similar utterances, such sentiments have not always been honoured. The problem of inadequate, lenient and inappropriate sentencing is discussed further in the final chapter.

In the USA, too, most of the remedies open to a battered wife fall under the civil law (Martin 1976: 10). Should a wife wish to instigate criminal proceedings, the screening process ensures that her case will almost inevitably be transferred to the family court, where the family court judge will decide whether it should go before a criminal court. Many violent husbands are dealt with by a peace bond or protection order. Since 1983, with the introduction of Misdemeanour Arrest Laws, the police have been allowed to arrest (a) if the victim complains, or (b) if the police witness the assault. Evidence from Stith (1986) and Bowles (1986), and others, suggests that, despite clear changes in policy, policy officers are only using arrest powers when they actually witness assault (see chapter 6 for a fuller discussion). Certain states in America, however, have recognized the importance of separately recording assaults on wives. The State of Ohio has been compiling such figures since 1979. Despite attempts across the states to pass legislation that would compel the police to keep separate records on domestic violence reluctance is strong (Jolin 1983: 453).

### *Rape*

*Rape on known women* As Adler (1987) and Temkin (1987) have indicated, most rape is committed on women known to their assailant and not by strangers. This fact has always functioned to nullify the allegation of rape to varying degrees. Police have been reluctant to bring prosecutions, jurors reluctant to convict, and judges contrite in passing the most lenient of sentences, all excepting in cases of rape accompanied by an unusual degree of violence.

However, the sentencing guidelines in *R.* v. *Billam* ( [1986] 1 All ER 985; 8 CAR(S) 48) have undoubtedly had an impact on sentences for rape between acquaintances. In *Billam* it was held that a rape committed without any aggravation should carry a sentence of five years, and aggravated rape should be assessed according to the presence of the following features: (1) violence; (2) the use of a weapon; (3) the repetition of the rape; (4) evidence of previous convictions for rape and/or violence; (5) the addition of further indignities and perversions; (6) where the victim is young or old; (7) the effect on the victim both psychologically and physically. So far sentencing guidelines in *R.* v. *Billam* have had an effect on the decision in *R.* v. *Green* ( [1987] CA 9 CAR(S) 133), where a sentence of six years was upheld on a man who raped his ex-girlfriend where the rape was accompanied by violence. In this case Green had previous convictions for violence.

*Rape on a spouse* The remedies available for a wife raped by a husband are few in law and even fewer in its practice. The notion of spousal immunity persists in, among other countries, Britain, Italy, Spain and West Germany. In the Soviet Union, France, Australia, Canada, Poland, Sweden and the other Scandinavian countries wives have some measure of protection. In the UK, few cases are brought and even fewer cases successfully prosecuted. Edwards (1981: 32–3) has shown that husbands were exonerated for using violence on wives in pursuit of their right to sexual consortium. The exemption of rape within marriage in English law was further defined and clarified in the decision of the judge in *R.* v. *Millar* ([1954] 2 QBD 282) who decided that a husband could not be found guilty of rape but could be guilty of common assault. The charge of rape was dismissed. Judge Lynsley likewise decided that a husband who raped a wife could only be guilty of common assault. Feminist researchers and lawyers in the UK and USA agree that forced sexual intercourse in marriage is a typical component of domestic violence. Mrs Z, in giving evidence to the (UK) Report of the Select Committee on Violence in Marriage (1975) recalled one particular incident of violence, in which she was stripped and beaten severely with a wet towel by her husband and his friends. The committee asked whether she had ever been raped. Replying, she said: 'No, I had to give in to what they wanted because I was so scared' (p. 25).

Diana Russell has documented the extent of marital rape in the USA, 'finding that of 930 of respondents who had been married, 14 per cent reported being raped and beaten by husbands' (1982). And a US survey conducted by the National Council on Battered Women included marital rape (*Gwinnett Daily News*, 2 May 1986). Laura X of the National Clearing House on Marital Rape in the USA claims that one of every seven wives has been raped by her husband (personal communication; see Laura X).

In 1980 the (UK) Criminal Law Revision Committee in its *Working Paper on Sexual Offences* conceded that the present law may sometimes lead to a failure of justice where a husband lives apart from his wife (1980a: 11). The working paper recommended that rape in marriage should be an offence to be prosecuted only by the Director of Public Prosecutions (p. 15, para. 42). In its final report on sexual offences, published in 1984, the Committee took this position: 'We would like to see the present law extended so that a husband could be prosecuted for rape where he and his wife had ceased cohabiting with each other' (1984a: 17). Some of the sentiments expressed in these deliberations have been reflected in recent cases.

Case law has shown that sexually abused spouses can bring a charge of rape against the aggressor if a decree nisi is in force and a non-molestation order has been made. Nevertheless, the following cases indicate that only in the most exceptional cases of violence will a charge be brought, and then typically of assault. Only rarely will a husband be found guilty. In the case of *R.* v. *Caswell* ([1984] CLR 111), Caswell had attacked his estranged wife, 'kicking her in the face and ribs'. After this violence, he forced her to suck his penis and then subjected her to intercourse against her will. She submitted, fearing further violence. He was charged with assault and pleaded guilty. In *Kowalski* (*Independent*, 9 October 1987) the Court of Appeal convicted a man of assault and indecent assault on his wife after forced sexual intercourse and fellatio at knife-point.

Scottish law on marital rape has been a little bolder. The marital rape exemption does not exist there, as the case of *HM Advocate* v. *Duffy* ([1983] SLT 7) indicates. In that case Lord Robertson put into case law the sentiments mooted in the CLRC's 1984 Report.

> I can see no logic in justifying such a law by making a differentiation between a man and woman who happen to have gone through a ceremony of marriage and ones who have not, and I do not understand why the mere fact that the marriage bond has never been formally broken should make any difference. To some extent it might be a question of degree, but I do not think that it can be affirmed as a matter of principle that the law of Scotland today is that a husband, in no circumstances, can be guilty of the crime of rape upon his wife. (Williams 1984: 28)

Are women any better protected in jurisdictions where the law relating to marital rape has been considerably revised? In three states in Australia (South Australia, Victoria and New South Wales) the law on marital rape has been revised. In South Australia, since 1976 a husband is liable if he uses violence, or gross indecency. In Victoria since 1980 a husband is liable if the couple are no longer cohabiting, and in New South Wales since 1981 and Western Australia since 1985 a husband's immunity was removed altogether (in the Sexual Assaults Amendment Act 1981, s. 61A). However, few successful prosecutions have been brought (Naffin 1984). In Canada, in 1983, section 143 (Rape) of the Criminal Code was replaced by three provisions: s. 246.1, Sexual assaults; s. 246.2, Sexual assault with a weapon or causing bodily harm; s. 246.3, Aggravated sexual assault. Under the terms of the new Act, men may be prosecuted for sexually assaulting their wives (see Begin 1987).

In the USA the marital exemption rule regarding rape has also come under fierce challenge from feminists. In at least 30 states men have been put on trial for raping wives. The first prosecution of marital rape was in Oregon, in a celebrated case brought by Greta Rideout, but it resulted in acquittal. In 1984 William Edward Piper was given a 14-year sentence in Dade County for raping his wife, and Daniel Steven Warren became the first man in Georgia to be convicted of raping and sodomizing his wife while the couple lived together. As the National Clearing House on Marital Rape documents, up to 1984 there were 154 cases of marital rape; 100 have gone to trial, and 89 men have been convicted (see Laura X).

Feminist activists, campaigners and scholars have started out with an analysis of the substantive law as the basis of their critique. Many laws mirror and reflect patriarchal privilege, and while the relationship between law and the patriarchal state is not implacable, laws regulating rape and assault against wives/cohabitees in the home mirror some of the worst excesses of the permission of male power and control over women. As I have already stated, reforming the substantive law is a basic ingredient of the struggle to bring about some measure of equality. Challenging the myth of gender neutrality is part of the task.

# 3
# The Police Role: Using Discretion?

## Introduction

Police response to the problems of partner violence, rape, prostitution and pornography is governed both by the substantive law regulating these behaviours and by the substantive law that circumscribes police response to all law-breaking. Police conduct is thus not only the product of individual police attitudes, but is constructed in accordance with formal rules which provide the legal ratification for much of what they do. Traditionally, studies of police discretion have focused on informal rules and processes, such as stereotypes of offenders, victims and locations, as they affect policing practice (see Skolnick 1966; Sacks 1972; Sudnow 1972). But policework cannot be reduced to an analysis of informal processes alone, for it is the law itself that shapes police action and extends or limits the exercise of their discretion.

In this chapter two questions are addressed. First, it is important to consider the formal rules (substantive law) governing at one level the decisions of chief constables (chief officers of police), and at another level the rules that govern officers in front-line policework, i.e. those about arrest and charge decisions. Second, it is important to realize that the statutory interpretation of these rules has permitted a wide discretion in the exercise of police powers. The substantive law and the discretion of chief police officers and individual officers has contributed to a policing profile that has focused on street crime and public order and treated domestic violence as 'domestic' and inconsequential. This marginalization of domestic violence as an area for policing is a consequence of the independence of chief constables and the staunch preservation of the right of individual officers to exercise (or not) their powers of arrest. In the US it has been possible to introduce mandatory arrest laws (Humphreys and Humphreys 1985) in respect of domestic violence. Actions have been brought against police departments for failure to enforce (see chapters 5 and 6). No such actions have been taken here and the question of police accountability to women's needs and interests remains largely unaddressed. Given the considerable discretion of police officers this area of policing is determined more by sophistry than by a response to the reality of the violence.

**The independence of chief constables**

Chief constables' decision-making in policing matters is affected by legal rules which facilitate the maximum discretion. How rigorously particular laws are enforced is a matter decided by the police and not the courts or the electorate. The police continue to have exclusive authority over these decisions, since they are defined as 'operational matters'; the views of the local community have no legal weight.

The role of the police in deciding on matters of operational policing is circumscribed by case law. In 1985 in a House of Lords debate on provincial police forces Lord Chesham stated that:

> no police authority or anyone else has any authority to interfere in relation to the enforcement of the law by the police . . . full responsibility for enforcement is a matter which is reserved entirely to the chief officer of police. In the exercise of this responsibility he is answerable to the law alone, and not to any public authority. That is the position both in the Counties and in the Boroughs. (Hansard, vol. 213, col. 47, 8 December 1958)

This assertion supports the autonomy of each police force in the way in which the law is enforced. The chief constable is his own master, accountable only to the law. The Royal Commission on the Police in 1962 enshrined the concept of police independence and stressed further that the chief constable 'is accountable to no one, subject to no one's orders'. This 'divine right' was further espoused in the deliberations in *R.* v. *Metropolitan Police Commissioner ex parte Blackburn* ( [1968] CA 1 All ER 763), where this absolute and divine right of chief constables to complete discretion in policing matters was a principle firmly established in precedent. In April 1966 an instruction issued to senior officers of the Metropolitan Police had read 'Confidential Instruction: Gaming in registered or licensed clubs. For the time being all applications for authority for an inside observation in licensed or registered clubs for the purpose of detecting gaming are to be submitted to A.1 Branch for my covering approval' (768). In practical policing terms this meant that no proceedings were to be taken against clubs for breach of gaming laws. Mr Bearman for the Metropolitan Police explained that the expense and manpower involved in prosecutions of this kind 'were not justified'. This excuse seemed inadequate to Albert Blackburn, who thought the lack of policing of the clubs to be a blatant abrogation of the duty of the police. He, worried that the law was not being properly enforced, had written to the Commissioner asking him to assist in prosecuting several London clubs, and finally moved for a writ of mandamus against the Commissioner.

The Court held that:

> It was the duty of the Commissioner, as also of chief constables to enforce the law, and, though chief officers of police had discretions (e.g., whether to prosecute in a particular case, or over administrative matters), yet the court would interfere in respect of a policy decision amounting to a failure of duty to enforce the law of the land. (763)

Lord Denning, Master of the Rolls, deciding the duty of the Commissioner of the Police, opined:

> I hold it to be the duty of the Commissioner of Police, as it is of every chief constable, to enforce the law of the land. He must take steps so to post his men that crimes may be detected; and that honest citizens may go about their affairs in peace. He must decide whether or no suspected persons are to be prosecuted; and, if need be, bring the prosecution or see that it is brought; but in all these things he is not a servant of anyone, save of the law itself. No Minister of the Crown can tell him that he must, or must not, keep observation on this place or that; or that he must, or must not, prosecute this man or that one . . . It must be for him to decide on the disposition of his force and the concentration of his resources on any particular crime or area. (769)

Denning also stated that 'there are some policy decisions with which, I think, the courts in a case can if necessary interfere' (769), although we are not told which ones! Lord Justice Salmon similarly opined that 'the police owe the public a clear legal duty to enforce the law' (771). Notwithstanding these views, the appeal was dismissed for technical reasons, although at least Lord Salmon seemed to concede that the exercise of discretion over the gaming laws in this particular area was not properly applied. On the one hand, the judgment in *Blackburn* (1968) makes it clear that the discretionary decisions of individual officers, not the policy decisions of chief constables, are matters in which the court may interfere; on the other hand, there may be some situations (it seems *Blackburn* wasn't one of these) when the court would see it fit to interfere with chief constables' decisions if there was a failure of duty.

Blackburn, however was not satisfied with this judgment, and took the police to task over another apparent failure to enforce the law. On this occasion (*R.* v. *Metropolitan Police Commissioner ex parte Blackburn* and another [1973] 1 All ER 324) he alleged that the police had failed to enforce the obscene publications laws. Albert Blackburn and his wife Tessa, the parents of five children, were concerned that, although legislation prohibiting the publication of obscene material had been passed in 1959, the police had neither seized nor destroyed these publications. Blackburn contended that efforts to prevent the sale of pornography were largely inefficient. In Soho 'hard porn' was openly on sale and 'soft porn' was available in newsagents. The applicants were concerned that the Metropolitan Police

Commissioner was not carrying out his duty of enforcing the law unless and until the Director of Public Prosecutions authorized such action.

The court held that an order for mandamus should be dismissed, and stated that it would only interfere in extreme cases. Lord Denning reiterated his earlier view in *Blackburn* (1968): 'In the carrying out of their duty of enforcing the law, the police have a discretion with which the courts will not interfere' (331). Lord Roskill agreed: 'It is no part of the duty of this court to presume to tell the respondent how to conduct the affairs of the Metropolitan Police, nor how to deploy his . . . resources' (338).

While it was made clear that the courts *could* intervene in policing matters, it was also intimated that they would be unlikely ever to do so. So who can persuade chief constables that certain laws should be heeded and certain behaviours regulated? Can anyone? What role do police authorities have in such matters? What role does the Home Secretary have? Again, it is the substantive law that circumscribes the position of police authorities and the Home Secretary. The duty of police authorities, according to the 1964 Act, is 'to secure the maintenance of an adequate and efficient police force for the area' (s. 4(1)). Following the Scarman Report on the Brixton Riots (1981), police authorities were obliged to make arrangements for obtaining the views of people in their area. And in 1982 the Home Office issued a circular giving recognition to such consultative committees, which was later enshrined in the Police and Criminal Evidence Act 1984.

The role of the Home Secretary, in accordance with the Police Act 1964, is defined as the interpretation of legislation, that is, translating the spirit and intention of parliament into working police practice. Yet, as Jefferson and Grimshaw point out, the Police Act makes a clear distinction between operational and financial matters, and it is only in financial matters that police authorities, the Home Secretary and presumably consultative committees have a role to play.

> In the case of operational matters, whilst successive Home Secretaries have been prepared to offer advice and general guidelines (via the practice of issuing circulars on general principles and procedures in the operational field and to employ their powers to call for reports or initiate inquiries on any police matters, they have not felt it appropriate to take responsibility for directing the application of the criminal law in particular cases, or for issuing instructions with respect to general policies of enforcement and prosecution. (1984: 20)

If the substantive law in these case law decisions allows the police maximum discretion in operational matters, how far can police authorities or consultative committees influence policing, and the policing of marital violence in particular? Unlike in the USA, where successful actions have been brought against the police for under-enforcement in domestic assault cases, no similar actions would be countenanced in Britain (see chapters 5 and 6). There is no mandatory policy nor uniformity in treatment from one force to another.

In 1986 a Home Office circular on '*Violence against Women*', issued to chief constables in England and Wales, indicated some measure of concern regarding marital violence. The circular (no. 69, p. 3) read:

> The Home Secretary recognizes the difficult and sensitive issues which may be raised for the family and the police in cases of domestic violence, and that opportunities for intervention by the police may in some circumstances be restricted by the reluctance of victims to provide evidence. He believes, however, that there must be an overriding concern to ensure the safety of victims of domestic violence and reduce the risk of further violence, both to the spouse and to any children who may be present, after the departure of the police from the scene of the incident. Police officers will be aware of the powers of arrest which are provided in sections 24 and 25 of the Police and Criminal Evidence Act (1984) and of section 80 of the 1984 Act, which provides for circumstances in which the accused person's spouse may be a competent and compellable witness.

No specific guidelines are laid down here; it is merely a reminder to chief officers of existing legislation. Nothing is said about policy or operational matters. The Home Office circular has left no one in any doubt at all that the informing opinion in *Blackburn* (1968, reiterated in 1973) regarding the total independence of each chief officer to decide on operational matters is secure. The demands of contemporary British feminist campaigners, together with the view of the 1975 England and Wales Select Committee on Violence in Marriage, for a national police force policy, could not be forced on the police even if police authorities or indeed the Home Secretary urged such a move. However, a national police force policy might come to fruition, in the future, through influence on chief officers by their own 'union', the Association of Chief Police Officers (ACPO). Yet so far ACPO's line on spousal violence has served to ratify the existing permissive discretion and the wide variations between forces, though it has responded to recent attempts to revise the police response to spousal violence in a fairly positive manner (see Home Office 1986: appendix). They suggest that there is a need for all chief officers to consider a review of training and procedures. Training 'should include insight into the nature and potential of domestic violence, as well as seeking to establish that officers know, and are able to communicate to victims, the wide range of options available to them in law. Officers should be aware that police have been criticized for "non-interference" ' (p. 16), and, with due regard to difficulties, helpful and unhelpful approaches should include seminars and lengthier training programmes where use should be made of expert knowledge and Women's Aid workers. Chief officers will also be asked to review their record-keeping arrangements. But ACPO offers no national policy for arrests in cases where physical injury has been inflicted. Simply, officers are asked to review their instructions and to consider whether they adequately cover appropriate responses to domestic violence. But in any event, as ACPO makes clear, 'the appropriate response to any incident must rest with the judgement of the officers directly involved' (see Home Office 1986).

Research by Bourlet (1988) indicates that only 9 out of 43 forces have any policy on spousal violence; and those 9 are advisory rather than mandatory. Chief constables could make a substantive impact here, but sadly they won't. In the absence of such moves, patrol officers, investigating officers, charge officer, front line and middle management continue to police marital violence as they have always done. Some chief constables argue that it is not their duty or prerogative to interfere with the arrest decisions of patrol officers, yet they do direct their officers' priorities, as we saw above. A policy directive on marital violence would certainly create the appropriate climate for the desperately needed changes in policing on the front line.

### Influences on front line policework

Practical policework involves not deciding operational matters, but deciding when and where surveillance and arrest are appropriate. This is of course firstly a matter of finding and arresting law-breakers. As policework is also about investigating allegations and gathering the necessary evidence to sustain a prosecution, judgements about the sufficiency of evidence and the subsequent court outcome inevitably inform police action at the outset as well as in subsequent stages of investigation. (In March 1988 a new system of crime-screening was introduced, directing police to channel resources into dealing with crimes likely to lead to prosecution and conviction (see chapter 6).) Policework also includes moral judgements, involving stereotypes of likely suspects and the plausibility of complainants' allegations. It is inevitable that the use of police discretion in practical matters results in an over-enforcement of some laws and an under-enforcement of others but the nature of these inconsistencies is a cause for concern. Over-enforcement or under-enforcement are not arbitrary or unintended consequences of unfettered individual discretion, but the result of policy decisions or the lack of them. The systematic over-enforcement of law where suspects are black, underprivileged and powerless is the result of police culture, but the under-enforcement of law with regard to marital violence is also a matter of police policy.

As we have already seen, the substantive law facilitates different styles of policing 'proactive' in public order situations and 'reactive' in spousal violence situations. When an officer is called upon to use discretion in marital violence cases, his or her perceptions of seriousness, culpability, motivation and intent vary in accordance with the particular prevailing conceptions of likely suspects and credible victims. Policing in the absence of policy (or a policy of maximum discretion) facilitates the making of individual judgements, often based on erroneous stereotypes.

*Public order: suspicion and the over-enforcement of law*

Public order situations allow for great police freedom where the substantive law often requires police evidence alone. Police 'suspicion' of loitering, breach of the peace, drunk and disorderly behaviour, and obstruction of the highway is sufficient evidence of the offence. In an increasing number of offences the police have become the key initiators of complaints and the chief prosecution witnesses. Box refers to this as 'vigilante justice'; the police acquire the habit of charging 'certain people with offences for which there is no real defence, such as being disorderly, resisting arrest, using threatening behaviour towards an officer, and obstructing the highway' (1987: 153). Sacks's observations of the American police define this informal process:

> If one feels that it is strange that the rates of crime vary with suspiciousness of the police, one probably has in mind crimes of violence or robbery as typical crimes. And these might be expected to be reported by the public. However, such matters as gambling, prostitution, dope-selling, depend for being listed in statistics on the ability of the police to locate arrestable persons. (1972: 445–6)

Researchers have agreed that suspicious persons are more often than not 'the aspiring juvenile "tough" and . . . the big-haired, unkempt "hippy" ' (Matza 1969: 192). Piliavin and Werthman (1967) see people who are 'out of place' as likely to arouse a sense of suspicion. For Adams, a police chief himself, it is 'people who do not belong'. He writes, 'Watch out for the girl who is pregnant or late getting home one night; such persons are notorious for alleging rape or indecent assault, do not give her sympathy' (1963: 28). All these images are:

> founded on a series of background assumptions concerning what is expected or typical or 'out of place', what particular features of persons or places indicate suspicion, and finally if and when a crime has been committed, what features indicate 'normal crime' in the sense that

> explanations and motivations for crime methods and locations take on a common characterization. (Edwards 1984: 124)

Police training manuals in the UK and USA continue to perpetuate certain stereotypes about 'real' crime, 'real' victims and 'real' criminals. Powis writes that 'it is the policeman's task to identify criminal types. This acquired knowledge will sink into the sub-conscious mind' (1977: 1). And yet I have been assured by police training officers that recent training also attempts directly to challenge the stereotypes about blacks, the mentally handicapped and women. Despite this the police are continually criticized for the harassment of black communities and the impact of improved training on practical policing seems (so far) to be negligible: black people are still two to three times more likely to be stopped and searched than whites (Willis 1983: 14). Smith and Gray (1983: iv: 141) in their study of the Metropolitan Police found that the police defined 'black people with woolly hair' as suspicious!

Public order has always been a key concern of the police, and their legal powers to deal with this have been extremely wide. Historically, the Public Order Act 1936 (s. 5, breach of the peace) has allowed for the arrest and prosecution of persons whom the police consider to have breached the peace. The definition is wide and the offence requires no witness, while the allegation is almost proof in itself. Experience has shown that the use of police discretion here frequently violates and infringes the rights of the individual. But the problem presented little difficulty to the Royal Commission on the Police (1962: 123, para. 419): 'In carrying out their duties the police may have to revoke the rights and liberties of others, and sometimes be tempted to do so without proper cause.' The Royal Commission however also recognized the levity with which discretion could be applied. 'Clarification of powers will help but the principal safeguard must be found in the requirements for and stricter application of the criterion of reasonable suspicion.' Unfortunately 'reasonable suspicion' in policing has not been defined, yet it forms the very basis of most police action, and much of the UK legislative response to arrest is founded on 'reasonable suspicion', ratifying 'proactive' policing. The Royal Commission on Criminal Procedure (1981) was aware of the problems of the almost infinite interpretation of reasonable suspicion, but it also stated that it is none the less impractical or perhaps impossible to try to define it. Consider, for example, how the Criminal Attempts Act 1981 endorses this power. The repeal of the much maligned 'sus' laws served only to grant a new stamp of credence to what had gone on before. The Vagrancy Act of 1924 gave the police the power to arrest 'every suspected person or reputed thief ... loitering with intent to commit an arrestable offence'. In the nineteenth century these powers became a way of controlling and containing working-class men and women, the latter being frequently arrested on suspicion of prostitution (Edwards 1981: 57). From the 1950s onwards they were extensively used by some police forces (e.g. West Midlands), particularly those with a high immigrant population (see Foot 1969). The Criminal Attempts Act of 1981 endorsed the criminalization of 'attempting' to commit a crime, where evidence had to be 'more than merely preparatory' (s. 1). However, 'even though the facts are such that the commission of the offence is impossible' (s. 1(2)), a person may nevertheless be convicted.

The Police and Criminal Evidence Act 1984 (s. 1) represents a return to the legitimation of hunches regarding who is a suspicious person and what is a suspicious setting. In section 1 a police officer is given the power to 'stop and search' if 'he has "reasonable grounds for suspecting" that he will find stolen or prohibited goods' (s. 1(3)), or if he has 'reasonable grounds for believing' (a) that he does not reside in the dwelling, or (b) that he is not in the place in question with the express or implied permission of a person who resides in the dwelling (s. 1(4)). In this way the Act provides a general power to make investigative stops. The 'sus' powers under the Vagrancy Acts of 1824 and 1848, the Misuse of Drugs Act 1971, and the Criminal Attempts Act 1981, and more recently under the Police and Criminal Evidence Act 1984, ratify 'proactive' policing, sometimes with contentious results, as it seems inevitable that these powers will be used randomly, arbitrarily or indiscriminately. R. Reiner writes:

> Suspiciousness is a product of the need to keep a look-out for signs of trouble, potential danger and clues to offences, it is a response to the danger, authority and efficiency elements in the environment, as well as an outcome of the sense of mission. Policemen need to develop finely grained cognitive maps of the social world, so that they can readily predict and handle the behaviour of a wide range of others in many different contexts . . . (1985: 91)

Before the 1984 Act, police in London could detain persons for the purpose of search under section 66 of the Metropolitan Police Act 1839. Figures supplied by the Metropolitan Police to the Royal Commission on Criminal Procedure for July 1978 and January 1979 revealed a total of 40,477 stops for July 1978, and 32,298 stops for January 1979; 12–13 per cent of those stopped were arrested.

For example, in Operation Swamp in Brixton, in April 1981, '943 stops were made and 118 people arrested, out of which 75 charges resulted, many for offences such as threatening behaviour . . . only 22 persons were charged for offences such as robbery, theft and burglary (Christian 1983: 35). Carole Willis in her research (1985: 94) found police figures to be a series of understatements. In a detailed survey of the use of stop and search based on 'stop' records in four police stations, she found a variety of reasons for these stops: 're movements', 'suspected stolen vehicle', 'suspected possession of drugs' and 'suspected possession of an offensive weapon'; few were specific about the statutory power under which they were conducted (p. 101). The individual and subjective basis of discretion and 'reasonable suspicion' is further reflected by the fact that black men and women were much more likely to be stopped than any other racial group. Black males aged 16–24 were likely to be stopped particularly frequently (p. 100). Discretion can lead to self-fulfilling prophecies. The police expect certain persons or groups to be more likely to engage in unlawful activities than others, and this presumption influences policing, determining who is watched and subsequently arrested and entered into official figures. Similar proportions of other people may be committing crimes, but fewer of them are arrested and so the official figures show them as 'less criminal'. Police policy can thus contribute to the amplification of the view that certain people are more likely to engage in unlawful activity. The objective justification for a 'stop and search' becomes apparent after the stop, yet the initial stop is based on subjective intuitive hunches. Police accounting for conduct on paper does not always reflect the real motivational basis for stop; it may simply be that an officer just doesn't like the look of a person. After a stop and search the discovery of a penknife or similar item becomes the legitimation, after the event, for the search in the first place. Case law has shown that the carrying of a penknife or a pair of scissors, for example, would be sufficient to justify a 'stop and search' and a prosecution.

The case of *R.* v. *Dayle* ( [1973] CA 3 All ER 1151) is significant. Here a distinction was made between an 'offensive weapon' *per se*, e.g. a flick knife, and other items that could be used as weapons; here the prosecution must prove intent to use them offensively. The defendant had been convicted for assault and the possession of offensive weapons (a car jack and a wheelbrace). In this case the conviction was quashed. But it has been pointed that that in many cases intent can be too easily established by 'verbalizing'. Christian (1983: 22) cites the following series of questions and answers between the police and a suspect from the submission of the Haldane Society to the Royal Commission on Criminal Procedure (1981). This conversation was the prelude to the arrest and subsequent charge of a person said to be carrying an offensive weapon. The conviction was later quashed.

*Police officer*: Do you carry your penknife to fight with?
*Dayle*: No.
*Police officer*: If you were attacked would you use it?

*Dayle*: I suppose so.
*Police officer*: Do you think you may get attacked?
*Dayle*: Probably.
*Police officer*: So you might use it then in a fight?
*Dayle*: Yes.
*Police officer*: I am arresting you for being in possession of an offensive weapon.

Many people of course carry innocently items which could be described as 'offensive weapons'. One boy who was a 'snappy dresser was locked in a police cell for two hours for carrying a silver headed cane' (Christian 1983: 23). In such cases, while police stereotypes of crime and criminals provide the initial motivation for action, the vagueness of the formal rules legitimate these informal processes. It is also the formal rules which legitimate the shift towards 'proactive' policing in the public sphere, which is not reflected in the policing of marital violence complaints. That stop and search powers are said to be based on objective grounds according to 'reasonable suspicion' overturns the reality that suspicion is not objective. Lambert (1986: 147) argues that the low proportion of stops that lead to arrests is explicable on the basis that 'reasonable suspicion' was probably absent, and the legal requirements to articulate reasons for stops are at odds with the operational use of stop and search powers. The Criminal Justice Act 1988, s. 140(1), extends the powers conferred on the police by PACE. Stops can be executed in respect of an officer's reasonable suspicion that the person is carrying 'an article'. It no longer must be proved to be an 'offensive weapon'.

*Private order: under-enforcement*

While the police have the discretion to over-enforce certain laws, they also have the discretion to under-enforce them. Just as stereotypes affect street policing, so they affect the police approach to domestic violence, but in the latter case the result is less intervention, rather than more. This is particularly apparent in cases of private violence between family members or partners, especially spouses, where the protection of victims is influenced by private attitudes regarding sex roles, appropriate conduct and family ideologies. Police officers' decision-making, in all matters, operates in the context of legal procedure, evidential constraints, and police culture and attitudes, as we have seen above. D.J. Bell, commenting on the parameters of police discretion, claims that: 'society should maintain a constant vigil on any government agency that decries the necessity and claims the expertise to utilize deadly force, but abandons women and children to abuse, mutilation, rape, torture and death under the façade of police discretion' (1985a: 309). This contradiction lies at the heart of the policing of public and private order. In spousal disputes the police are neither a 'force' nor a 'service'. Their response, unlike in other categories of crime, is styled by the offender's attitude to the police and by police perceptions of the complainant.

In the same way as police officers subscribe to stereotypes about 'real' crime and 'real' criminals, conventional police wisdom similarly accommodates its stereotypes of real and legitimate or false and illegitimate victims. These particular assumptions about victims are sustained and perpetuated in wider social attitudes, medical cultures, police culture, and legal culture, attributing blame to some victims while exonerating others.

In addition, individual officers' decisions in cases of domestic assault are affected not only by the victim and the officer's perception of her role, but also by class and race stereotypes of both victim and offender, which shape his/her attitude about the likely guilt of the offender and innocence of the victim. For example, police may be less willing to protect poorer women and black women, whom they may perceive as less deserving and precipitative. Such commonly held views are conflated with perceptions of the normality of domestic violence between individuals in particular groups and social strata. Police officers generally come to regard domestic assault as a 'normal' occurrence in run-down inner-city neighbourhoods, where victims because of their powerlessness or culture may be seen to have forfeited their right to protection. For example, domestic violent assault committed against Asian women by Asian men is often seen as 'a family matter'. Police officers are caught here between the political tide which encourages respect for ethnic minority culture, understanding of the need for privacy and appreciation of the values of other communities, and the police role which requires officers to protect all individuals regardless of race or culture. This conflict often explains their lack of action when Asian women call for help. The view that spousal violence is related to alcoholism, to unemployment and to stress factors, too, continues to absolve middle-class men of blame for wife-beating, reinforcing the stereotype that 'real' wife-battering is related to race and social class alone.

Police training manuals in the UK and in the USA continue to reinforce such subjective judgements and stereotypes, despite the advent of more recent training programmes designed to counteract and challenge just these fixed perceptions. The belief that most domestic disputes are non-violent is affirmed in J. English and R. Houghton's police training manual widely used as a text book on police training: 'Basically police officers become involved because of their duty to ensure that there is no disturbance of the peace and, upon occasions, the forms of violence which are used are sufficient to cause serious injury if there is no intervention' (1981: 375). English and Houghton go on to state the popular characterizations of domestic disputes and violence as incidents confined to poor neighbourhoods, where the batterer drinks and where the victim, often if not always, later withdraws the charges. Binney et al. also found this message in training manuals and force instructions which insisted that 'the officer's role is to preserve the peace . . . in dealing with family disputes the power of arrest should be exercised as a last resort. The officer should never create a police problem when there is only a family problem existing.' (1981: 20) English and Houghton's instructions state that these situations require in the main the intervention of a social worker rather than the criminal law (p. 380).

In the United States, police training manuals have mirrored similar stereotypes. In a training guide by Frank Vandall the officer is required to assess the impact of his action on the offender rather than to respond objectively and protect the victim. 'Before invoking the criminal process however, the officer should consider several negative results that flow from such an action. The most serious factor to be considered is that the physical arrest record may contribute to the offender losing his present employment' (1976: 27). Police training manuals are not without a victimology which attributes blame to the victim; accordingly women who have been the subject of violent attacks occasionally become more aggressive when police officers arrive. It is precisely these attitudes which have led to the systematic under-enforcement of the law in dealing with domestic violence.

In both the US and the UK police policy-makers and senior officers recognize the importance and essential contribution good training has to play in the formulation of the police response. Indeed John Alderson has argued most forcefully for the recognition of the social services aspects of policing and an effort to tackle the underlying social causes of crime as well as the symptoms. Yet while senior officers argue for this progressive approach, rank-and-file officers have openly and vociferously resisted the service role. Tensions exist between senior management and the rank and file, and also within ranks, about the duties of the police in domestic situations. Evidence from the Metropolitan Police Department in its submission to the Report of the Select Committee on Marital Violence (1975) read:

> Whereas it is a general principle of police practice not to intervene in a situation which existed or had existed between husband and wife in the course of which the wife had suffered some personal attack, any assault upon a wife by her husband which amounted to physical injury of a serious nature is a criminal offence which it is the duty of the police to follow up and prosecute.

Yet it has also been pointed out by Scutt and others that 'the police are possessed of a discretionary power not to prosecute' (1980: 725). Discretion to arrest or to caution male violent and male sex offenders is influenced, to some limited degree, by a moral perspective: that is to say by the extent to which 'she' deserved it and whether 'his' behaviour was justified.

In assessing police handling notice of marital violence complaints, researchers agree that the protection of victims depends as much on their perceived (subjective criteria) as it does on legal evidence of assault (objective criteria). Oppenlander (1982), in a study of 596 police investigations of arguments and assaults drawn from 5,688 observations of patrol officer and citizen encounters, found that officers often did not arrest, although there were legally objective grounds for doing so. McLeod claims the prioritization of such moral judgements above legal criteria: 'Individual officers' biases and perceptions of spousal assaults perhaps play the major role in shaping law enforcement response to domestic violence' (1983: 397). The Women's National Commission in London, in their report on *Violence Against Women* have similarly espoused this view:

> Perhaps the greatest fault in the traditional police response to domestic violence is not best described as an unwillingness to act, but over-willingness to assume the 'judgement of Solomon'. There is evidence that police do have judgemental attitudes to the behaviour of women victims which they may consider contributory to the man's violence e.g. if they think the woman is 'nagging', hysterical', or 'a sluttish housewife'. (1985: 52)

Chatterton (1983: 211) also recognizes the prevalence of this tendency not to enforce the law in practical policing. Banton argues cogently that, contrary to police claims that they are governed by the rule of law (discussed in chapter 2), they are, more often than not, 'governed much more by popular morality . . .' (Banton 1964: 146). This 'popular morality' is saturated with particular views regarding gender; as Stanko found:

> Decisions to arrest or not to charge a suspect with a crime, decisions to charge a suspect with 'disorderly conduct' rather than assault, or decisions to refer 'incidents' of male violent behaviour to the social services instead of the criminal court all affect how men's threatening or violent behaviour comes to be defined as criminal or non-criminal . . . (1985: 104)

As Chatterton explains further, the legal victim did not always prove to be a moral victim. He develops a model in which he identifies the four combinations of these tendencies in which the legal evidence and constructs of moral blameworthiness are in accord or at variance, and shows the impact this has on arrest decisions (figure 3.1). Chatterton

| From a moral perspective | | From a legal perspective: Should be arrested | From a legal perspective: Should not be arrested |
|---|---|---|---|
| | Should be arrested | Type 1 | Type 4 |
| | Should not be arrested | Type 3 | Type 2 |

Type 1 evidence is sufficient to arrest and suspect is morally blameworthy

Type 2 evidence is insufficient to arrest and suspect is not morally blameworthy

Type 3 evidence is sufficient to arrest but suspect is not morally blameworthy

Type 4 evidence is insufficient to arrest but suspect is morally blameworthy

Figure 3.1 *Arrest decisions: moral and legal perspectives (Chatterton 1983: 210)*

discusses in some detail one case he attended where the moral blamelessness of the husband and the moral blameworthiness of the wife governed the officer's decision not to arrest from a moral perspective, though from a legal perspective evidence for arrest was more than sufficient. In the case in question a neighbour reported the incident to the police. The wife's visible injuries consisted of a swollen lip and a swelling under the eye. She stated that her husband had attacked her and that she was prepared to make a statement and testify in court against him. Admitting the assault, the husband said that he had given her a 'banjoing' but that she had asked for it. He explained he had been out at work all day, since 6.30 am, and when he came home his children had not had tea and did not know where their mother was. The police officer noted that 'there was no fire in the place despite the fact that it was a cold night, and the unwashed breakfast pots were still on the table. There was a bundle of dirty washing in the corner of the room ...' (pp. 211–12). The police officer took the woman into the front room and talked her out of her complaint. The husband was given a warning and the officer entered the incident in his pocket book and in the Charge Office Journal. The entry read 'Domestic dispute. Parties advised.' The officer in conversation with Chatterton explained his decision not to arrest by referring to the moral characteristics of the father, whom he considered a good worker and provider, counterposed against the mother who kept a slovenly home and was difficult and 'mouthy'.

Smith and Gray also found evidence in their survey of police officers (1983: iv. 100) of the interference of a moral perspective in the policing of domestic violence disputes. In general, assaults or threats of assault seem to invoke sympathy and concern from police officers if the victim is thought to be weak or defenceless, but not if she is thought to be strong or not entirely blameless. Similarly, in the investigation of rape complaints the use of discretion had led to an under-enforcement of the law. Here, as in domestic violence complaints, men are frequently exonerated and women blamed because a moral rather than legal perspective intervenes.

Chambers and Millar (1983) found that in the investigation of rape complaints aspects of 'her' moral character weighed heavily on the police assessment of her credibility and affected their subsequent decision about whether to prosecute. Credibility was established by assessing (a) her way of life, (b) her respectability, and (c) her criminal record. They discovered that the police officer's general orientation is not really conducive to a fair handling of complaints of rape and victims in considerable distress (p. 81). Quoting W.B. Sanders (1977), who writes:

> In developing information, detectives encounter sources they take to be possibly unreliable. They meet people who intentionally lie about themselves or others. This, they believe, is to be expected since the lies may enable the teller to avoid legal sanctions. Further, detectives believe that even well-meaning witnesses tend to be inaccurate in their description of people, things and events . . .

Chambers and Millar agree that this orientation may be positively damaging, as officers are naturally sceptical. 'I am of the opinion that Mrs M. is an inveterate liar and quite capable of inventing such a story' (pp. 82–5). As Chambers and Millar (p. 87) were soon to discover, police dichotomize incidents into 'good' and 'bad' cases, based not just on the legal features of the case, but (as Chatterton describes in his discussion of assault cases) in accordance with the character of the complainant. Thus the moral perspective rather than the legal perspective prevails. Cases which were considered 'good' or 'real rapes' consequently exhibited, firstly, overwhelming evidence from a legal perspective, and secondly, a 'blameless' complainant (the moral perspective). Listed below are some of the criteria necessary to a 'real' rape.

'respectable' complainer attacked by stranger(s);
complainer is severely beaten up;
complainer is attacked by assailants wanted by or known to the police, for crimes of violence (especially if against women);
assailant uses weapon;
assailant apprehended at scene of crime.

Le Doux and Hazelwood (1985), in their study of police attitudes and beliefs towards rape in the USA, found that, while officers are not typically insensitive to the plight of rape victims, they nevertheless remain suspicious of women who have had a previous relationship with the assailant, and women who 'provoke' rape through their appearance or behaviour. The researchers found, too, that some officers still agree with the statement that 'Nice women do not get raped', or 'Most charges of rape are unfounded.' The stereotypes of 'real' and 'legitimate' victims, as opposed to undeserving illegitimate victims operate not only in a conceptual framework of patriarchy, but against a backcloth of imperialist and racist assumptions. Untried and untested assumptions prevail in popular legal, police and everyday consciousness, which uphold class divisions, white supremacy, and the superiority of 'civilized' culture. For example, black men are considered innately more aggressive, more sexual and more lacking in self-control than whites; the demands of Asian culture require the submission of women and exonerate male control in all its forms. Black and Asian women lose out on protection because of racist and cultural perceptions, but they lose out even more because their protection is seen as of lesser importance. Angela Davis indicates the dilemma of black women seeking protection: 'If black women have been conspicuously absent from the ranks of that contemporary anti-rape movement, it may be due, in part, to the movement's indifferent posture towards the frame up rape charges as an incident to racial aggression . . .' (1982: 173) (i.e. the stereotyping of rape as being by black men on white women). These moral aspects considerably dilute and compromise legal rules, which take second place to decisions about blameworthiness.

### Police perceptions of their role

The substantive law provides a framework within which the police operate and use their discretion. There are two distinct approaches among those who want to see better protection for women in domestic assaults. First, there are those reformists and Left realists who argue that officers' discretion in decision-making can be influenced by training, 'designing-out' stereotypical attitudes.

Second, other argue that the police respond to formal rules; hence changing formal police policy on relevant issues is the only way of changing police behaviour. In North America well-established research traditions have examined the impact of policy on police attitudes and practices. One, focusing on police policy on deterrence, is examined in chapter 6. Another, which focuses on changing police attitudes through training programmes, has been explored by Berk and Loseke (1981), Walter (1981), Homant and Kennedy (1985), Stith (1986) and Breci and Simons (1987). These studies have examined the perceptions officers hold of their role in calls to domestic violence, and the effect this has on policing strategy. Walter starts from an interactionist standpoint, evaluating the perceptions and practices of officers in their response to domestic violence. He explains:

> Important in determining how the domestic disturbance call will develop, is the perception the officers hold of their role in such calls. Individuals do not simply respond to stimuli they encounter, instead, they construct a definition of the situation which places all events into a perspective based on their orientation towards the world and the manner in which they perceive their position in everyday life. (1981: 43)

Walter interviewed 41 officers who handled domestic disturbance calls in a small north-eastern city in the USA with a population of 75,000. He examined the perception officers had of such calls and the policy strategies they subsequently adopted. He investigated every domestic disturbance which was called into the station during a one-month period (there were 56) and matched each call up with the officers handling the case. Family members were also contacted (78 of them) and interviewed. The study revealed that officers believed that alcohol was a significant factor in the occurrence of violence, and indeed often a cause of it. Furthermore, officers believed that alcohol abuse was a family problem, since wives were often seen as the initial cause of husband's drinking, or at least at fault for being with the drinker! 'I will tell you what the problem is, they [the wives] want to blame anyone but themselves. Very frequently it is the wives' fault, to this extent; they marry those people that they know are drunks' (p. 246). A large percentage of officers did not believe that they should intervene in family disputes unless actual violence was committed. Walter found that officers disliked these calls and, having family problems of their own, strongly identified with the conflict family.

> *Walter*: How do you feel about these calls?
> *Officer*: If there is no violence, I feel that it is just a private matter and I have no right being there. I know that I have my own problems with my wife and I settle them myself. I wouldn't want anyone else to butt in. That's the way I feel about other people. Even if I threaten my

> wife – which I don't usually do – I would not consider that sufficient reason for somebody to butt in; because I wouldn't really do my wife any harm, and I think that's true of nearly all of these husbands. They are really no different from me or anybody else. (p. 247)

Contrary to these police officers' commonsense impressions of the triviality of such cases, as the statistics for homicide in chapters 2 and 4 demonstrate, it is just this kind of 'trivial' family disturbance that escalates into serious and grievous violence and homicide. Walter found that during the year there were four murders in the city, in which wives who had been repeated targets of their husbands' violence retaliated and killed their tormentors. He identified three styles of policing in domestic disturbance calls: (a) para-marriage counsellor; (b) referee; (c) not legitimate. The 'para-marriage counsellor' officer spent a lot of time at the disputant's home. Often the officer would drive the husband round in the squad car until he 'cooled off'. The majority of officers, however, saw counselling as way beyond them and outside the policing function. Their role was one of peace-keeping 'referee' (p. 15). 'I just go in as a neutral observer. I try to reason with the people' (p. 253). Finally, over four-fifths of the officers believed they had no legitimate role at all to play in domestic disturbance. Domestic calls were nuisances to be avoided. 'Now this is the worst call I get – domestic disputes. I hate to get a call like that!' (p. 2).

Evidence from other researchers similarly suggests that domestic calls are the most stressful and frustrating. Some interesting work in the United States, examining police perceptions of their work role and individual attitudes, and personal stress and its impact on action and response to domestic violence has been investigated by Sandra Stith (1986). Stith argues that, while police officers have a unique opportunity to assist victims and to intervene in the cycle of violence, in most cases this opportunity is thrown away. Stith tested seven hypotheses:

1. Whether police officers with violence and conflict in their own marriage respond more negatively.
2. Whether police officers who approve of men controlling women respond more negatively.
3. Whether police officers who are more sexist respond more negatively.
4. Whether police officers who report more stress in their lives respond more negatively.
5. Whether police officers with more stress in their marriage respond more negatively.
6. Whether younger and more educated officers respond less negatively in sum.

7 Whether 'The police officer's response to victims of domestic violence is predicted from his age, education, reported level of stressful life events and mental stress, his attitude towards mental violence and his use of violent conflict tactics in his own marriage' (p. 8).

Stith distributed questionnaires to 240 law-enforcement officers in three sheriff's and four police departments in north-east Kansas. The final sample, excluding those who did not respond and those who did not meet the research criteria, was 72 (p. 9). Stith found that personal approval of marital violence by officers is significantly related to anti-victim response, and the more an officer believes that violence in marriage is justifiable or acceptable the more likely he is to respond negatively (p. 16). Stressful life events, marital stress, age and education did not significantly affect police response.

In a later study conducted by Breci and Simons (1987), data were collected from four law-enforcement agencies. Questionnaires were distributed in each department to officers on all three shifts dealing with domestic disturbances, and 242 were completed. The findings were that officers were against the introduction of tougher laws, and were only more likely to arrest when department policy actually backed up training in this direction.

*Policing domestic violence: a study in London and Kent*

As described in the Introduction, the author, Armstrong and others conducted a study of police attitudes to spousal violence at two divisional police stations in the Metropolitan Police District and one divisional station in Kent (Edwards 1986b; Bourlet 1988). Interviews began in November 1984 and continued throughout 1985 and into January 1986. Sixty-two men and women were interviewed, including officers from patrol duties and criminal investigations, ranking from police constable to inspector. Respondents were encouraged to disclose attitudes to, and experience of, policing domestic incidents and assaults. Interviews lasted from one to two-and-a-half hours. The purpose of the interview was to examine those 'subjective and situational' contingencies that an officer's discretion in (a) responding to the initial call, (b) attending at the scene, and (c) the subsequent investigation and prosecution. The police officers' perceptions of spousal violence incidents tended to reflect both private and organizational attitudes to violence in the home. Spousal violence, where assault occasioning actual bodily harm was apparent, was considered a private matter, and it was expected that the complainant would in any event withdraw her allegation.

Reiner, in his investigations of policework, found that 'Domestic disputes are a common sort of call regarded as "rubbish" by many police officers; "with domestic disputes, the husband and wife going hammer and tongs, you have got to separate them, calm them down before you go. And you are not doing a policeman's job, you are doing a socialist's [*sic*]" ' (1985: 95). Front line officers in the London and Kent interview survey similarly saw domestic disputes as low status work. Most patrol or beat officers held negative attitudes towards it. Some said that police officers should not be involved in what was essentially, 'a waste of time'! Although most officers formally accepted intervention in marital violence calls as part of their role, their own privately held attitudes reflected feelings of reluctance, frustration, ambiguity and disdain for 'service' work. 'It depends on your attitude to policework and whether we should be chasing hardened criminals or offering a service and helping people' (Officer no. 1 DK); 'A lot of them are a load of crap and a waste of time' (Officer no. 4:1:48).

A minority of patrol and beat officers and most CID, middle management and senior officers held a rather more serious view, or else verbalized one. 'Society in general tends to knock the arse of domestics saying "it is only another bloody domestic", then again they say, it is only a shoplift, but it is still a theft, then again a domestic can become a murder, as I know only too well' (Sergeant no. 10:5:54). In the case that follows, although the woman was seen as the aggressor there was no doubt in this officer's mind of the disastrous course of some so-called 'domestic incidents'.

> It wasn't the first time that she assaulted him, but there he was, nearly dead. But he refused to prosecute, when we saw him in hospital. What had happened was that he had arrived home drunk, argued and threw a bowl of water over the wife, and she in anger just broke and stabbed him . . . she had had enough . . . we fully expect a murder in that house one day. (Officer no. 18:1)

Rank-and-file officers felt ambivalent, understandably so as they were not always wanted at the scene, particularly if the aggressor was still present. 'You get a piggy in the middle feeling at times, you get let in, but none of the parties are pleased to see you' (Officer no. 1:1:1). 'When we got to the address, they did not want us in. The woman had cuts on her arms . . . the man present was trying to bandage her up. They more or less told us to clear off, in fact they said "fuck off" ' (Officer no. 13:1). The ambivalence and consequent negative response of the police to spousal or partner violence cases arise, then, not simply as a result of ideological views about the triviality of the private sphere, but from certain practicalities of the task. Feeling they can't intervene helpfully, police frequently respond by withdrawing from these situations, rather than intervening further and trying to restore some peace. In street violence the police also encounter the problem of complainants' later reluctance to give evidence or otherwise co-operate further. This difficulty, however, does not deter police from making arrests. A key difference is that while police 'enjoyed' dealing with street crime, domestic violence was seen as a bore. This attitude was enhanced among rank-and-file officers in the absence of clear guidance and example from senior management (some of whom held contradictory views). One officer straight from training school felt particularly uneasy about handling this type of call. His unease resulted not only from the instrinsic difficulties of dealing with spousal and partner violence cases, but also from the contradictions and tensions between the styles of policing advocated at training school and the styles found at divisional stations. At the end of the day, survival for the young officer meant accountability to his station sergeant rather than loyalty to the *mores* of training school or progressive policing. Describing the intrinsic difficulties of such calls, one young officer remarked: 'It is very frustrating that we get sent to some of them in the first place . . . and it is infuriating when the same woman calls us weekly, but is still living there, and also when they withdraw charges' (Officer no. R1:45:5).

*Non-enforcement of the criminal law* As Chatterton has argued 'one of the most extensively documented facts about police work is that police under-enforce certain laws and jealously protect the discretion which that implies' (1976: 113). The exercise of discretion in arresting an offender for breaching a civil non-molestation injunction or for committing a criminal assault on a wife or cohabitee is influenced, according to the officers interviewed in the London study, by the seriousness of the injuries (legal, objective, *prima facie*) and by the preparedness of the complainant to prosecute (legal procedure). As I have already shown, these judgements are made in a context where moral considerations regarding blame and justification and family ideology come to influence the police decision. Turning to the seriousness of the injury, this consideration is necessary, but not sufficient to result in an officer making an arrest, while the willingness of the complainer to press charges was regarded as of foremost importance. In the absence of complainer commitment, the police initiated independent action only when the violence inflicted was unusually severe (here the public interest factor presided), or when the aggressor had threatened the police and behaved belligerently. In the latter case the object of the arrest was not to ensure protection of the complainant, but to enforce public subordination and compliance with police authority.

When officers decided to take no action, this was the result of a presumption of complainer withdrawal, and this presumption was stronger when the parties concerned were cohabiting. In the London/Kent study there were *no* formal prosecutions where spouses or cohabitees were living together. The presumption of complainer withdrawal resulted in the emergence of four distinct policing styles, all favouring the avoidance of criminal law remedies: (a) non-arrest; (b) deferring police recording during 'cooling off'; (c) using other sanctions, such as 'breach of the peace'; (d) recourse to civil remedies. Table 3.1 shows the frequency of each style among the sixty-two officers questioned.

First, officers expressed a reluctance to arrest in domestic cases, presuming a later withdrawal which would then negate all the work that had been done. This presumption was based on informal advice from other officers, as well as personal experience.

> There is a lot of work and you take statements, make a pocket book entry, nick someone, then there's the worry of everything being tickety boo for court, that takes about 16 hours; only for the husband or wife to say thanks but no thanks. You think all that bleedin' 'ard work is going out the window. (Officer no. 3:4:57)

> There are a lot of officers who lose interest when she says that she docs not want to prosecute. (Officer no. 19:1)

> If he has beaten her up and she is willing to charge, we will arrest him. At the station, she will often withdraw. (Officer no. 14:1)

> In the ambulance on the way to the eye hospital, she told us she wanted him prosecuted. We got a statement from her. We arrested him, he was remanded in custody, but one week later she withdrew the complaint. (Officer no. 18:1)

> I am reluctant to arrest, usually because of the withdrawing. It creates a hell of a lot of work for no good reason. (Officer no. 22:1)

Table 3.1 *The effect of individual police officers' perceptions of likely complainer withdrawal on styles of policing in the London and Kent study, 1984–1986*

| | Effect on police response | | | | | | | |
|---|---|---|---|---|---|---|---|---|
| | | | (c) Other measures | | | | | |
| | (a) | (b) | | | (d) | | | |
| Police area | No arrest or prosecution | Delay action | Breach of the peace | Criminal damage | Civil remedy | No effect | No answer | Total |
| London[a] | 15 | 6 | 4 | 1 | 8 | 4 | 6 | 44 |
| Kent[a] | 7 | 2 | 2 | nil | 1 | 4 | 2 | 18 |
| Total | 22 | 8 | 6 | 1 | 9 | 8 | 8 | 62 |

[a]These are two Divisional police stations in the Metropolitan Police District and one in Kent.

*Source*: Edwards 1986b; Bourlet 1988.

Other officers referred to the practical limits to the use of arrest in domestic cases.

> We arrested him, got to court, he got weighed off in court and the next day he's back living in the house. You think what's the bloody point. (Officer no. 9:2:53)

> After an argument . . . the husband who has struck his wife has in my opinion lost control of himself by hitting her. The wife is protected by the law but it is seldom practical to arrest the husband. (Officer no. 4:1:48)

Some divisions in London respond to the difficulty of complainer withdrawal by the routine use of the 'no crime' (see chapter 4). From a policing point of view, this seems the best way to deal with a complaint made but later unsubstantiated. The advent of the compellability provision in the Police and Criminal Evidence Act (1984) may have some impact on the use of the 'no crime', although this is likely to be limited.

Why do women make a formal complaint, make a statement, sign a charge sheet, and then some while later withdraw the allegation? Many women explain their withdrawal in terms of feelings of fear, powerlessness, and helplessness (see chapter 5) but the police generally had other perceptions – which influenced their attitude to the victim concerned. Police explanations for withdrawal emphasized woman's fickleness, rather than her fear of further violence, homelessness and poverty, all of which frequently follow if she takes legal steps to protect herself. The majority of police officers interviewed were unable to understand how, as one officer put it, 'She screams she wants him nicked, then the next day she wants him back' (Officer no. 1:2). The kind of pressures that prevented a nineteenth-century woman from prosecuting the man she lived with, both economic and emotional, persist today. Senior officers were more open to the argument that women withdrew complaints because of fear.

> I have known strangulations happening, then, on reflection, the victims change their minds and back out, perhaps it is the fear of attending court . . . then of course there is the fear of retaliation. (Officer no. 2:4)

> A case at . . . we will always remember involved a man who had knocked 'seven bells of whatsaname' out of his wife and he was still going bananas when we got there. In fact, it was touch and go whether the wife died. The beatings she had had on the head . . . we thought she would be left a cabbage. The wife was in such a bad state the hospital would not let us get near her. Later in that day she made a withdrawal! (Officer no. 33:2)

Although, as we have seen elsewhere, the anticipation of the complainant's withdrawal is the major reason given by police to justify their own reluctance to prosecute, many indicated that when the couple are living together, they regard prosecution as 'morally', though not 'legally', inappropriate. One officer explained:

> Normally, it is when the husband and wife are estranged and the husband has broken in, in some way. If they were living together I would only arrest where there was a GBH or danger of the violence continuing or getting worse. (Officer no. 7:1)

In practice, though many situations contained the potential of escalating after the police had left, the police still displayed considerable unwillingness to act. The only type of situation that resulted in arrest in this study, as with others, was one in which violence continued after the police had arrived or the aggressor was 'stroppy' with the police. Officers relied on their own presence and ability to calm things down. If these attempts failed, arrest would follow, but even then the arrest might not be for assault. One officer explained:

> I seldom arrest, and I use Breach of the Peace if I can get them out of the house. Inside the house is more difficult, but I would arrest if fighting was likely to continue in my judgement. Actually, I have always been able to calm things down, maybe I have just been lucky. (Officer no. 8:3)

Another officer reiterated this sentiment, saying that those charged would not necessarily be charged with assaulting a wife. This officer said that he had used the power of arrest once in a 'domestic'.

> only once, he was hitting the wife, breaking things, making allegations against the children. There was no way I could leave him there. (Officer no. 9:1)

But he did not arrest for assault:

> . . . so it was a criminal damage arrest.

Why do the police not arrest for the crimes committed? One sergeant explained that the possibility of a complainer withdrawal was a major influence here too.

> *Interviewer*: Do you think the perceived possibility of complainer withdrawal might influence the way in which you deal with a case?
>
> *Sergeant*: Well, yes. From that experience you try and find other ways and means of dealing with the situation without involving the wife as witness.
>
> *Interviewer*: What other ways do you have of dealing with such incidents?
>
> *Sergeant*: Well there is threatening behaviour for one, or if the incident happens in the street you can use Breach of the Peace. So you might encourage the man into the street. Of course if we charge him with threatening behaviour, for example, that does not prevent the wife substantiating a charge of assault at a later stage. Breach of the Peace is very useful to us indeed. First, it does not involve the wife as witness and secondly it allows for a cooling down period by getting 'chummy' to court. (Officer no. 33:15)

These sentiments were reiterated by another (female) officer:

> Breach of the Peace can often be used to remove the man from the home: it really is a safety net when there is nothing else you can actually do, but you feel that there is a need to give the woman some further protection. It does remove him from the house and it means we can lock him up overnight. (Officer no. 23:2)

Chatterton (1976) found that police often used the law to achieve ends other than arrest for the crime committed, referring to the practice as 'resource charging'. The London study found the same practices: one officer remarked:

> Domestics are not really criminals, so Breach of the Peace enables us to detain the man overnight, allowing a cooling off period on both sides. (Officer no. 31:3)

> The majority of domestics you go to . . . most want someone to talk to, they have a moan and then think we've done a wonderful job. You're not looking for an arrest at a domestic. You are looking to sort it out. (Officer no. R1: 45:2)

Another strategy developed by officers in the course of marital violence investigations was the use of an informal 'cooling off' period, which was standard practice in one of the two London stations studied. Here, after the complainant had actually decided to press charges officers would wait some time, up to two days, before a crime sheet was filled in. This delaying tactic was based on the belief that women frequently withdraw charges in the hours immediately after an allegation. Practically, the idea seems reasonable, but it has serious results for the recording of crimes. If a complaint is withdrawn before it has been recorded, then there is nothing to clear up or to 'no crime'. In effect it never existed. As one officer remarked,

> If it is a serious assault, well you usually give them a couple of days to think about it, then call back and invariably they don't want to take it further. (Officer no. 15:1)

*Enforcing the civil law* As table 3.2 shows, police in the London study did not consider injunctions effective in granting women protection unless they had a power of arrest. When there were breaches of injunctions with a power of arrest that power was seldom enforced. The granting of injunctions, with and without a power of arrest, by the courts created problems for policing (see chapter 2) First, officers were unanimous in stressing that injunctions without a power of arrest were 'useless', 'a waste of time' and 'not worth the paper they are written on', no more than a caution or a ticking off. Injunctions granted with a power of arrest gave them the authority to

Table 3.2 *Police evaluation of civil orders in the London and Kent study, 1984–1986*

| Police area | Generally seen as useful | 'With power of arrest' seen as not effective | 'Without power of arrest' seen as waste of time | No comments | Total |
|---|---|---|---|---|---|
| London[a] | 6 | 1 | 20 | 17 | 44 |
| Kent[a] | 4 | nil | 11 | 3 | 18 |

[a]These are two Divisional police stations in the Metropolitan Police District and one in Kent.
*Source*: Edwards 1986b; Bourlet 1988.

arrest if they saw fit. In practice, however, few officers actually arrested men where non-molestation injunctions or protection orders with a power of arrest had been clearly breached. For example, when ouster injunctions were in force and men had returned to the matrimonial home, women were frequently blamed for inviting them back. Men were rarely if ever held responsible for returning to the matrimonial home or accepting the invitation. It was considered the woman's responsibility to uphold the injunction, although the order was made against the man and often involved his undertaking. Where women were considered to have allowed men to return, for whatever reason, the police felt they had forfeited their right to protection when the man became violent, difficult or abusive. One male officer remarked

> from my experience a lot of women have actually spoiled it for the rest. They get an injunction and then when the injunction is granted, they invite the man back in, I mean I was called to a disturbance the other day. He is there on a Sunday. He said 'I took her out for a meal on Friday' and she says 'OK you can come back for the weekend', a lot of them actually use this and then when they have had enough of them they say 'out' and invoke the injunction.

This moral perspective is reflected by another officer, who remarked:

> It is not always correct to arrest the man for breach of an injunction . . . she might actually have contacted him or some situation like that. (Officer no. 28:4)

## The interaction of the formal and the informal in police work: classification

The substantive law, police policy and individual police officers' attitudes to marital violence result in an under-enforcement of the law. This occurs by a gradual process in which violence against wives is edged out of the criming process and criminal investigation.

The first contact a victim makes with the police is crucial to the definition of the case. A call for assistance in a marital violence incident passes through a series of selective meshes in which the incident is reclassified, and the danger or imminent crisis often downplayed. A senior UK police officer told me of a 'domestic' he had attended. Answering a call over the car radio assigned 'domestic dispute', he arrived at the scene to be told by other officers already there 'They are in there.' Entering the room, he found that both the man and the woman involved had fatally stabbed one another. Just another 'domestic dispute'! This classification disadvantages both the victim and the police.

How far do attitudes affect the police response from the start, and how far do police practices and procedures facilitate the perpetuation of attitudes that lead to relegating partner violence to the lowest policing priority? One of the key figures in the police organization, crucial to determining the nature and speed of the police response to a call from the public, is the dispatcher or radio controller. Studies both in the UK (Ekblom and Heal 1985) and in the USA (Grassie et al. 1978; Sumrall et al. 1981) have explored the screening of calls at this stage, focusing on domestic assault response, and found that dispatchers screen and divert domestic assault cases, or else accord them a lower priority. Important work in this area was conducted some while ago in the USA by Raymond Parnas.

Parnas (1967) has shown how calls to the communications centre are initially screened, and as a result may be proceeded with no further; police response 'may end with the dispatcher simply rendering or referring the caller elsewhere'. Parnas also finds that, while the role of the dispatcher is relatively unnoticed, yet the initial attitudes and actions of officers on the beat will be guided by the dispatcher's information. And the classification of the incident will depend, not only on the information given to the dispatcher by the public, but also by the dispatcher's attitude to the problem. 'A call that is apparently concerned with violence (e.g. "a neighbour is beating his wife") is often classified by the dispatcher as a domestic disturbance rather than as a battery' (p. 924). Through this definitional process, some domestic violence incidents may not even reach the station message book. The later work of Stanko (1985: 109) demonstrates the continuing diversion of such cases and their trivialization. In the UK, Faragher (1985) explored the role of the dispatcher in the allocation of response and drew similar conclusions.

In the Metropolitan Police, until the introduction of Computer Aided Despatch in a select number of stations since 1986, once a message was received by the communicator/dispatcher after a 999 call, the incident was assigned to one of a number of possible computerized categories, Domestic (05), Disturbance (06), Assault

(07), and then relayed by the teleprinter from the central information room at Scotland Yard to the local station. Similarly, calls to individual stations were categorized by officers or civilians using a wide range of descriptive shorthand, including criminal assault; assault; civil dispute; disturbance, domestic; argument, civil; altercation, domestic; family row; fight; etc. The speed of the police response and the prioritization of the reported incident were reflected at the outset by the computer categorization of the incident or the descriptive shorthand used by the controller/dispatcher. Since categorization of incidents requires specific recording practices to be followed, both here and in US certain classifications are often avoided because a written report is expected to follow. McCabe and Sutcliffe found that:

> There is, however, some evidence, notably in the area of domestic violence and offences by those who are thought to be mentally ill, that incidents brought to the notice of the police, in the belief that there was in them some criminal ingredient, are redefined in a way which avoids police action or even police record. (1978: 5)

This 'early exiting' or mortality tendency has been referred to by other researchers as 'cuffing'. Here, domestic complaints of various kinds, including both arguments and incidents involving violence, have been reported to the police by the complainant but not recorded in the station message book, and the incident has been dealt with there and then over the phone by the communicator or dispatcher. In my study of the Metropolitan Police in 1984–5 (see Introduction), the use of 'cuffing' in the two divisions investigated was exceedingly rare, but it was not unknown (Edwards 1986b). Some of the police officers interviewed were men working in the communications room. It is clear from the following reply that on occasions the dispatcher may consider it appropriate to deal with a call over the telephone without sending a patrol car to investigate.

> *Interviewer*: Do you always send a mobile unit to attend a call?
> *Police dispatcher*: Yes, I always do. Unless you happen to know the family and then you might be able to deal with it over the phone. We have a number of very excellent trained telephonists who have been dealing with this for many years and often can deal over the phone with this situation. For example, a woman called up last week, her husband drinks and he regularly beats her up. He would hit her and then he went out. Well she just wanted to talk. I was on the phone for about 20 minutes just talking to her.

The benefits of 'cuffing' from the police point of view are that it facilitates the widest possible use of discretion, avoids paperwork, and avoids the use of a patrol car to attend the call.

The second problem at this stage is that of the precise

'classification' of the incident. Parnas (1967: 927) found that a 'disturbance' classification was often preferred because a case report was not required when such a classification was made. The 1984–5 study of the Metropolitan Police in London (described in the Introduction and more fully in chapter 4) found that spousal violence was classified at the outset in such a way as to ensure the self-fulfilment of the prophecy. A complainant might call the police indicating that her husband was hitting her. The radio controller/dispatcher would then fit or reclassify that information into one of a fixed number of categories including 'disturbance', 'assault' or 'criminal damage'. Police also preferred to write up the calls they had attended in the station message book with the shorthand NCPA (no call for police action), even when officers had spent considerable time advising one or both of the parties. Officers in interview explained that if they noted the incident as 'NCPA and advice given', which was a more accurate description of their activity, they would then be required to complete further paperwork in the form of an Incident Book Report. This would involve them in time-consuming record-keeping. Smith and Gray also found that 'the police tend not to record messages when they do not think that action is required' (1983: 91). Chambers and Millar, in their study of rape in Scotland (1983), found this practice even more pervasive, reporting that it was a routine feature of the way in which police handled rape complaints.

The use of police discretion in dealing with marital violence leads to the under-enforcement of the law. Decisions to arrest or enforce the law in cases of both criminal assault or civil breaches depends not only on a 'legal objective' and 'legal prosecutorial' perspective, but also on the 'moral perspective' of the police. In both criminal and civil practice women are frequently seen to forfeit their right to protection because of moral presumptions about them. Enforcing the criminal law is influenced not only by objective criteria, that is evidence that the law has been broken or an existing injunction breached, but also by whether the victim is in some way responsible. In addition, complainant withdrawal is a major reason given by police for not proceeding with action against offenders. In the absence of a police policy directing officers to arrest where there is physical assault or a breach of an existing injunction, private attitudes will continue to edge out and redefine male violence against women, treating it as inconsequential.

The impact of police attitudes on their recording practices has been touched on here. The next chapter explores this issue further, bringing out the various stages in the process of an incident's handling by the police by which its importance can be progressively devalued, and showing how police attitudes can impact on recording practices.

# 4
# The Extent of the Problem: How Widespread is Domestic Violence?

## Introduction

The focus of public interest in the crime debate has been the unanswerable question - how big is the crime problem, and how serious? Traditionally attention has homed in on the phenomena of street crime, burglary, robbery and violence against the person. The victimization of women in these crimes and especially their victimization by male spouses and partners has rarely been acknowledged. Instead, as Stephen Box argues, 'Selective deployment patterns adopted by the police ... focus on certain parts of urban areas ... they also concentrate on "public" places where "idle" hands spend most of the unoccupied days and nights' (1987: 152). The crime figures of greatest interest are those on street crime. Hence the powers of the police are widened, with the result that more 'offences' of public order and street crime are generated. By contrast, violence in the private domain between family members remains under-recorded, while the recording system itself legitimates what is in effect a systematic tampering with the figures. The resulting apparent low level of violent crime in the home nurtures the widely held ideology that marital violence is not a problem.

Crime figures are important as a barometer of order or disorder. To the political Right they are politically expedient, reflecting societal breakdown, while to the political Left they are an artefact of policing, state definitions and repressive practices. Both these polarized positions are dangerous in their simplicity. Crime figures serve important political functions and are used for the furtherance of certain political ends, such as the justification of more laws and more repression. They serve as the basis for constructing a variety of criminal 'realities', the process of construction for some classes of statistic being more prone to systematic tampering than others. Crime figures are also part of the evidence for police effectiveness, and have an important significance for police forces, particularly the clear-up and detection rates.

What is *real* about crime, however, is the experience of victimization. During the 1970s victimology, victim surveys and studies of particular groups of victims began to force a consideration of this issue onto public agendas. In the USA the growing recognition of victims led to a movement which prompted legislation. Clearly, no longer could the crime problem be kept under wraps when victims of crime were becoming more vocal. It also became clear that victims of crime were (like offenders) frequently from poor neighbourhoods, powerless and vulnerable groups, the aged and young women. ' "Street" crime is primarily an intra-class and intra-racial phenomenon, media stereotypes to the contrary . . . the victims of street crime are overwhelmingly poor people' (Platt 1981: 18 ). The contribution of left-wing realism, in an attempt to rescue the crime debate from stalemate, was to recognize that 'crime is crime' (Cohen 1985; Lea and Young 1984). This recognition helped to expose the reality that criminal victimization hits the most vulnerable (Kinsey, Lea and Young 1986: 71). The appreciation of victimization is of paramount relevance to feminist scholars and to the feminist movement. The struggle has always been characterized by a concern for victims of domestic violence and victims of rape. Feminists in the 1960s found themselves preaching to a world not yet ready to recognize the victimization of women in rape and marital violence, in street crime and in the criminal justice process. The male voices now awakened to class differences in victimization were then mute on the question of women's victimization, which was predominantly seen not as a victim issue, but as a women's issue that nobody except feminists wanted to know.

The problem of victims is now on the political agenda. In the USA and the UK there are victims' support schemes, and in the USA laws have been passed to promote victims' rights. The feminist movement has always recognized that crime hits the weakest and the poorest, so it is not surprising that they view with suspicion the Left realists' claims to breaking new barriers when they ignore gender. Left realism has also failed to address the problem (for some while a concern of Left feminist realists) of the particular weakness of crime statistics on domestic violence.

As we have seen, certain sectors of society are less protected than others; crimes against the working class or against ethnic minorities are regarded as less serious than others. These perceptions influence both operational decisions regarding deployment and response, and recording practices. It is not possible to talk helpfully in general terms about police under-recording or 'no-criming' tendencies, as such generalizations ignore the political shadow cast by the prioritizing of crimes. The extent of under-recording and 'no-criming' will vary not just between individual complainants according to class, race, etc., but also between different categories of crime.

Crime figures on particular crimes reflect, then, different and specific distortions, the result of a general problem affecting all figures and the uneven impact of police discretion in criming and recording practices. Crime figures proclaim that armed robbery is on the increase, and maybe this proclamation contains a grain of truth. At the same time crime figures indicate that violence against wives is hardly a problem at all. Yet the figures for different crimes are not always subject to the same influences. For example, taking the crime figures at their face value, the number of woundings and assaults has almost doubled between 1974 and 1984 (62,000 to 112,000); robbery has almost trebled (8,700 to 24,900); and rape has increased by just under a third (1,050 to 1,430) (Walmsley 1986: 3). Yet, in 1981 about 6 per cent of recorded offences of wounding and serious assault related to violence between spouses (Walmsley 1986: 28).

This chapter focuses on the differential impact of policing styles on the production of specific offence statistics. The attempt is to look specifically at 'off-street crime', that is violence against female spouses or cohabitees. It is time to rescue concern about partner and spousal violence from being the exclusive province of feminism and locate it centre-stage within the mainstream law-and-order debate. Part of that endeavour is to reveal the distortions, and how they occur.

First, the wholesale dismissal of the reality of spousal violence and the impact on women's lives must be seen in the context of the increasing concern with street crime, and the recording and clearing-up practices used in street crime. Second, we examine the homicide figures, which are less prone to systematic distortion than those for assault, for the dead cannot be 'no crimed'. Third, in turning specifically to the problem of spousal violence, routine police investigatory practices are seen to contribute to the fallacy that spousal violence is not a problem. Fourth, an examination of police recording and clear-up procedures shows how the systematic distortion of statistics on violence against partners is achieved.

## Recording and clearing up non-domestic crime

Public knowledge about the extent of crime is derived from police statistics. Public fears and anxieties about crime are exacerbated by selective media portrayal, which produces an *uneven* heightened awareness. Government figures or police statistics depend for the most part on the reporting of crimes to the police by the public, but recent public order legislation will increase the slice of the crime cake in which the police are the complainants, and so the ambit of police discretion will widen.

When a member of the public reports an incident to the police, the police decide whether the incident amounts to a crime and whether the crime/incident should be recorded. In the UK the basic official crime statistic is represented by 'notifiable offences recorded by the police', while in the USA it is 'crimes known to the police'. This however does not reflect the 'real' volume of crime known to the police, and certainly in no way reflects the volume of crime committed. 'Notifiable offences recorded by the police' and 'crimes known to the police' are 'real' reflections of the number of incidents the police decide to record as 'crimes'. As the Home Office, in the annual publication of UK crime figures, accedes: 'For a variety of reasons many offences are either not reported to the police or not recorded by them and so changes in the number of offences recorded do not necessarily provide an accurate reflection of changes in the amount of crime committed' (*Criminal Statistics* 1985: 15).

This problem has long been recognized by criminologists such as Kitsuse and Cicourel, who write: 'rates of deviant behaviour are produced by persons in the social system who define, classify and record certain behaviours as deviant' (1963: 135). The relationship between police definitions and recording practice is not a universal one. While in the UK, for example, police forces are issued with guidelines on how these statistics are to be compiled, decisions are taken locally with regard to whether a reported incident occurred, if it occurred whether it is appropriate to record it, and if appropriate whether to 'crime' it, and if so, under which crime classification. Comparisons between different forces' crime rates tell us less about the impact of local police decisions and procedures on crime than about these various definitional judgements.

The decision to include an incident in the category of 'notifiable offences recorded by the police' is influenced both by the intrinsic nature of the incident or conduct, and by an officer's prospective presumption about the likely fate of the incident at the prosecution stage. With the advent of the crown prosecutor (discussed in chapter 6), this consideration may have even more bearing. The latter consideration is also guided and informed by the organizational goal, and the strength of the endeavour to clear up and detect crime. Clear-up and detection rates are regarded as barometers of police performance. The clear-up rate is derived from the number of offences initially recorded and the number of those cleared up either by prosecution, detection, caution or admission. The police have good reason to ensure that those crimes initially entered as 'notifiable offences' have more than a reasonable prospect of being cleared.

Kinsey, Lea and Young (1986) maintain that crime is rising, but it is clear that variations in police recording practices cannot be ignored in assessing the situation. It is street crime that seems to be rising the fastest.

*Classifying crimes*

Just as there are wide variations between forces about whether an incident is recorded as a 'notifiable offence', there are also inconsistences about which of a number of criminal categories is considered the most appropriate. The experience of Brixton, London, in 1981 illustrates the impact of a heightened police awareness and anxiety about street robbery on the classification of theft from the person. It is well known that officers' use of discretion in Brixton led to certain incidents being recorded as 'robberies' which might otherwise have been recorded as 'thefts'. In 1981, the evidence of the Metropolitan Police to the Scarman Inquiry stated that while Brixton during 1976–80 accounted for 35 per cent of all crimes in 'L' district (Lambeth), Brixton accounted for 49 per cent of all 'robbery and other violent theft' in Lambeth. In the Metropolitan Police area as a whole 'robbery and other violent theft' rose by 38 per cent, while from 1976 to 1980 in Lambeth it rose by 66 per cent, and in Brixton by 138 per cent. Lord Scarman readily accepted this presentation of crime figures, and Brixton was identified as 'unique in terms of its violent street crime' figures. This resulted in a greater police deployment, and a more visible police presence on Brixton streets. Blom-Cooper and Drabble (1982) were less ready to accept this crime profile as a reflection of 'real' crime, instead preferring to explain the rate as a dependent variable. They argued that the 'unique level of street crime' theory could only be supported so long as the categories of 'robbery and other violent theft' and 'other theft and handling' are kept separate since 'L' district had a comparatively low incidence of simple theft. Firstly, they argued that 'theft from the person' was possibly being categorized in Brixton as 'snatches', and being classified together with 'other violent theft', while in other police areas such incidents were categorized as 'simple theft'. Secondly, the increase in police deployment may have led to a rise, though probably only a marginal one, in the crime figures. They concluded that the police stereotype of Brixton as a high crime area actually led to the apparent amplification of 'robbery and other violent crime'.

Crime figures are not only determined by objective evidential ingredients, and by force policy and practice, but also by the subjective perceptions of individual officers about precisely what type of person commits what type of crime (Sudnow 1965). Such factors may also have helped the Metropolitan Police in Brixton to perceive their 'unique' crime profile. Burrows (1986: 11), in his research on burglary, further reveals the extent and nature of this problem, arguing that the variations between forces' crime figures can be explained by examining the way in which they exercise different criteria in making a judgement about what kind of conduct falls into one of several offence categories. He found that in Clapham, London, incidents 'no crimed' or crimed as acts of 'criminal damage' might be recorded in other areas of the same force and in other forces as burglary (see table 4.1).

The Metropolitan Police are turning to the use of a variety of charges in order to achieve convictions of women who are known prostitutes. Research by the author indicates that known prostitutes are variously charged with loitering and soliciting (Street Offences Act 1959), gross indecency in a public place and obstructing the highway.

The question of definitional assignment not only influences the rising crime rate, as in Brixton, but also the declining rate of some other offences, certain sexual offences being a notable example. While the number of rapes recorded has increased since 1975, from 1,040 to 1,842 in 1985 and 2,288 in 1986, the rate of indecency between males has fallen. Interestingly, in both these sexual offences, decreases and increases in recorded cases can be accounted for by changes in police recording practices. Offences may not be recorded, or they may be given a different definitional assignment. Variations between police forces in recording practice must also be assessed in the light of policy, and the operational decisions of police constables. For example, while the populations of Bedfordshire (507,054) and Cumbria (487,038) are roughly comparable, the rate of notifiable sexual offences for Bedfordshire (at 248) is almost twice that recorded for Cumbria (132). See table 4.2 below.

*Clearing up crime*

Successful investigative performance and police efficiency have always been assessed, mistakenly, in terms of high clear-up rates and high levels of detection. Judged in this way the police are bound to fail. James Anderton, Greater Manchester's Police Chief, has said: 'To suggest as some have, that a falling crime detection rate and a rising level of crime indicates a lack of police dedication is an appalling travesty of the truth when judged against all known results and recorded facts' (1981: 2). Clear-up rates overall are declining, as Kinsey, Lea and Young note: 'Between 1973 and 1983 the percentage of crimes cleared up by the police in England and Wales fell by 10 per cent' (1986: 21), while clear-up rates for different types of crime vary enormously.

Table 4.1 *Variations in burglary classification in seven police forces, based on experiments from Clapham cases*

| Actual classification in Clapham | Metropolitan Police 1 | West Yorkshire Police 2 | Other forces 3 | 4 | 5 | 6 |
|---|---|---|---|---|---|---|
| No crime | Burg. | Burg. | Burg. | Burg. | Burg. | Burg. |
| Criminal damage | A/Burg. | A/Burg. | A/Burg. | A/Burg. | Burg. | Burg. |
| Criminal damage | CD | A/Burg. | A/Burg. | A/Burg. | CD | A/Burg. |
| No crime | NC | A/Burg. | Burg. | Burg. | Burg. | Burg. |
| No crime | NC | Sus. Occ. | Burg. | NC | Burg. | Burg. |
| No crime | Burg. | Theft | Burg. | Burg. | Burg. | Burg. |
| Criminal damage | CD | CD | CD | CD | A/Burg. | CD |
| No crime | Burg. | Sus. Occ. | A/Burg. | Burg. | Burg. | Burg. |
| No crime | NC | A/Burg. | Burg. | Burg. | Burg. | Burg. |
| No crime | NC | Agg. B. | Burg. | Burg[a] | Agg. B. | Agg. B. |
| Criminal damage | CD | CD | A/Burg. | A/Burg. | CD | CD |
| Criminal damage | Burg. | A/Burg. | Burg. | Burg. | Burg. | Burg. |
| Criminal damage | CD | A/Burg. | A/Burg. | A/Burg. | A/Burg. | A/Burg. |
| Criminal damage | CD | CD | A/Burg. | Burg. | CD | A/Burg. |
| No crime | NC | Burg. | Burg. | Burg. | Burg. | Burg. |

Burg.: Burglary (dwelling); A/Burg.: Attempted burglary; Agg. B.: Aggravated burglary; CD: Criminal damage; NC: No crime; Sus. Occ.: Suspicious occurrence.

[a] Burglary, but more serious wounding offence would be charged.

*Source*: Burrows 1986, p. 20, table 3.2.

The first divide is between police complainant and public complainant crimes. For example, crimes dependent wholly on police evidence (prostitution, indecency between males, going equipped for stealing, public order offences) have an almost 100 per cent clear-up rate. Crimes which involve members of the public as chief complainant have lower clear-up rates, particularly crimes of burglary, theft from the person and robbery. But how are crimes 'cleared up' according to the book? Once an incident is reported to the police, and once the incident is identified as a crime, the desired end-product for the police and public alike is to have the matter 'cleared up' by one of the following legitimate methods. First, the police may charge or summons the offender to appear before a court with a view to prosecution. Secondly, if the suspect admits to the offence, the police may give a formal caution as an alternative to prosecution. Thirdly, if the prisoner, in the case of those already sentenced, admits to the commission of other offences, these additional offences may be taken into consideration in any future sentencing. The greatest room for latitude in clearing up crime exists in those cases so cleared 'otherwise without proceedings', according to Burrows and Tarling (1985: 89). They point out that this is probably the least researched and least understood area.

> To complete the returns police forces apply the counting rules agreed with the Home Office Statistical Department in respect of the number of crimes cleared; but in respect of the methods by which these clearances are achieved [which the Statistical Department do not require], no counting rules exist.

They argue:

> clear-up rates can simply be a reflection of the strategies pursued in particular forces ... because of the political repercussions that the publication of clearance statistics can engender, there is pressure on the police to manipulate these statistics to indicate either success or struggle against 'impossible odds'. (p. 82)

Much research has been done indicating the wide variation between forces as to the methods used for clearing crime. For example, the increasing use of cautioning is generally promoted in accordance with the Criminal Justice Act 1969, Home Office Circulars on Cautioning (70/1978 and 14/1985), and the Attorney General's *Guidelines on Prosecution* (1983), yet wide variations can be observed between forces, especially in terms of juveniles, race and ethnicity and class (see Ditchfield 1976; Landau 1981; Landau and Nathan 1983; Farrington and Bennett 1981; Fisher and Mawby 1982; Mott 1983; Laycock and Tarling 1985; and Giller and Tutt 1987). Laycock and Tarling (1985: 85) examined cautioning practices for 42 police forces and the Metropolitan Police. Force policy towards adults in the Metropolitan Police at the time of the study stressed: 'Where there is clear evidence of other than a very trifling offence, use of the caution is not justified and the only consideration should be whether to prosecute or not' (1985: 85). In dealing with juveniles, however, policy in all forces has encouraged cautions for juvenile first offenders. The Home Office in its consultative document on cautioning expressed some concern over these wide variations, and recommended 'a basis for some consistent and effective police cautioning practice' (1984: 2). The UK Attorney General's *Guidelines on Prosecution* (1983), closely in accord with the recommendations of the Royal Commission on Criminal Procedure (1981) regarding prosecution, set out some indicators. One of the key criteria is that evidence should be sufficient to support a prosecution, applying the test of whether a conviction was more likely than an acquittal. Clearly the Attorney General envisaged that cautioning also has a part to play in the disposal of adult offenders (see Home Office 1984: 4). The Royal Commission and the Attorney General's guidelines actually ratify the use of a caution when: (a) the penalty may be trivial, i.e. conditional or absolute discharge; (b) there has been a delay; (c) the offence is not grave and the complainant wishes that no action be taken.

While most research has focused on the role police discretion has to play in deciding whether to caution or to prosecute, the use of cautioning by the police may also be seen as a means of 'weeding out' cases in which they consider a prosecution inappropriate. In this respect the use of the caution varies not only in accordance with age, race and class but with the offence committed, and perceptions of the culpability and moral blameworthiness of the offender and the strengths of the prosecution case. Table 4.2 shows the numbers of notifiable sexual offences recorded by the police for 17 of the 44 police areas in England and Wales, together with the rate of each force's use of caution. Figures for the number and percentage cleared up are given for Greater Manchester and the Metropolitan Police District only. What is abundantly clear on the basis of this information alone is that enormous diversity exists in the use of cautioning between forces. Lincolnshire and Wiltshire, on the one hand, have a cautioning rate of 30 per cent, compared with the Metropolitan Police and City of London, which have rates of 3 and 5 per cent respectively. Since sexual offences include a wide range of activities, ranging from consensual ones (e.g. sexual intercourse between a boy of say seventeen and a girl under sixteen) to non-consensual acts of sexual violence, cautioning practice will vary enormously within these categories, depending on particular force policy on homosexuality, rape and unlawful sexual intercourse.

Table 4.2 *Sexual offences: variations between selected police forces in England and Wales in the use of a caution, 1984*

| | Notifiable offences recorded | Cautioned No. | Cautioned %[a] | Cleared up No. | Cleared up %[b] |
|---|---|---|---|---|---|
| Avon and Somerset | 533 | 56 | 11 | | |
| Bedfordshire | 248 | 71 | 29 | | |
| Cambridgeshire | 263 | 71 | 27 | | |
| Cheshire | 307 | 37 | 12 | | |
| Cleveland | 231 | 60 | 26 | | |
| Cumbria | 132 | 17 | 13 | | |
| Derbyshire | 532 | 75 | 14 | | |
| Devon and Cornwall | 557 | 111 | 20 | | |
| Dorset | 198 | 32 | 16 | | |
| Durham | 263 | 48 | 18 | | |
| Essex | 484 | 66 | 14 | | |
| Gloucestershire | 110 | 17 | 15 | | |
| Greater Manchester | 1,012 | 73 | 7 | 673* | 66* |
| Lincolnshire | 249 | 74 | 30 | | |
| City of London | 19 | 1 | 5 | | |
| Metropolitan Police District | 3,053 | 102 | 3 | 1,627† | 53† |
| Wiltshire | 214 | 64 | 30 | | |

[a] Cautioning rate: those cautioned as a percentage of all offences recorded.
[b] Clear-up rate: crimes followed by prosecution/caution as a percentage of offences recorded.
*Source*: *Criminal Statistics* 1984, vol. 3, *Supplementary Tables*, tables S.3.1 (p. 8) and S.3.7(A) (p. 178); *Manchester Chief Constable's Report (1984); †London Commissioner's Report (1984).

Furthermore, the Attorney General's *Guidelines on Prosecution* (1983) indicate that a caution might be the appropriate response 'when the girl or youth has been a willing party to the offence. Account should be taken of his or her age, the relative ages of the parties and whether or not there was any element of seduction or corruption' (cited in Home Office 1984: 33).

Variations between forces in the use of the caution for burglary offences are just as wide as those for sex offences (table 4.3). Dyfed/Powys is top of the league at 6.8 per cent, while the Metropolitan Police District and City of London are at the bottom, with the lowest percentage use of the caution (0.8 and 0.2 per cent respectively). Again, bearing in mind the low use of the caution for sexual offences and burglary for the Metropolitan Police District, we find that their overall 'clear-up' rate in all offence categories is down compared with the average figure for England and Wales (28 per cent for 1984). Further information is needed about the use of methods of clear-up, including cautioning, prosecution, and taking offences into consideration, as well as about the use of the 'no crime' as a means of disposing of problem cases.

Table 4.3 *Variations between police forces in England and Wales in the use of a caution for burglary offences, 1984*

| | Notifiable offences recorded | Cautioned | |
|---|---|---|---|
| | | No. | %[a] |
| Avon and Somerset | 116,833 | 166 | 0.9 |
| Bedfordshire | 8,004 | 248 | 3.0 |
| Cambridgeshire | 6,172 | 99 | 1.6 |
| Cheshire | 12,776 | 254 | 1.9 |
| Cleveland | 14,070 | 145 | 1.0 |
| Cumbria | 6,442 | 160 | 2.4 |
| Derbyshire | 10,516 | 216 | 2.0 |
| Devon and Cornwall | 13,324 | 405 | 3.0 |
| Dorset | 5,525 | 89 | 1.6 |
| Durham | 11,479 | 191 | 1.6 |
| Essex | 13,776 | 327 | 2.3 |
| Gloucestershire | 5,746 | 86 | 1.4 |
| Greater Manchester | 83,448 | 869 | 1.0 |
| Hampshire | 18,756 | 369 | 1.9 |
| Hertfordshire | 6,596 | 92 | 1.3 |
| Humberside | 17,438 | 271 | 1.5 |
| Kent | 15,769 | 212 | 1.3 |
| Lancashire | 19,301 | 500 | 2.5 |
| Leicestershire | 10,917 | 231 | 2.1 |
| Lincolnshire | 5,875 | 253 | 4.3 |
| City of London | 954 | 2 | 0.2 |
| Merseyside | 53,885 | 564 | 1.0 |
| Metropolitan Police District | 168,900 | 1,441 | 0.8 |
| Norfolk | 7,846 | 142 | 1.8 |
| Northamptonshire | 7,871 | 413 | 5.2 |
| Northumbria | 51,057 | 684 | 1.3 |
| North Yorkshire | 8,518 | 113 | 1.3 |
| Nottinghamshire | 18,878 | 358 | 1.8 |
| South Yorkshire | 25,372 | 356 | 1.4 |
| Staffordshire | 13,509 | 165 | 1.2 |
| Suffolk | 4,673 | 177 | 3.7 |
| Surrey | 6,656 | 85 | 1.2 |
| Sussex | 16,080 | 201 | 1.2 |
| Thames Valley | 20,902 | 350 | 1.6 |
| Warwickshire | 6,204 | 89 | 1.4 |
| West Mercia | 11,229 | 304 | 2.7 |
| West Midlands | 77,626 | 1,283 | 1.6 |
| West Yorkshire | 46,599 | 648 | 1.3 |
| Wiltshire | 5,214 | 136 | 2.6 |
| Dyfed/Powys | 2,681 | 183 | 6.8 |
| Gwent | 4,941 | 157 | 8.1 |
| North Wales | 8,665 | 181 | 2.0 |
| South Wales | 26,443 | 378 | 1.4 |

[a] Cautioning rate: those cautioned as a percentage of all offences recorded.

*Source*: *Criminal Statistics* 1984, vol. 4, *Supplementary Tables*.

We have seen that there are wide divergences between forces in terms of cautioning as a means of clearing up sexual offences and burglary, and it is certain that similar variations exist with regard to (a) whether domestic violence incidents are recorded as crimes, (b) if they are recorded as crimes, what crime classification is chosen, and (c) whether such cases are cleared up by a prosecution or caution, or erased by the use of a 'no crime' classification.

## Recording and clearing up assaults

In cases of wife murder, the offence is reported and the offender prosecuted and convicted. Cases of wife assault, by contrast, are rarely reported by the victim and seldom recorded as crimes by the police. Official figures are inevitably inaccurate and seriously underestimate the extent of the problem. Yet this underestimation occurs not only through the under-reporting by wives and under-recording by the police: government research continues to assume that statistics can be taken at face value, thereby denying that violence against women in the home is a grave problem. For example, the Home Office, in a *Statistical Bulletin* (no. 29, 1986) and research study conducted by Walmsley (1986), treats official police statistics as non-problematic.

Walmsley's analysis was based on data derived from 18 police forces about crimes of violence, excluding homicide. On the basis of these police statistics, which he regarded as 'real' and non-problematic, he concluded that males were five times more likely than females to be victims of serious woundings. In minor woundings, males were three times more likely to be victims than females, while in cases of robbery (theft from the person) otherwise known as 'mugging', males were twice as likely as females to be victims. One in five woundings occurred in dwellings, and half of these victims were male. This study suggests that women are far less likely to be victims of serious and of minor woundings than men, but Walmsley's analysis underestimates the true extent of women's victimization at the hands of men known to them.

Walmsley explains this finding by attributing blame to the victim for her reluctance to report: 'Little is known about the incidence of domestic violence, because most of it does not come to the knowledge of the police' (p. 28). But women's failure to report is *not* the only reason why so little is known. Firstly, the police initially fail to record such incidents as crimes, and secondly, where they decide to record the incident as a crime, at a later stage it may be erased in a legitimate process by being written off as a 'no crime'. The justification for this typical procedure is found in the complainant's unwillingness to prosecute. The 1984–5 London study described in the Introduction found that in the Metropolitan Police area an estimated 7,144 crime reports were initiated in 1985 involving spouses and cohabitees (my estimate). Statistics from the Metropolitan Police submitted to the Home Office for the purpose of official publication indicate a much lower figure – 380 cases (Metropolitan Police statistics for 1986). The shortfall can be explained by the systematic application of the 'no crime' classification, which facilitates the legitimate disposal of cases when a complainer withdraws the allegation. Walmsley seriously fails to address the issue of the validity of statistics by taking official figures derived from police statistics as unproblematic.

Other studies by feminists have taken, by contrast, the victims' experience of violence, rather than police statistics, as a starting-point for estimating the extent of violence. Large-scale victimization surveys have incorporated a consideration of spousal violence into their questionnaires. Kinsey in a study of crime in Merseyside (1985) found that while few women experienced physical attacks by strangers, they experienced other kinds of threatening behaviour on the streets, including kerb-crawling and sexual harassment. If one starts out by examining police statistics on personal violence, these additional forms of behaviour which encroach on a woman's feeling of safety are immediately lost. MacLean, Jones and Young in a study of crime in Islington (1986) noted that women are less likely than men to feel safe at home and are more at risk from domestic violence and theft from the person. They found that 'crimes which are for the most part directed at women are not usually effectively dealt with by the police . . . domestic assaults are down-crimed or ignored' (p. 5.2).

### Recording and clearing up homicide: who is most at risk?

Studies on homicide have traditionally started out by comparing the different rates for different countries (see Williams and Flewelling 1988). The rate for the UK is 1.2 per 100,000 population, and for the USA 7.12. Presented in this way, homicide becomes homogenized; the overall rate cannot take account of the variability of risk according to rural/urban area, class or sex, or indeed according to victim/offender relationship. A crude crime rate assumes that each member of the population is equally at risk (Deane 1987: 216), yet if one simply breaks down the figures by area, one finds that for 1987 one third (210) of all homicides in England and Wales (610) involved people from the Metropolitan Police area, one police force out of 43. The rate of homicide in London was 3.0, whereas in Cleveland (well known for the 1987 child sex-abuse scandal) the number killed was 5, giving a rate of 0.89. Doerner (1975: 95) found the same wide variability in the USA. The overall homicide rate was 6.28; in Tennessee it was 19.95, and North Dakota 0.39. When we disaggregate the overall homicide rate into more refined categories on the basis of the relationship of victim to offender, the victimization of spouses and female cohabitees becomes overwhelmingly apparent (see Gibson and Klein 1961, 1969).

Homicide figures in the USA and England and Wales present very different profiles of who is most at risk, where, and from whom (see Edwards 1986c). In the USA unpublished data from the Supplementary Homicide Report collected as part of the Uniform Crime Reporting Program indicated that 12,582 women aged 18 and over were killed in one-to-one homicides between 1980 and 1984. As many as 52 per cent of these women were killed by husbands, male cohabitees and boyfriends.

England and Wales Home Office figures (supplied to the author) reveal that those persons most at risk are female spouses, ex-spouses, cohabitees and ex-cohabitees, and the most likely aggressor is a male spouse. Home Office data reveal that for 1982, 1983, 1984, 1985 and 1986 the chances of becoming a victim of homicide are only slightly greater for males than for females. In 1982, 314 males were killed compared with 262 females. In 1983, the ratio was 255 to 277, in 1984, 303 to 240, in 1985, 306 to 257 and in 1986, 350 to 260. What was especially significant, however, was the divergence in victimization between males and females for the categories of stranger, friend, and spouse (see table 4.4 for a detailed examination for 1982 only).

Looking first at the chances of becoming a victim of spousal homicide, women were nine times more likely than men to be victims in 1982 (104 to 12) and in 1983 (87 to 10), seven times more likely in 1984 (97 to 14) and in 1985 (100 to 15), nine times in 1986 (109 to 12) and four times in 1987 (83 to 19). Male chances of being killed by a stranger were the highest, at six times that of females in 1982, and three times that of females in 1983, 1984 and 1985. It is to be noted, however, that there has been a very small but nevertheless steady increase in the number of females killed by strangers. The chance of a man being killed by a friend or associate is between two and three times that for females for all four years. Women's chances of being killed by a husband or a male friend, compared to the chances of being killed by a stranger, are ten to one for 1982, seven to one for 1983 and eight to one for 1984 and 1985.

In 1982, 21.2 per cent of all homicides were committed against wives/female cohabitees/heterosexual lovers by their male partners. In 1983, the figure was 20 per cent, and in 1984, 18.8 per cent, although the proportion of husbands killing wives (lovers excluded) in 1982, 1983, 1984, 1985 and 1986 has remained constant at about 18

Table 4.4 *Homicide: a comparison of male and female victimization, 1982*

| | Female victims | | | Male victims | | |
|---|---|---|---|---|---|---|
| Victim | No. | % of female victimization | % of all | No. | % of male victimization | % of all |
| *Family* | | | | | | |
| Daughters | 34 | 13 | 6 | | | |
| Mothers | 11 | 4 | 2 | | | |
| Wives | 104 | 40 | 18 | | | |
| Sons | | | | 27 | 8 | 5 |
| Fathers | | | | 14 | 4 | 2 |
| Husbands | | | | 12 | 4 | 2 |
| Other family | 5 | 2 | 1 | 12 | 4 | 2 |
| Lovers | 18 | 7 | 3 | 9 | 3 | 1 |
| Sub-total | 172 | 66 | 30 | 74 | 23 | 12 |
| *Friends* | | | | | | |
| Friends | 46 | 17 | 8 | 106 | 34 | 19 |
| Associates | 5 | 2 | 1 | 13 | 4 | 2 |
| Sub-total | 51 | 19 | 9 | 119 | 38 | 21 |
| *Not acquainted or unknown* | | | | | | |
| Strangers | 16 | 6 | 3 | 93 | 30 | 16 |
| Relationship unknown | 23 | 9 | 4 | 28 | 9 | 5 |
| Subtotal | 39 | 15 | 7 | 121 | 39 | 21 |
| Total female | 262 | 100 | 46 | | | |
| Total male | | | | 314 | 100 | 54 |
| Total | 576 | | | | | |

*Source*: Figures supplied by kind permission of the Home Office Statistical Department.

per cent of the total homicide rate (see table 4.5) (Edwards 1986c). The message to be drawn from homicide figures is clear. The safest place for men is the home, and home is, by contrast, the least safe place for women. If women are most vulnerable from spousal homicide (which accounted for around 40 per cent of all female homicide victims in 1982, 1983, 1984, 1985 and 1986, we have no reason to believe that they are not similarly at risk from men known to them in terms of other violence against the person, including attempted murder, wounding and assaults. (See chapter 6 for an examination of some recent findings on this point.)

In the USA, studies of homicide have similarly shown that the wife/spouse/cohabitee is significantly represented in the overall homicide victimization profile, and also overwhelmingly represented in the female victim category. Marvin Wolfgang (1958: 212–13) examined patterns in criminal homicide from 588 cases that occurred

Table 4.5 *Homicides of female spouses in England and Wales, 1982–1987*

| | All victims | Female victims | Female spouse victims | Spouse as % of all victims | Spouse as % of all female victims |
|---|---|---|---|---|---|
| 1982 | 576 | 262 | 104 | 18 | 40 |
| 1983 | 482 | 227 | 87 | 18 | 38 |
| 1984 | 543 | 240 | 97 | 18 | 40 |
| 1985 | 563 | 257 | 100 | 18 | 39 |
| 1986 | 610 | 260 | 109 | 18 | 42 |
| 1987 | 635 | 240 | 83 | 13 | 35 |

*Source: Criminal Statistics* 1982–7.

in Philadelphia between 1 January 1948 and 31 December 1952. Of the 588 victims, 100 (17 per cent) were spousal. Of those 100, 53 were wives and 47 husbands. Yet the number of wives killed by their husbands constituted 41 per cent of all women killed. MacDonald, commenting on Wolfgang's findings, remarked 'the relative danger to women increases when the homicide rate is low. Thus the percentage of female victims in England (57 per cent of 551 criminal homicides) is higher than in the United States (24 per cent of criminal homicides in Philadelphia)' (1961: 74).

As in other areas, it has been feminist criminology and not radical criminology, Left realism or radical victimology that has focused attention on the significance of wives as victims in the overall homicide figures, as a reflection of the disastrous course spousal violence may run. Studies by the US Police Foundation (1976) and Jolin (1983) found that men who went on to kill wives had often been convicted of assaulting them on previous occasions.

An important area of research has examined the extent to which violent partners are also violent against non-family members. Flynn (1977), in a study of abused women, found that at least one third of the assailants had previous records of other types of criminal assault. White and Straus (1981) found that men who were violent toward wives were arrested and/or convicted for a 'serious' crime at almost twice the rate of non-violent spouses. Fagan, Stewart and Hansen (1983: 54) found that more than half of spouse abusers are violent with others as well as with their partners; 46 per cent of spouse-abusers had been previously arrested for violence. A study conducted by the Home Office indicated that 43 per cent of suspects of homicide within the family had previous convictions for violence (*Criminal Statistics* 1986: 60).

If we compare homicide figures for England and Wales and the USA in 1981 (table 4.6), some clear differences in the distribution of

Table 4.6 *Homicide offences known to police in England and Wales and the USA by relationship of offender to victim, 1981 (percentages)*

| Victim's relationship to suspect | England and Wales | USA |
|---|---|---|
| *Acquainted* | | |
| Spouse | 22 | 9 |
| Lover/former lover | 5 | 3 |
| Son or daughter | 12 | 2 |
| Parent | 4 | 1 |
| Other family | 5 | 5 |
| Friend, acquaintance, other associate | 27 | 35 |
| Sub-total | 75 | 55 |
| *Not acquainted or unknown* | | |
| Stranger | 19 | 15 |
| Unknown | 6 | 30 |
| Sub-total | 25 | 45 |
| Total | 100 | 100 |
| N | (517) | (20,053) |

*Source*: Information adapted from *Criminal Statistics, England and Wales* 1981, table 4.4, p. 70; Jamieson and Flanagan 1983, table 3.64, p. 391.

homicide emerge. Curiously, although the aggregated England and Wales homicide rate is low compared with that of the USA (1.2 to 7.5 for 1987), spousal homicide forms a far higher proportion of all homicide in England and Wales than it does in the USA. This is borne out in a smaller study in the USA conducted by Wilbanks (1983) in Dade County, Florida, where the sample size compares with the England and Wales annual figure (see table 4.7). In 1984, 543 victims were killed in England and Wales compared with 569 in Dade County for the year 1980. In Dade County almost equal proportions of wives kill husbands as husbands kill wives, and spousal homicide constitutes a much smaller proportion of the overall homicide rate than it does in England and Wales, where dramatically higher numbers of husbands kill wives than wives kill husbands. Again, homicides of sons or daughters as a proportion of the homicide rate are far higher for England and Wales than for Dade County. Are we in the UK especially violent to our loved ones?

The differences in female homicide victimization in England and Wales and the USA are undeniably curious. England and Wales figures suggest that almost as many women are murdered as are men; this is not the case in the USA, where since 1964 about 76 per cent of homicide victims are males and 24 per cent females. In the profile of spousal homicide in England and Wales, women are overwhelmingly the victims, and male victims are a rarity. The US figures for 1982 and

Table 4.7 *Homicide in Dade County, Florida, 1980, and in England and Wales, 1984*

| Relationship of victim to offender | Sex of offender: Male DC | Male EW | Female DC | Female EW | Unknown DC | Unknown EW | Total DC | Total EW |
|---|---|---|---|---|---|---|---|---|
| Spouses | 18 | 97 | 17 | 14 | 2 | nil | 37 | 111 |
| Other sexual partners/lovers | 38 | 13 | 12 | 2 | 2 | nil | 52 | 15 |
| Parents or sons/daughters | 13 | 53 | 4 | 38 | nil | nil | 17 | 91 |
| Other family | nil | 14 | nil | nil | nil | nil | nil | 14 |
| Friends/acquaintances | 167 | 158 | 7 | 8 | 6 | nil | 180 | 166 |
| Crime partners | 122 | nil | 2 | nil | 28 | nil | 152 | nil |
| Other associates | nil | 16 | nil | 3 | nil | nil | nil | 19 |
| Strangers | 188 | 77 | 4 | nil | 24 | 2 | 216 | 79 |
| Unknown | 7 | nil | 1 | nil | 19 | 48 | 27 | 48 |
| Total offenders | 553 | 428 | 47 | 65 | 81 | 50 | 681 | 543 |

DC: Dade County.
EW: England and Wales.
The total number of victims was 569 (DC); 543 (EW).
*Source*: Wilbanks 1983, table 2, p. 11; *Criminal Statistics, England and Wales* 1984.

1983 demonstrate that husbands kill wives and wives kill husbands in almost equal proportions. In 1982, 3.4 per cent of all homicide victims were husbands, compared with 4.8 per cent wives. In 1983, 3.9 per cent were husbands and 5.5 per cent wives (US Department of Justice 1984). In England and Wales 18 per cent of all homicide is against wives compared with 2 per cent against husbands. How can these differences be explained? Women who have killed husbands in England and Wales have mostly used either guns or knives, and in nearly all cases have waited until the husband is asleep or otherwise incapacitated (Edwards 1985b, 1987a). The restrictions on availability and use of handguns in the UK is a significant factor; a wider availability of handguns would result in an increase in the homicide rate overall and, arguably, a significant increase in the number of women killing violent husbands. Figures for England and Wales in 1983 indicate that wives shot husbands in 8 per cent of cases, compared with 58 per cent of cases for the same period in the US. These differences also have to be considered against the backcloth of a much lower clear-up rate for homicide in the States, where in 1982 and 1983 in 28 per cent of homicides the suspect was unknown. This compares with 7 per cent in England and Wales.

This examination of spousal homicide figures puts violence in the home centre-stage in the mainstream crime debate (see O'Brien 1988). While homicide causes the deaths of 100 wives/cohabitees in the UK each year, thousands of women's lives are deeply affected and shattered by domestic assault, yet the size and seriousness of this problem is uniquely fudged and distorted. How this happens and is legitimated is a matter of increasing concern.

**Police dispositions of marital violence**

The process of defining and recording incidents as crime is, as we have seen in chapter 3, a process inextricably bound up with the nature of the police investigatory process, including both policy and individual decisions regarding surveillance, deployment of officers and resources and prioritization of certain crimes for policing. Police statistics on crimes of violence against women in the home are so low that they convey the message that violence against wives is a rare and trivial event. They also indicate that prosecutions frequently fail. From the outset, an officer's stereotype of domestic violence cases precludes an awareness of the potential seriousness of many of these cases, which helps to explain the styles of policing adopted.

Criticism of this police response has centred on their intransigence over arresting suspects for domestic assault. As American research has shown (e.g. Sherman and Berk 1984a, discussed in detail in chapter 6), arrest is imperative in order to deter the use of violence and its repetition, and ultimately prevent homicide. The need for change in this area has led researchers in America, the UK and elsewhere to focus specifically on how the distortion of figures for offences of rape and domestic violence has come about. On the whole, American studies have tended to lead the way, and findings from Left feminist scholarship and liberal academic research have broadly concurred. Feminist scholars Nan Oppenlander (1982) and Maureen McLeod (1983) and liberal scholars William Wilbanks (1983) and Daniel Bell (1984a, b, 1985a, b) have variously explored the operational responses and recording practices of the police, drawing similar conclusions.

In the United Kingdom studies on the operational response and recording practices of police in rape cases paved the way for similar enquiries into police response and recording practices in domestic violence. As in the USA, the studies have been conducted by people from a broad political spectrum, from liberal academics to liberal-minded police officers. In 1980 Richard Wright, from the Institute of Criminology in Cambridge, published the results of an investigation of police recording practices in rape cases. In 1985 Ian Blair, a police officer with the Metropolitan Police in London, published a study of the police response to rape in the capital. In Scotland, G. Chambers and A. Millar (1983) of the Scottish Office conducted studies on investigatory and prosecution practices in sexual assault cases. Bedfordshire police in 1976 conducted their own 'in house' research into police dispositions, and Dobash and Dobash (1984) and Faragher (1985) conducted studies broadly addressing domestic violence. These studies have emphasized some of the specific characteristics of police response to violence against women, and the specific construction of violence against women as a crime problem.

*American studies of police dispositions*

Both Bell and Oppenlander found, as other studies have done (see chapter 3), that the police were reluctant to arrest the offender, and when they did, it was usually in respect of some offence other than the assault for which attendance had been requested. Data for Bell's studies were based on records of domestic disputes and violence known to the police made available annually in the Ohio report on domestic violence which collates all recorded incidents of family violence, following the Amended Substitute House Bill 835 (1979), which provided for a four-year period within which law enforcement agencies were required to report incidents of domestic dispute and violence to the Bureau of Criminal Identification and Investigation (see Ohio Attorney General 1981: 9). His work includes an exploratory study of Ohio's data for a twelve-month period in 1980 (1984: 25) and a multi-year study of recorded violence from August 1979 to December 1981 (1985: 301). During 1980, 55,933 incidents were reported to Ohio police, from a population of 10,797,000. Of these incidents, 13,215 (24 per cent) criminal complaints were filed, while the police initiated action independently in 3.6 per cent (477) of these cases. In 5,292 cases (10 per cent of the total) an arrest was made under the Domestic Dispute and Violence Program, Ohio Revised Code S. 3113.32A which defines a domestic dispute, and S. 2919.25 which defines the appropriate action. In a further 2,008 cases (4 per cent), an arrest was made under other sections of the Ohio Revised Code. In 8,662 cases (15 per cent) the result involved referral to other agencies, such as social services or women's shelters, or to the civil process. In an overwhelming number of cases, 39,971 (71 per cent), a total absence of action was evident. The Ohio data indicated that the majority of assaults were spousal: 79 per cent on wives and 8 per cent on husbands. Family abuse constituted 21 per cent, where mothers were victims in 4 per cent of cases, fathers in 2 per cent, children in 7 per cent and other family members in 8 per cent. Clearly, as Bell concludes, the police are reluctant to arrest, to make reports or to take any kind of action, unless the victim initiates the complaint.In addition, he concluded that police officers were inadequately trained in counselling and referral techniques. Attempts at mediation often exacerbated the situation. The distortion of crime figures followed from the use of police discretion, based on a police culture which traditionally recorded violence in the home as non-criminal. Violent assault against wives was not part of the crime problem.

Oppenlander (1982) similarly examined the police investigatory process, and the nature of the police response to domestic violence in three metropolitan areas: (a) Rochester, New York; (b) Tampa–St Petersburg, Florida, and (c) St Louis, Missouri, for an eleven-week period starting in May 1977. The database included 596 police investigations of arguments (disputes without physical contact) and assaults (including threats) for both domestic (including relatives, ex-spouses and cohabitees) and non-domestic (unrelated persons) disputes. From the outset Oppenlander found that police discretion and procedural mechanisms facilitated the gradual construction of domestic assault as a non-crime problem, through diverting cases out of the criminalization route. First, less than half of the domestic cases were dispatched as an assault, being described instead as 'family trouble', while 60 per cent of non-related disputes were dispatched as assaults. Second, patrol officers were slower in arriving at domestic disturbances than at arguments between unrelated disputants. Third, the police arrested in few cases, although there were clear legal grounds to do so. Of 180 domestic arguments, the police arrested in 8.9 per cent, while only 4 per cent of 110 non-domestic arguments resulted in arrests. Seventy-nine cases of domestic assault involved 22 per cent arrests. Of 227 non-domestic assault cases, over 13 per cent resulted in arrest. This might indicate that domestic incidents were taken seriously, were it not for the fact that there were *twice* as many injured victims in domestic compared with non-domestic cases, and so the proportion of arrests in domestic cases might have been expected to be much higher.

A central finding of Oppenlander's research was the fact that in spousal cases arrests were made not in respect of protecting the victim, but in respect of protecting public peace and order, or else punishing the offender for his recalcitrant anti-police behaviour. In a high proportion of domestic assault cases arrests were made for drunkenness or resisting an officer. As this case shows, an assault charge might be brought, as an afterthought, only if the suspect was hostile to the police.

> The domestic suspect was drunk and hostile. He referred to the officers as 'the law', taunted them, and refused to leave the house of his girlfriend, who looked bruised and scraped. Though he finally did leave, he continued yelling at the officers in the street, threatening to 'beat their heads'. The primary officer then placed the man under arrest for public drunkenness. When the suspect threatened to kill the officer at the police station, he added the charge of simple assault (of the female victim). (Oppenlander 1982: 456)

*British studies of police dispositions*

A number of studies of policing domestic violence have emerged. In July 1975 the Report of the Select Committee on Violence in Marriage recommended that 'Chief Constables should review their policies about the police approach to domestic violence. Special instructions about this difficult and delicate subject should be given to all new recruits, and regular written guidance should be issued by the Chief Constable in the form of advisory leaflets.' It was further recommended that where there was evidence of injury the suspect should be arrested and the abused woman conveyed to a place of safety. Since 1975, there have been few specific instructions and no regular written guidance from chief constables, few suspects have been arrested and few abused women conveyed to a place of safety. However, after the select committee's report, one police force scrutinized its own recording, investigatory and prosecution practices by conducting a small 'in house' research project.

Over a six-month period, from 1 February to 31 July 1976, Bedfordshire police monitored all reported cases of domestic violence, although their report doesn't make clear what criteria were used for inclusion. This suggests that, in conformity with traditional police practice, only the more serious cases were classified as 'domestic violence'. According to the police report, 288 acts of violence in the home came to police attention. Of the 288 cases, in 184 (63.9 per cent) the complainant withdrew the original allegation. In the remaining 104 cases (36.1 per cent) an arrest was made and prosecution proceedings commenced. The Bedfordshire Police report concluded by defending their existing practice not to arrest and/or prosecute where women had withdrawn the allegation.

Further studies from a radical perspective have tended to confirm that policing practice and the decision to arrest are variables dependent on a complainant's willingness or reluctance to prosecute. However, evidence regarding the real reluctance of the complainant is contradictory. Dobash and Dobash (1980) found little evidence to substantiate the finding that complainers were reluctant to prosecute: out of 933 cases examined in Scotland, only 6 per cent of women dropped the charges (see Stanko 1985: 122–9 for a detailed discussion). The finding of the London policing study (Edwards 1986b), on the other hand, was that complainers' reluctance to prosecute was cited by the police in nearly all cases as the reason for not proceeding further.

The contradiction is also found in studies of withdrawals at the prosecution stage. Wasoff (1982) found little evidence to support the view that complainants withdrew allegations at the prosecution stage. By contrast, Sanders (1988a) found this to be the main reason influencing a decision not to prosecute in four out of five domestic assault cases.

Like Oppenlander, Dobash and Dobash (1984) found the police reluctant to arrest unless they themselves were verbally abused. In a more recent study conducted by the Policy Studies Institute in London (1987) into domestic and non-domestic disputes a similar reluctance to arrest was revealed, even in cases when participants asked for an arrest to be made and their injuries amounted to assault.

*The London Policing Study* The most comprehensive study conducted so far in the UK is the London Policing Study, undertaken by the author and colleagues from the Polytechnic of Central London at two divisional police stations in the Metropolitan Police District (see Introduction). The study was based on an analysis of police dispositions (449 at Hounslow and 324 at Holloway) drawn from a total of 24,637 and 18,250 police records (station messages) (see figures 4.1 and 4.2), taken on a daily basis for six months during 1984 and 1985. The criteria for inclusion of cases followed Bell's definition of domestic violence disputes:

> A domestic dispute is any quarrel, altercation, or strife, including domestic violence between family or household members. Domestic violence occurs in domestic disputes when a person or persons cause or attempt to cause physical harm to another family or household member. (1985b: 303)

'Spousal incidents' included disputes between boyfriend and girlfriend, cohabitants, and husbands and wives. Family incidents were defined as assaults or threats by parents on children, children on parents or between siblings. The study found a police tendency towards diverting cases away from criminalization, by avoiding making arrests (rendering advice rather than arresting in assault cases), referring parties to other agencies, and in most cases doing no more than attending the call and stopping any violence actually in progress. In the two stations, slightly different patterns of reporting by the public and police recording practice were found.

Holloway police station in the London Borough of Islington covers a population of approximately 75,000. During the period of study, from August 1984 to January 1985, 449 domestic incidents were identified, though undoubtedly a larger number of such incidents came to police attention. As we have seen in earlier chapters, police initial classification and dispatching practices utilize a variety of computerized codes, and discretion is used in classifying domestic assault and disputes either as 'disturbances' or into the more specific category of assault. It is certain, therefore, that additional domestic

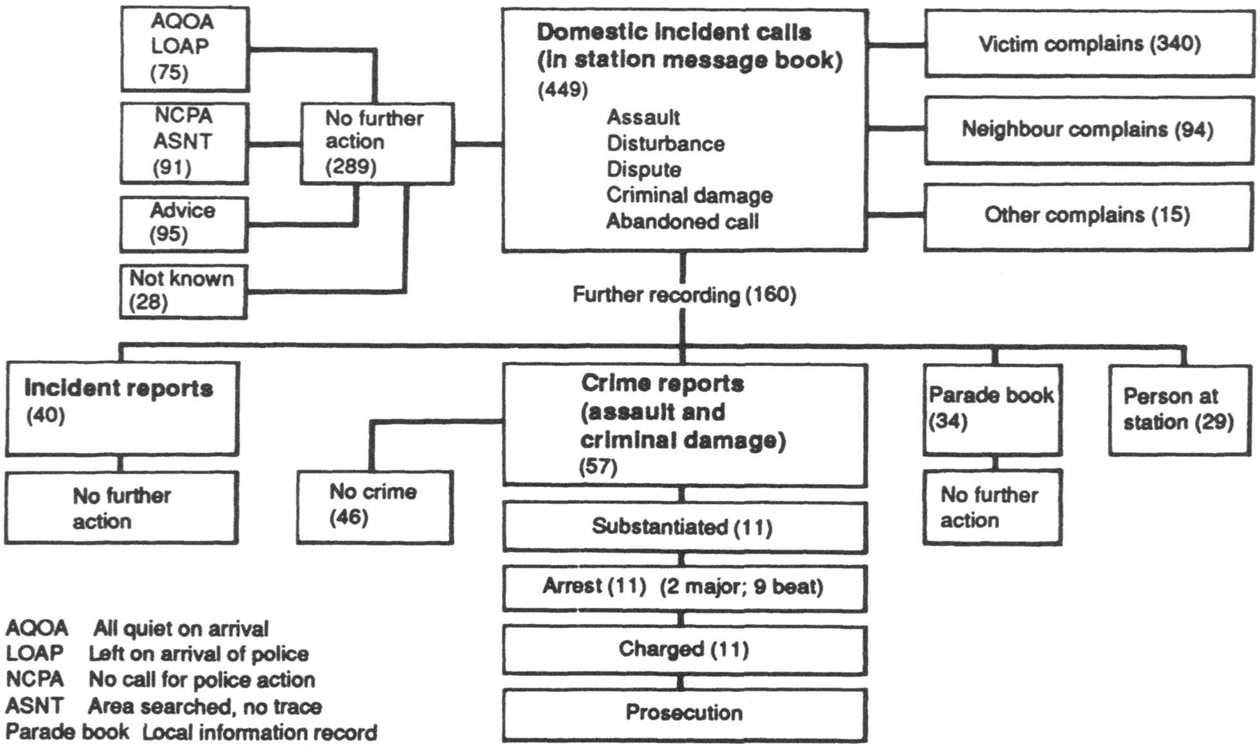


Figure 4.1 *Policing domestic disputes: Holloway, London, 1984–1985*

disputes and assault were reported to the police, but went unobserved by the researchers either because of 'cuffing' or because ambiguous assignment prevented identification. Of the identifiable sample of 449 cases, 85 per cent were spousal (i.e. between cohabitees or ex-cohabitees). Excluded from this spousal category were those cases where incidents had arisen out of quarrels between present and past husbands, present and past wives, or similar permutations. Of the 85 per cent of spousal incidents, a very small and insignificant proportion involved women as offending parties. These, however, were incidents in which women were also the victims of assault and where men counter-filed charges against them. A total of 2 per cent implicated women as offenders.

Who complained? Victims of assault and disputes complained in 340 (76 per cent) of cases. Neighbours or bystanders reported in 109 (24 per cent) of cases. How did the police respond? Of the 449 cases, 363 (81 per cent) were completed by the police at the scene. With no action other than incident reports or parade book entries (40 and 34) in some cases. A further 29 cases (6 per cent) were regarded as dealt with after a visit to the station, while in 57 cases (13 per cent) a crime report was filled out. Of these, 20 cases were regarded as serious and recorded as major crimes, and 37 were regarded as less serious and recorded as 'beat crimes'. Of the 20 major crimes, 18 (90 per cent) were later 'no crimed' (written off); only 2 (10 per cent) were proceeded with up to a prosecution. Of the 37 'beat crimes', 28 (76 per cent) were 'no crimed' and 9 (24 per cent) proceeded with further. However, not all 9 cases including beat crimes and major crimes actually reached formal prosecution, some dropping out before. Warrants were issued for arrest in 4 cases; arrests were made in 3 cases (1 suspect was detained in custody and 2 released on bail); and in the 1 remaining case, the police reduced the charge and proceeded with a 'breach of the peace' action, the complainant not wishing to proceed with an assault charge. The outcomes were trivial for all cases reaching court, and are discussed in chapter 6.

In a further 40 cases (9 per cent), although a crime report was not completed the police deemed the incident of sufficient seriousness to be recorded in an incident report book. In many of these cases police recorded that a common assault had occurred. The legal criterion for common assault is bruising or reddening. Yet in 29 (72.5 per cent of the 40) cases recorded as incidents, police recorded details of more serious assaults. Officers recorded visible evidence of assault: bruising, cuts, swellings following strangulation attempts, and injuries sustained in an attack with a weapon. Nevertheless such cases were recorded in an incident report rather than a crime entry which arguably would have been more appropriate. It is not known what proportion of these cases resulted in victims applying either for a non-molestation injunction or a personal protection order, or else pursuing an action for common assault in the magistrates' court. It is unlikely that many women actually took any action themselves when we look to the figures for criminal and civil proceedings in London. A total of 6,080 women were recorded by the police as being advised about civil remedies in the metropolitan area alone in 1985 (my estimate). In 1985 in England and Wales a mere 1,362 men were prosecuted in the magistrates' courts for the offence of common assault on men, or women, or children. In addition, in 1985, 13,020 injunctions were granted in the county courts and 6,770 applications for personal protection orders were made in the magistrates' courts. Taken together, these figures for the whole of England and Wales represent only three times the number of cases advised by the police in London alone. It must be concluded that few women advised by the police about remedies actually pursue civil or criminal actions themselves.

Of all the 449 calls for assistance, physical violence was recorded by the police as a feature in 86 cases, reported either in crime reports (57) or in 29 out of the 40 incident report book entries. Moreover, the absence of any detailed reporting in the remaining cases does not exclude the possibility that violence might have featured in them. Yet, although clear evidence of violence was apparent in 86 cases, in only 11 out of 449 assaults and arguments reported (2.4 per cent) was the case proceeded with to prosecution. These 11 constituted 12.7 per cent of the 86 recorded physical assaults including crime reports and incident reports where violence was recorded. During this period, 16 injunctions with a power of arrest were on file, including 13 non-molestation/exclusion orders granted by the county court in accordance with the 1976 Act, while 3 personal protection/exclusion orders were granted in the magistrates' court in accordance with the 1978 Act.

Turning to the second police area under study, a similar profile of complainer reporting, police recording practice and prosecution emerges. The population of the area served by Hounslow Police Station is 65,007. During the period of study (July–December 1984), 324 incidents of physical assault and altercation were identified as having been reported (see figure 4.2). A total of 288 cases, 89 per cent, were spousal, and 36 cases (11 per cent) related to family matters. The victims of the assault, altercation or threat complained in 244 cases (75 per cent), while bystanders (principally neighbours or friends) alerted police in 80 cases (25 per cent). A total of 279 cases (86 per cent) were dealt with at the scene, and 9 cases (3 per cent) involved visits to the police station. Of all incidents reported, a total of 36 (11

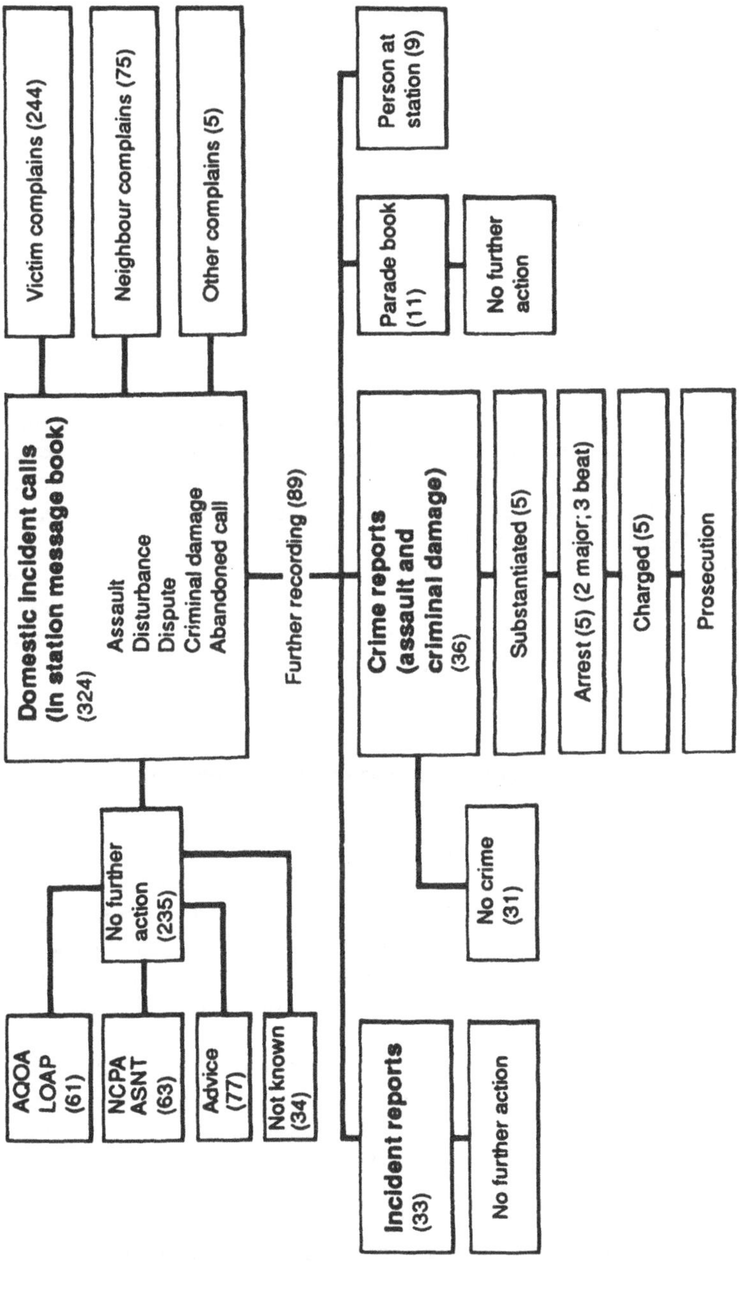


Figure 4.2 *Policing domestic disputes: Hounslow, London, 1984*

per cent) were made the subject of a crime report. This included 3 major crimes; 2 were proceeded with and 1 'no crimed'. Of the 33 beat crimes, 30 were 'no crimed' (91 per cent) and 3 proceeded with (9 per cent). Court disposals in these cases were trivial. A total of 33 incidents were recorded in the incident report book, of which 19 were recorded as involving physical injury (57 per cent). It is not known what proportion of these cases resulted in women taking civil action to obtain an injunction or charge with common assault. Out of 324 calls for assistance, 5 cases (1.5 per cent) were proceeded with. Expressed as a proportion of all recorded physical assaults (55), 9 per cent of cases were proceeded with. A total of 11 injunctions were in force during the research period, 10 from the county court and one from the magistrates' court.

The difference in public reporting and police recording practices in the two areas is not especially marked. Cases of violence in Holloway tended to be more serious, reflected in the greater proportion of major crimes recorded and a lower proportion of 'no criming' overall. Although both race and class variables may have affected these discretionary decisions, it was not possible to examine the extent of possible race bias, as information on the racial identity of victims and offenders is only systematically available in crime reports. An analysis of crime reports indicated that Afro-Caribbean, Asian and white groups were roughly equally represented. The above profiles of cases emerge as a result of the use of officers' discretion at certain pivotal points in the process of dealing with an incident, from first complaint onwards.

### Recording violence against women: the use or abuse of 'no crime'

Let us turn now to a consideration of the routine management of discretion in the police processing of domestic violence incidents. Official figures of spousal/partner violence tend to be much lower than is suggested in research, including the London Policing Study. This reduction begins with the dispatcher who allocates calls to patrol or investigating officers who then attend the scene. How does this distortion occur?

When cases of domestic assault are made the subject of a crime report, the initial decision to record an allegation of assault as a crime does not automatically imply that these assaults are finally classified or cleared up as crimes. Only a very small proportion of crimed cases result in an assault classification and the arrest and prosecution of the offender. Instead, more typically in cases where a crime report is initiated, at some later stage the crime is likely to be erased without trace through a 'no crime' reclassification. Officers' book-keeping methods account for this routine practice, on grounds of either insufficient evidence or complainer withdrawal. Skolnick found that when a domestic offence had occurred the patrolman (usually with the advice of his sergeant, even if the offence appears serious) might decide not to write it up as a crime.

> It was a very quiet evening for crime. Only one interesting happening - a call that an assault had been committed. After some time trying to find the house - in one of the courtyards of a city project - Sergeant L. and I arrived on the scene after one of the 'beat' patrolmen . . . We walked into a poorly furnished house. A large, rather handsome Black man was seated on a couch daubing his ear with a towel and being aided by a five or six year old boy. The man looked dazed and the Sergeant inquired brusquely as to what had happened. (He knew already; before we entered the patrolman told us the man had been cut on the ear by his wife, and also that the man didn't want to file a complaint.) 'She cut me' the man mumbled . . . 'Nothing really happened, she just came at me with the knife; I was drinking, she came at me with the knife.' Before leaving the Sergeant made sure the man didn't want to file a complaint. (1966: 171)

Skolnick explains that typically no offence report is made out for such an incident - where the matter is within the family and there is no complainant. He further suggests that if the family had been white, the police response might have been different and the offence taken more seriously. Such events, however, are routinely diverted out of the criminal justice process with the compliance of patrolmen who record such offences in assignment reports and not in crime reports.

The use of the 'no crime' classification, particularly in domestic violence situations, varies considerably from one police force to another. The Metropolitan Police have traditionally applied the 'no crime' in difficult or ambiguous cases. McClintock, in his classic study of the Metropolitan Police, questioned the commonly held assumption that all prima-facie cases of violence reported to the police were automatically recorded. He found that domestic assault cases in particular were likely to go unrecorded.

> A woman aged 31 went into a police station late at night and complained that she had just been beaten up by a gang of thugs and robbed. She had a cut across the left eyebrow as well as slight grazes on her face and hands. She had obviously been drinking fairly heavily. On interview she was recognized by a member of the local CID as having been previously convicted of larceny and soliciting and her criminal record showed that she was a woman of low repute, 'associating with thieves and prostitutes'. She reluctantly withdrew her first story when it was pointed out that she was still in possession of her handbag, which contained more than £3. She

> then said that she had been beaten up by J.N. because she had refused to give him money. Her new story was that he had kicked her in the shin and then pushed her so that she had fallen in the gutter and had cut her head on the kerbstone. J.N., who was known to the police as a thief, was interviewed; he admitted that he had spoken to her but denied committing the assault. 'She asked me home but I sees she was the worse for gin and told her that drink would be her end but I never touched her.' Next morning when confronted with this other account of the incident she said 'You know J.N.'s a b . . . liar. He did attack me.' However, later in the same interview she said she did not really know what had happened the night before. In the end she left the police station in a rage shouting that she didn't want anything more to do with J.N., the police, the magistrates or anyone else . . . The offence that was recorded for statistical purposes was one of assault occasioning actual bodily harm. On application to a senior officer the case was marked down as a 'no crime'. If the police had accepted L.V.'s story the crime would have remained on record as assault occasioning actual bodily harm, but it would have had to remain as not cleared up because the victim refused to cooperate with the police. (1963: 63)

However, it would not be true to say that the use of the 'no crime' classification was exclusively reserved for domestic cases where complainants withdrew complaints. Researchers have also found instances of the use of this category for other offences. Coleman and Bottomley in their investigation of this 'no criming' practice in rural and urban police forces found considerable variations between forces and categories. 'Most typicaliy they involved property reported stolen but subsequently found by the complainant . . .' (1976: 341–2). McCabe and Sutcliffe (1978) in their study of policing in Oxford and Salford found further differences. In Oxford during 1974, 617 (6 per cent) out of a total of 10,116 crimes known to the police were classified as 'no crime', while in Salford 205 (1 per cent) out of a total of 12,994 were similarly classified. Burrows (1986: 20), in his study on burglary, found wide variations between the classifications of incidents (see table 3.11 in Burrows). Finally, Steer (1981: 58), in a study of police recording practice in Oxford, discovered that the 'no crime' classification was used where the complaint could not be substantiated. 'Complaints that cannot be substantiated' run the whole range from situations in which evidence is weak because the injury is not visible to the officer to those in which the injury is apparent but the complainant does not wish to prosecute. Forces disagree about the proper use of 'no criming'. In cases where 'the guilt of the offender is clear but the person refuses to give evidence', Steer argues that the crime should be recorded as 'crime detected but not proceeded with' (p. 59). In a case from Steer's study the following incident was classified as a 'no crime', and police recorded their reason for the decision as 'Insufficient evidence to charge'. A woman had alleged that her husband, from whom she was separated, had assaulted the children, causing one actual bodily harm, an offence which he denied. Steer's view was that this should have been recorded as an undetected crime.

*'No criming' rape*

'No criming' may be police practice in a range of difficult cases. Research in police recording of rape cases suggests that 'no criming' is particularly used in cases of rape and domestic violence. A 'no crime' classification weeds out cases and treats them as if they had not occurred at all. In 1984 a total of 1,433 crimes of rape were recorded by the police in England and Wales. By 1985, this figure had risen significantly to 1,842, by 1986 to 2,288 and by 1987 to 2,471 (*Criminal Statistics* 1987). Taking crime figures at their face value, the statistics suggest that more women are at risk from rape than ever before. And, an examination of regional crime figures shows rape in London to be increasing at an alarming rate: 269 rapes in 1980, 256 in 1981, 285 in 1982, 317 in 1983, 365 in 1984, 570 in 1985, 824 in 1986 and 732 in 1987 (*Reports of the Commissioner of the Police of the Metropolis*). The idea that the rise in recorded rapes, particularly from 1984 to 1985, resulted from a heightened public confidence in the police's ability to deal with them sympathetically, thus encouraging more women to report their victimization, was an eagerly promoted interpretation. Yet the increase in cases recorded is in fact the result of several factors, most significantly perhaps recent improvements in police recording practices. These changes arose as a direct consequence of the findings of Ian Blair's study on rape (1985).

Blair, a senior police officer, examined the problems of sexual offence investigation in England and Wales and in the United States, and produced a series of recommendations for policing policy. He recommended that the British police learn from the US experience (p. 73), and outlined the need for improved medical procedures, specialist units, better trained officers, and procedural changes in methods of interview. A major thrust of his work was a critique of police recording practice. He gingerly let the 'cat out of the bag' in pointing out that high 'clear up' rates do not necessarily reflect sound police practice. He argued that as far as rape is concerned the 'clear up rate is likely to drop as a result of improvements in police methods', and 'the high detection rate in Britain is likely to be at least in part, an artefact of police recording practices' (pp. 73–4). Such bold statements from a senior officer certainly challenged the views of those chief constables in England and Wales who had preferred to present high clear-up rates as the sugar-coated almond of success. Blair, not without considerable courage, went even further: 'high detection rates seem to go hand in hand with police recording practices aimed at disposing of crimes in the interest of administrative convenience' (Blair 1985: 60).

Blair was right. While in 1984, 68 per cent of all recorded rapes in England and Wales were cleared up, with the introduction of the new recording practices in the Metropolitan Police District the clear-up rate for England and Wales fell to 64 per cent in 1985, though they rose back up to 71 per cent in 1987 (*Criminal Statistics* 1984, 1985 and 1987, table 2.9, p. 35). In the Metropolitan Police area alone the clear-up rate was 54 per cent for 1984, 49 per cent for 1985 and 49 per cent for 1987. The number of rapes prosecuted in England and Wales in 1984 had been only 657; 46 per cent of all 1,433 rapes officially recorded by the police. In 1985 only 826 rapes were prosecuted, constituting 45 per cent of all 1,842 rapes officially recorded by the police, and in 1986 925 cases out of 2,288 (46 per cent) were proceeded with. In 1987 1,046 out of 2,471 (42 per cent) cases were proceeded with. In looking at these figures we should be mindful of the fact that in court the charge is sometimes reduced to one of indecent assault (Walmsley and White 1979; Adler 1987; *Home Office Statistical Bulletin* 1989).

Similar criticisms had been made by researchers working for the Scottish Office with a greater degree of independence and freedom than a police inspector. Chambers and Millar regard the use of the 'no crime' as systematic tampering. They write, 'The term no-crime is used in this study to describe the technical reports to ensure that those which do not turn out to be criminal incidents after investigation are excluded, and do not appear in the records of official statistics concerning the number of crimes made known to the police' (1983: 38). The studies conducted by Wright (1980) and Chambers and Millar (1983) show 'no criming' to be used routinely. Chambers and Millar (1983: 10, 38) found that almost one quarter of all cases in their study were 'no crimed' by the police. Almost half (48 per cent) of all undetected cases were no crimed. Wright (1980) examined 384 rape allegations made to the police from 1972 to 1976 in six English constabularies (Cambridgeshire, Hertfordshire, Bedfordshire, Northamptonshire, Essex and Norfolk). Of those allegations, 175 were classified as rapes, 80 as attempted rape, 37 as group rape, and 92 (23.9 per cent) were written off as 'no crime'. Wright acknowledges that some of these 'no crime' cases were false allegations, but also concedes that a significant proportion represented true rapes. Consider the following 'no crimed' case.

> In one case, for instance, police officers discovered an immigrant woman and an Englishman having intercourse in a car park. The woman immediately complained to them of rape. The police classified this

> incident as 'no crime', pointing out in their report that the woman probably alleged rape because she was embarrassed at being discovered in such compromising circumstances. What they did not mention (though the information was contained in the police records) was that the man and woman were found lying on a bed of broken glass and, according to the police surgeon's report, both had received several cuts. (1980: 101–2)

Figures for Thames Valley Police (a force exposed for its unsympathetic handling of rape complaints in an embarrassing television documentary in 1982) revealed that in 1980, 94 cases were reported, 62 recorded and 32 withdrawn (34 per cent), while in 1981, 76 cases were reported, 37 recorded and 39 withdrawn (51 per cent) (*Guardian*, 20 January 1982).

Blair's (1985: 60) own analysis of final dispositions of rape allegations in the United States reveals that the detection rate may well be largely an indication of the policy pursued in relation to classifying allegations as withdrawn or unfounded, rather than the 'true' rate.

### *Recording spousal and partner violence in London: 'no call for police action'*

In the UK, having attended the scene of a call, a police officer is required to make out a written report. Most cases of domestic assault and altercation result in the officer making a radio call back to the station, where the incident is then recorded 'No call for police action'. Seventy per cent of all calls from the public in domestic cases in the London study were recorded in this way. The use of 'no call for police action' as a police shorthand neither does justice to police time and energy expended, nor does it accurately describe what assistance has been offered. Yet in their view the use of 'no call for police action' is legitimate in circumstances where the attendance of the officer at the scene of the call is sufficient in itself. Police perceptions of such incidents are that they are trivial, and do not involve physical violence. However, we do not know this, and no research has been conducted on the precise range of situations encountered by the police which are later written off in this manner. The London policing study found that 'No call for police action' described situations in which the complainer did not want any further police intervention, but may have been assaulted, and cases in which there was no evidence of assault, as well as cases in which there was an argument or assault but both parties were extremely hostile to police presence. 'No call for police action' was also used where the dispute was a particularly difficult one.

Of the 773 calls attended by police officers in both locations (Holloway and Hounslow), 73 were written up more fully as incident report book entries, 93 were written up as crimes, and several further incidents were written up in the occurrence book (or 'person at station' book). It was often difficult to work out why one officer considered a call warranted an incident report book entry while another officer, after a similar incident, did not, or how the rather more important decision was made between 'criming' an incident or recording it in another way, avoiding the use of a crime category. Significantly, the use of the incident report book or occurrence book usually avoided further police action and any further paperwork. The arbitrary nature of recording is also borne out in other studies. Consider for example the appropriateness of recording the following incident in the police occurrence book rather than in the crime book, reported in the research conducted by McCabe and Sutcliffe in Salford: 'A young woman came to the counter late on a Saturday evening. She said she had been attacked by her husband and was afraid to go home' (1978: 25).

The London study also found evidence of the occurrence book being used to record domestic assaults which might more appropriately have been recorded as crimes. Domestic assaults were also found recorded in the Person at Station Book, where the offender may be cautioned rather than charged with an offence. This is an entry from a person at station book consulted in the London study.

> On Saturday 5 January, 11.50 pm at Red Rd, at the junction with Green Rd, a car with two female occupants was driven at, by two occupants of a Rover car. The car has apparently already got damaged on the near side. It was driven on the wrong side of the road and forced the females' car to stop. The driver of the car was armed with a knife with a blade about 4" long with a 6" handle. He cut the younger female's cheek with a swipe telling her he was going to cut her ear off. He stubbed his cigarette out on her face and he pulled her necklace from her neck and lunged at her with a knife but was stopped by the second male occupier of the Rover car. Immediately prior to this he drove the car directly at the girl, edging progressively towards her pushing her backwards. The incident lasted approximately twenty minutes. Any officer who may have any information with regard to either the identity of the owner of the car or occupier of the vehicle, will they please contact DS Grey at White Police Station.

Clearly, this case might also have been recorded in the crime book. In most cases it would have been likely to be crimed. However, consultation of the crime book indicated that no decision was taken to include it there.

Of the 773 calls made to the police during the six months' investigation period in both locations, many involved women who had experienced quite horrifying violence. More extensive documentation of the nature of the violence was available for 166 cases, which were made either the subject of a crime report (93 cases) or the subject of an incident report (73 cases). Clearly, in some cases women who have been physically assaulted are diverted out of the criminal process at the earliest possible stage, their attacks being recorded not as 'crimes' but as 'incidents'. Of those cases initially written up as crimes, the majority are 'no crimed' at the next stage. These cases are not trivial episodes, as conventional police and public perceptions have led us to expect; instead they involve varying degrees of physical assault.

While it is certainly true that a few cases were indeed minor, or else could be differentiated from cases crimed on the bases that an injunction was in force or civil proceedings for divorce in progress, in about half of all cases recorded as incidents physical injuries were apparent. Curiously, in these cases the degree and the nature of the injury was comparable to the degree and nature of injuries sustained by women in crimed cases. Why then were some cases crimed whilst other, almost identical, cases were made the subject of an incident report only? It was the difference in prospect of prosecution, rather than anything about the violence, which impinged on officers' decision to crime or to write up the case as an 'incident'. First, in cases recorded in an incident report, complainants seemed unwilling to press charges or to want further interference from the outset. Although similar reluctance was also evident in most cases that *were* crimed, it generally only emerged at a later stage. One could conclude that some officers, realizing that the complainant was not going to take the case any further, preferred to write off the incident at the earliest possible stage, rather than write it up as a crime, which would then necessitate a follow-up and possibly further enquiries.

### *No prosecution, no crime*

Violence against wives and cohabitees is probably the most sensitive of all crimes to 'no criming', as researchers looking more generally at the 'no crime' classification for all crimes (McCabe and Sutcliffe 1978; Steer 1981) have found. We have no means of identifying cases of spousal violence from other assault in England and Wales. The relationship of offender to victim is not a component of the statistics that are available to us. Nevertheless, the tiny proportion of cases of domestic assault that are crimed come to constitute a high proportion of offences of violence known to the police in the Metropolitan Police District. According to the Commissioner's Report, 40 per cent of those cases recorded involved assaults where the victim and assailant were known to each other (Commissioner of the Police of the Metropolis 1985: 90).

Table 4.8 *Physical injuries recorded in incident reports, Holloway and Hounslow, 1984–1985*[a]

| | Nature of incident | | | | | |
|---|---|---|---|---|---|---|
| Incident category | Injunction | Trespass | Locked out | Threats to hit | Threats to kill | Child abuse |
| Common assault | | | | | | |
| Holloway | — | — | — | — | — | — |
| Hounslow | — | 1 | 1 | 1 | 1 | — |
| Common assault or breach order | | | | | | |
| Holloway | — | — | — | — | — | — |
| Hounslow | — | — | — | — | — | — |
| Assault | | | | | | |
| Holloway | — | — | — | — | — | — |
| Hounslow | — | — | — | — | — | — |
| Domestic dispute | | | | | | |
| Holloway | — | 1 | 1 | — | — | 1 |
| Hounslow | — | — | 1 | 1 | — | — |
| Husband/wife dispute | | | | | | |
| Holloway | — | — | 2 | — | — | — |
| Hounslow | 3 | — | 1 | 3 | — | — |
| Family dispute | | | | | | |
| Holloway | — | — | 1 | — | — | — |
| Hounslow | — | — | 1 | 1 | — | — |
| Trespass | | | | | | |
| Holloway | — | — | — | — | — | — |
| Hounslow | — | 1 | — | — | — | — |
| Other civil dispute | | | | | | |
| Holloway | 1 | — | — | — | — | 2 |
| Hounslow | — | — | — | — | — | — |
| Total | | | | | | |
| Holloway | 1 | 1 | 4 | — | — | 3 |
| Hounslow | 3 | 2 | 4 | 6 | 1 | — |
| Both | 4 | 3 | 8 | 6 | 1 | 3 |

[a]Six-month sample: August 1984–January 1985 for Holloway; July–December 1984 for Hounslow.

A total of 175 cases of violence (including domestic and non-domestic) for Holloway for the period August 1984 to January 1985, and 85 cases for Hounslow for the period March to September 1984 were recorded and examined for incidence of 'no criming', together with the reasons given by the investigating officer for this decision. In cases of spousal violence in which the husband or male cohabitee had assaulted the wife or female cohabitee, 90 per cent of cases at Hounslow were 'no crimed' compared with 69 per cent at Holloway.

Table 4.8 *continued*

| Nature of incident | | | | | | | | | |
|---|---|---|---|---|---|---|---|---|---|
| Physical injury | | | | | | | | | |
| | Visible | | | | | | | | |
| Not visible | Fist to face | Kick | Choke | Leg injury | Weapon | Both parties | Grab/ drag/ rip | Sexual | Total |
| 10 | 9 | — | 2 | 2 | — | 2 | — | 1 | 26 |
| — | 5 | 2 | 2 | — | 1 | — | 1 | — | 15 |
| — | — | — | — | — | — | — | — | — | 0 |
| — | — | — | 1 | — | — | — | — | — | 1 |
| — | — | — | — | — | — | — | — | — | 0 |
| — | 1 | — | — | — | — | — | — | — | 1 |
| — | 1 | — | — | — | — | 1 | — | — | 5 |
| 1 | — | — | — | — | — | — | — | 1 | 4 |
| — | — | — | — | — | — | — | — | — | 2 |
| — | — | — | — | — | — | — | 1 | 1 | 9 |
| — | — | — | — | — | — | — | — | — | 1 |
| — | — | — | — | — | — | — | — | — | 2 |
| — | — | — | — | — | — | — | — | — | 0 |
| — | — | — | — | — | — | — | — | — | 1 |
| 2 | — | — | 1 | — | — | — | — | — | 6 |
| — | — | — | — | — | — | — | — | — | 0 |
| 12 | 10 | — | 3 | 2 | — | 3 | — | 1 | 40 |
| 1 | 6 | 2 | 3 | — | 1 | — | 2 | 2 | 33 |
| 13 | 16 | 2 | 6 | 2 | 1 | 3 | 2 | 3 | 73 |

When the physical evidence of assault is apparent and the identity of the suspect is known, it is the reluctance of the complainant to prosecute which results in police 'no criming'.

Of all 'no crimed' cases at both locations, in 40 per cent the violence was perpetrated against a girlfriend rather than a wife. In these cases the complainant can be compelled to give evidence. Even here, however, cases still did not proceed. Cohabitation seemed to be an overriding factor in the complainant's decision to drop charges and in

Table 4.9 *'No criming' in cases of family violence, criminal damage and theft in Holloway and Hounslow, 1984–1985*[a]

| Victim/offender relationship | Offence as recorded | Subject of crime report | Crimed No. | Crimed % | No crimed No. | No crimed % | Recorded reasons for no criming: Unknown | Victim unwilling to substantiate | Insufficient evidence | Venue |
|---|---|---|---|---|---|---|---|---|---|---|
| *Male on female (spousal)* | | | | | | | | | | |
| Holloway | ABH | 36 | 11 | 31 | 25 | 69 | 1 | 22 | 1 | 1 |
| Hounslow | | 25 | 2 | 8 | 23 | 90 | 1 | 17 | 4 | 1 |
| *Female on male (spousal)* | | | | | | | | | | |
| Holloway | ABH | 2 | — | — | 2 | 100 | — | 2 | — | — |
| Hounslow | | 2 | — | — | 2 | 100 | — | 2 | — | — |
| *Father/son or son/father* | | | | | | | | | | |
| Holloway | ABH | — | — | — | — | — | — | — | — | — |
| Hounslow | | 7 | 1 | 14 | 6 | 86 | — | 6 | — | — |
| *Female/female acquainted* | | | | | | | | | | |
| Holloway | ABH | 5 | — | — | 5 | 100 | 1 | 4 | — | — |
| Hounslow | | 6 | 1 | 17 | 5 | 83 | 1 | 3 | — | 1 |
| *Male/male unacquainted* | | | | | | | | | | |
| Holloway | ABH | 132 | 66 | 50 | 66 | 50 | 4 | 54 | 8 | — |
| Hounslow | | 45 | 23 | 51 | 22 | 49 | 1 | 17 | 4 | — |
| *All* | | | | | | | | | | |
| Holloway | Criminal damage | 493 | 296 | 60 | 197 | 40 | 20 | 65 | 112 | — |
| Hounslow | | 161 | 128 | 71 | 33 | 29 | — | 17 | 15 | 1 |
| *All* | | | | | | | | | | |
| Holloway | Theft | 1,120 | 960 | 86 | 160 | 14 | 6 | 80 | 74 | — |
| Hounslow | | 393 | 325 | 83 | 68 | 17 | — | 29 | 21 | 18 |

ABH = assault occasioning actual bodily harm.

[a]Six-month sample: August 1984–January 1985 for Holloway; March–September 1984 for Hounslow.

the police decision to 'no crime'. Even so, in 38 per cent of cases 'no crimed' the victim and aggressor were not residing together. Clearly, then, for a significant proportion of these cases (where complainants were not residing with aggressors and were not bound in marriage and were therefore compellable witnesses), police arguably had no reasonable grounds for not pressing charges.

Violence between males outside the family, including violence between acquaintances and males unknown in both areas, were far less likely to be reclassified as a 'no crime' even when the complainant was unwilling to press charges. Fifty per cent of all recorded crimes of violence between males were dealt with in this way; although this rate was much lower than that for spousal cases (around 80 per cent), it is still much higher than the 'no crime' rate revealed in other studies for other police force areas.

Turning to a consideration of the 'no crime' in dealing with minor thefts in both Metropolitan Police districts studied, we find that it was used much less frequently than in domestic and non-domestic assault. In 14 per cent of theft cases in Holloway the offence was 'no crimed', compared with a slightly higher rate for Hounslow of 17 per cent. Interestingly, while in domestic and non-domestic cases the offence is 'no crimed' in an overwhelming number of cases because of the victim's reluctance to prosecute rather than an insufficiency of evidence, in theft cases the reasons for the 'no crime' were roughly equally divided between an insufficiency of evidence and the withdrawal of the charge by the complainant.

Criminal damage cases had a higher degree of no criming than did theft cases, but still registered a lower rate than domestic and non-domestic assaults. In Holloway 40 per cent of cases recorded as criminal damage were later written off as 'no crimes', compared with 29 per cent of criminal damage cases in the Hounslow district. Like domestic assault, criminal damage in many cases involved criminal damage within the household. The main difficulty here is that in many cases the offender was smashing up his own property – which he has every legal right to do. In this respect in case law the decision in *Summers* v. *Summers* ([1986] 1 FLR 343) has shown, even in injunction applications, that evidence of a husband 'smashing the house to bits' is not considered sufficient to oust him from his own property, since it is not evidence of this physical violence. Overall the 'no crime' in London is used for disposing of cases where the victim is unwilling to substantiate the allegation, and as this reluctance typically characterizes violent assault between intimates and those acquainted it is certainly the case that such violence, whatever the relationship of victim to suspect, is seriously under-recorded.

What is the nature of the spousal violence that is being 'no crimed'? The following cases are drawn from the London study.

'The victim spoke to her husband about his driving without a licence, then an argument followed where he hit her in her head with his fists and then with shoes and threatened to throw acid in her face. She sustained injuries in the manner of bruising to the right forehead. The matter was later no crimed, the complainant wishing to withdraw the allegation. (Case no. 1)

Suspect punched victim in face whilst drunk. He is her common law husband. (Case no. 2)

Victim had an argument with former boyfriend which resulted in him breaking a vase and assaulting her. She sustained injuries - nose bleeding and bruising. (Case no. 14)

She stated that her boyfriend assaulted her, punching her and kicking her about the body and face. (Case no. 16)

The victim had an argument with her ex-boyfriend who was still living in the squat - he hit her over the head with a wine bottle, causing a cut to her right ear. (Case no: 19)

After a row the boyfriend assaulted the woman by punching her in the face. (Case no. 20)

Following an argument he pushed her on the floor, put his hand over her mouth and punched her on the left side of the face. (Case no. 28)

The victim's separated husband argued over custody, pushed her to the floor and punched her on the left side of the face. (Case no. 37)

The victim was bruised all over the body. Her injuries were caused by her ex-husband. He persuaded her to get into his car and assaulted her as follows: 4" square bruising left arm, 4" square bruising left thigh, bruising to arms, legs and torso and head. (Case no. 26)

Cases made the subject of a major crime report were more serious, as one might expect, often involving the use of objects to inflict violence. Even so, 'no criming' was still used if the complainer withdrew the allegation. The following major crime was 'no crimed':

Miss X had been living with her boyfriend at the address. He has beaten her up before whilst drunk, but she has never taken any action. This evening he was drunk and during an argument he hit her with a broom handle, causing a 4" bruise to the left leg and a 2" cut to the left forearm; left eye is 'blight' and a 2" bruise on the head above the left eye. Miss X does not wish any action to be taken. (Case no. H19)

Kent and South Wales Constabularies, like many others, claim to adopt a policy of recording all domestic cases as crimes - even those in which the complainant is not willing to substantiate the allegation at a later date. Other similar incidents of violence where the complainant is unwilling to proceed are recorded as crimes 'as endorsed - Detected . . . as per force policy'. It has not yet been possible to conduct research in these areas to assess the truth of these claims. Certainly, most police forces would vigorously deny the use of the 'no crime' for anything other than a genuine error in recording. In reality, as various researchers have discovered, 'no criming' is a routine feature of recording in many forces.

## Conclusion

Spousal or partner violence has never been seen as a central issue in the crime debate. It is a private event, occurring largely behind closed doors. The substantive law regulating personal violence, while in its content applying to domestic violence and non-domestic violence equally, in its form, particularly in terms of prosecution criteria and evidence, has reinforced a reluctance to intervene and prosecute in cases of violence against women. The problem is compounded by the reluctance of the complainer to prosecute, once having made a complaint. This probability justifies police non-intervention and prosecution avoidance. These difficulties translate into police culture, permeating every level, including police recording practice. This kind of violence against women, above all other crimes in some police force areas, can be almost totally erased from records.

Police organizational goals have traditionally placed an exceedingly high value on detecting and clearing up crime. Technically, most domestic assaults are capable of being detected, and they are also capable of being cleared up. The Home Office in 1980 made it clear that when the guilt of the offender was clear, even though the complainant did not wish to prosecute, charges could be brought. The guilt of the offender is clear in many of these cases, although the suspect may not make an admission. According to this Home Office guidance the majority of domestic cases 'no crimed' in London could be crimed and actually cleared up. More urgently, whatever the possibility of clear-up, crimes should be properly recorded. Is spousal violence and all violence against women more vulnerable to bad recording practice because of the low prioritization of violence against women (especially in the home), or is it that bad recording practices follow automatically from the widespread reluctance to prosecute (based on expectation of acquittal)? It is clear that victims *are* reluctant to prosecute. But if the police accorded this matter a higher priority, they would not tolerate the erosion of crimes in such a systematic manner.

The proper collection of figures on spousal violence is crucial to setting this problem in the centre of the general crime debate, and to arousing not only public concern, but a new police interest in the problem. At the moment police forces are not required to keep separate statistics on domestic assault, and no separate statistics are published. If the figures are not open to public scrutiny, there is no incentive or pressure to do anything about bad record-keeping practices.

# 5
# Women's Experience of Violence and Protection

## Introduction

Women who experience violence in marriage or in a cohabiting relationship, or rape by acquaintances or by strangers, then find themselves unwilling actors in another form of 'violence' – the undoubted harm engendered by the criminal 'justice' process. In this process the defendant is innocent until proven guilty, and this fundamental pillar of justice is rigorously guarded. By contrast, in cases of violence and sexual violence the position of the complainant is unique. Rape complainants and domestic violence complainants are accused and maligned, and in the adversarial contest they find that their conduct is 'on trial'. While the double victimization of the rape victim has been well documented (Weis and Borges 1973; Griffin 1971; Edwards 1981), the double victimization of spousal violence complainants is less well known (Bowker 1984).

Fewer men plead 'not guilty' to domestic violent assault than to rape, but blaming the victim is nevertheless frequently the basis of any explanation offered to the court by the defendant in mitigation. Women's motives for silence have been widely documented (e.g. Radzinowicz and King 1978), and women victims who know their aggressors have many reasons for fear (see Gelles 1972). First, they fear retaliation. Walker (1979) found that violence often escalated when a woman called the police. Binney, Harkell and Nixon found that even when men were prosecuted they were left free to assault wives/cohabitees again. One woman remarked:

> He was charged with actual bodily harm, common assault and unlawful assault. He got fined, bound over and was given a suspended sentence. It was useless because he wouldn't pay the fine and I had to. They threatened to take the furniture if I didn't. And it didn't stop him beating me. (1981: 15)

Second, both parties frequently have a joint interest in the property, whether it is a council tenancy or privately rented or owned. Women, whether as wives or cohabitees, may be economically dependent on men. If the man is employed, he may be supporting her and any children of the family (at one stage the Government were considering paying family credit through the man's pay packet); if he is unemployed, state benefit (social security, now income support) is usually paid to him as head of the household. Women do not call for help because of this burden of dependency, as Townsend noted in his study on poverty: 'wives have restricted access to resources, except through their husbands' (1979: 781). Women's dependence on men is an institutionalized feature of society.

Pahl has further examined the inequality of income distribution in the family which forces women into dependency (1985; see also Homer, Leonard and Taylor 1984: 5). In the UK, changes to the state system of income maintenance that became operative in April 1988 have further institutionalized this dependency. First, the old system of help for urgent needs - single payments - was abolished. In its place the Social Fund has been substituted, meaning that help to meet urgent needs must be applied for and assistance may be offered on a loan basis, to be recovered from future state benefit. Women desperate to leave home to escape from violence may be dissuaded from so doing, as they will be totally destitute. Second, the old system of income supplement to families whose earnings are low, a supplement usually paid to the mother, has been replaced by 'family credit'. These measures will force women further into dependency.

There is also the problem of housing. Under the Housing (Homeless Persons) Act (1977), local authorities have a statutory obligation to battered women. However, research conducted by Binney, Harkell and Nixon (1981), Homer, Leonard and Taylor (1984), Bryan (1984) and Logan (1986) found that local authorities had developed their own interpretation of the law as to whether they considered the battered wife had a legitimate 'housing need', or whether she was 'intentionally' homeless. In addition, many housing departments required proof of a cohabitee's violence, in the form of a court injunction or criminal conviction. Some authorities advised women to apply for an ouster injunction through the civil courts as a means of solving their housing problem.

As we have see in previous chapters (especially chapter 4), official figures on crimes reported to the police represent only a minute fraction of the extent of the problem. Some women report their victimization elsewhere - to rape crisis workers, self-help groups, Women's Aid, doctors, hospital staff, friends, or family. Many women remain forever silent. The number of women who officially reported violence to the police in the Metropolitan Police District alone in one year was estimated at 58,000. Yet, as we shall see from studies later in this chapter, only about half of all women accommodated in refuges have contacted the police. MacLean, Jones and Young (1986), in their study of crime and victimization in

Islington, London, found that only 27 per cent of women victims reported to the police or to Women's Aid. Borkowski, Murch and Walker (1983) found that many victims of violence and sexual assault preferred to report to social workers and general practitioners, a fact confirmed by Andrews (1987) in another study in Islington. MacLean, Jones and Young (1986) also found that, when women were physically injured, just under half contacted doctors. We cannot know the full extent of the problem.

Since the 1960s women have been researching, interviewing and writing about women victims of marital violence. Many studies conducted in women's refuges and elsewhere have been published in mimeographs, in radical women's journals, and as self-produced pamphlets. In the USA, UK and Europe women researching spousal violence have constantly tried to force a recognition of this problem upon a largely intransigent academic orthodoxy. These studies have been largely ignored by academics, and it is only with the advent of large-scale empirical victimization surveys that the problem of wife-battering is being seen as worthy of statistical recognition.

The notable exceptions to this wall of silence have not emerged from radical criminology, but from victimology. *Victimology: An International Journal*, edited by Emilio Viano, formed a vanguard in this realization. By 1977 Viano's journal was highly influential in bringing an awareness of the victim to the door of academic enterprise. And the assimilation of feminist scholarship on these issues was integral to its growth. Yet victimology as a tradition within or outside criminology had no internationally established status.

In recent years, unfortunately, large-scale victimization surveys have served to eclipse the problem of violence against women in a new way. Victimization surveys are now in the main the product of establishment criminology. The interests of establishment research do not lie with victims of spousal violence. Victimization surveys homogenize all kinds of victimization into one category, and cannot therefore address the specificities of particular classes of victimization. Labour-council-funded victimization surveys in Islington and in Liverpool have professed a concern about violence against women; yet this has been regarded with suspicion by feminists, who distrust the sudden interest in victimization of people from a tradition that has had no history of concern for the problem.

Women have been conducting research about women's reporting, women's fear and women's experience of violence for over two decades (e.g. Pizzey 1974; Hanmer 1977; Pahl 1982). But studies of battered women inside or outside refuges have never been considered important to traditional criminology or to anthropology.

**Victimization surveys**

The problem of non-reportage and the unreliability of official crime data have provided two of the major incentives for conducting victimization surveys, both here and in the United States, in the pursuit of the 'real' victimization rate. In the USA, victimization surveys were launched in the early 1970s under the banner of the National Crime Survey, government-sponsored research. In Britain the first national victimization survey was launched in 1981: the British Crime Survey, directed by the Home Office. The first of the National Crime Surveys was conducted between 1972 and 1975, and the second, still continuing, US national survey has been running since 1982. The current US household sample is about 60,000, involving 136,000 individuals. The British Crime Survey (1983) was based on a much smaller study of 11,000 households in England and Wales and 5,000 households in Scotland. Victimization surveys are not without their intrinsic problems, proving incomplete and inaccurate. For example, the British Crime Survey found few victims of domestic violence or of sexual offences. Ten per cent of assault victims were women who had been assaulted by their present or previous husbands or boyfriends. And only one attempted rape was uncovered (Hough and Mayhew 1983: 21). Hough and Mayhew explain that 'the assailant may have been in the room at the time of the interview' (1983: 21). Later studies have attempted to overcome some of these reporting difficulties by ensuring that interviewers are better trained, that more interviewers are women, that wherever possible interviews are conducted in private, and that notions of what is violent and what is threatening behaviour are more widely explored.

Two types of victimization survey have emerged in response to the problems encountered in the British Crime Survey. First, there are studies of localities, inspired by left-wing police monitoring units within Labour councils, which examine all kinds of victimization and for which violence against women is just one of several concerns. Secondly, there are studies of localities by left-wing radical feminists, with specifically address the problem of violence against women.

Young (1988: 172) sees the former as a step forward for radical criminology, and regards such studies as 'radical victimization studies', but incorrectly groups the feminist surveys on violence against women with the more general studies of all victims conducted by the Left. Richard Kinsey (1985: 49), in a study of crime in Merseyside commissioned by the Merseyside County Council, examined questions relating to policing priorities in the area, and included some consideration of women's fear of crime and women's victimization. Police officers were asked whether they thought some of their work could be better done by other agencies. A total of 63 per cent of officers gave examples of tasks they felt could be better undertaken by other agencies, and spousal disputes were the most frequently mentioned. MacLean, Jones and Young (1986), in a study commissioned by Islington Council, were also concerned to examine this question of violence against women. Their Islington Crime Survey found that 694 assaults against women had been reported as having occurred in the year of study. The feeling among feminist critics is that such macro-victimization studies cannot adequately address the problem of violence against women, and the inclusion of this issue on the general agenda is tokenist.

The second type of victimization study is represented in a series of UK studies, for example one conducted in Leeds by Jalna Hanmer and Sheila Saunders (1983), a study conducted in Wandsworth, south London, by Jill Radford (1987) and another conducted by women in the Police Monitoring Unit of the Labour Council in Manchester (1987). These studies specifically address the question of violence against women in a broader sense than its more legalistic definition followed in the British Crime Survey. In these studies women themselves are asked to define what they fear and what they consider threatening. These studies are also significant in their criticism of traditional methodology. The work of Hanmer and Saunders (1983, 1984) is particularly representative of this critical stance. (See also Oakley 1981; Stanley and Wise 1983; Smart 1984; and Cain 1986.) The victimization surveys conducted by women on women have all started out from what they describe as a feminist perspective. This approach is similar in many respects to the earlier interactionist research tradition observable in the work of Whyte (1943) or more recently in the work of Campbell (1984). Here the preference is clear for data that come directly from women 'telling it like it is', rather than collecting women's responses to a series of structured questions which may have little relevance to their lived experience.

Hanmer and Saunders (1983) interviewed 129 Leeds women about their experiences of violence. Over half of all women interviewed reported experiencing some form of threatening, violent or sexually harassing behaviour. While certain acts, for example 'flashing' and verbal abuse, were not seen as inherently violent, they were nevertheless regarded as potential preludes to behaviour which might involve rape or severe injuries, and were therefore alarming.

Jill Radford conducted a similar small-scale survey in Wandsworth in 1984. A total of 314 women were asked questions about their perception of safety in public places, and among others, their opinions of self-defence for women. Radford's findings complement the earlier Yorkshire study. Eighty-eight per cent of the respondents said their neighbourhoods were not safe at night-time, and 25 per cent said they were not safe during the day (J. Radford 1987: 30). These perceptions had fundamental effects on women's social behaviour, acting as a curfew. Women became 'street-wise', developing strategies of avoiding men and keeping to well-lit streets, and some carried objects for self-defence.

In 1986 the Manchester City Council Police Monitoring Unit distributed a questionnaire to all households receiving the *Police Watch* magazine, and received 1,841 replies. In July 1987 the magazine published the preliminary results of their findings. Replies revealed that women considered threatening a much wider range of male behaviour than the official definitions of violence against women included. Sexual assault was reported by 226 women, 152 reported rape, 311 reported assault, 43 reported racial attack, 587 reported indecent exposure, and 648 reported indecent suggestions (pp. 8–10). A significant finding in both types of survey is the extent of the fear of crime.

*Women's fear of crime: is it related to 'real' risk?*

One of the major findings of the victim surveys is the scale of women's fear of crime (see Hough and Mayhew 1983: 23). It is important to recognize that there is nothing new about this problem, and that it was not 'discovered' by the US National Crime Survey or the British Crime Survey. Women's behaviour has always been circumscribed by a fear of crime, as feminist researchers and writers have identified and discussed throughout history (Jacobs 1961: 30). Researchers are divided about how far the fear of crime is related to real risk, and the issue has influenced the interpretation of their findings.

Hough and Mayhew in their first report on the 1981 British Crime Survey, found that 'in some areas, fear of crime appears to be a serious problem which needs to be tackled separately from the incidence of crime' (1983: 26). In a more detailed analysis of the British Crime Survey, Maxfield (1984) found that fear of crime alone had real consequences for modes of living, behaviour, and social activity. Women's fear of crime, Hough and Mayhew argued, was disproportionate to their chances of victimization. Consider for example the fact that data from the first British Crime Survey (Hough and Mayhew 1983: 21) showed that those most at risk from personal violence were male, under 30 years old, single, widowed or divorced, spent several evenings out a week, drank heavily and assaulted others. According to Gottfredson's findings from the British Crime Survey, those who stay in and around the home are least likely to be victims of personal crimes.

Hough and Mayhew concluded that fear is much higher among women than among men for all ages, and that fear increases with age for males and females alike (1983: 21–4). Fear had certain definable consequences for women: it reduced their feeling of safety and had real effects on behaviour, ranging from avoidance behaviour to restricting travel and leisure pursuits. 'Women and older persons less often go to pubs and are more generally fearful' (p. 33). The second British Crime Survey (Hough and Mayhew 1985) found that 30 per cent of women over 60 felt very unsafe in comparison to 16 per cent of women between 30 and 40 and 14 per cent of younger women. But violence and sexual offences against women were grossly underestimated (1985: 9); despite questions about sexual attacks that were put to interviewees, the British Crime Survey (No. 2) recorded only 11 such cases out of 6000 women interviewed.

As Hanmer and Saunders (1983) and Stanko (1985) have recognized, official definitions of violence depend on male perceptions of harm and dangerousness. Official 'crime' categories cite violence with a weapon as more serious than an assault with feet, hands or clenched fists. They exclude the unwelcome advances of kerb-crawlers, however frightening or obscene, as well as harassment, intimidation and other less physically apparent expressions of violence, yet all these produce fear.

Homicide figures indicate that women who stay in and around the home are more likely to be killed than those on the street. The British Crime Survey assumed that since few women reported victimization, few women had in fact been victimized, relying on a direct relationship between reporting and victimization. This led them to conclude that women's heightened anxiety about crime related not to real risk but to largely unlikely events. Hough and Mayhew speaking of rape victims, argue that people tend to overestimate the risks of being victims of violent crime, but accede: 'this does not necessarily mean that women are worrying about nothing. In general one would expect rape to have a very serious impact on victims' lives and there is nothing irrational in worrying about an occurrence which may be very unlikely to happen' (1985: 21). In fact no one can yet assess the real likelihood of rape, but it is clear that most rapes are perpetrated by men known to the victim, and that women routinely encounter other less drastic kinds of sexual intimidation. As Kinsey acknowledges, 'Even this, more realistic approach however, appears to underestimate the actual experience of sexual and other forms of harassment experienced by women' (1985: 41).

The studies conducted by Islington and Liverpool councils did find that women were more at risk from violence than was apparent from the British Crime Survey, and they acknowledged that, just as women's risk of victimization is masked from official statistics, it is similarly masked from some victimization surveys. After all, why should any woman be inclined to talk on the doorstep or in her living room to an interviewer she does not know about an incident she has already decided not to discuss? How can any macro victim survey expect to be much more successful in eliciting intimate and painful details than official crime investigators at the time of the crime?

In Kinsey's study in Merseyside, of the 39 per cent of respondents who 'worried a lot' about crime, 27 per cent worried about the possibility of burglary, 17 per cent worried about muggings and 15 per cent about attacks by strangers. Men and women were both asked about 'risks for women who go out in this area after dark'. Over 33 per cent of male and female respondents believed that it was 'fairly likely that something would happen' (Kinsey 1985: 38–40).

All studies, from varying political perspectives, agree about the impact of the fear of crime. Women lock up, stay in and avoid public life (Skogan and Maxfield 1981: 195). The police are similarly influenced by media presentations of violence against women, or else respond to women's heightened fear. Advice from the police to women over the years has been 'stay at home', Don't go out at night alone', etc., and MacLean, Jones and Young (1986: 5.12) found that 37 per cent of all women never go out after dark (see also Kinsey 1985: 43). Hindelang, Gottfredson and Garofalo (1978: 203) found that 52 per cent of their sample in Boston and Chicago limited or had changed their activities because of fear. However, they concluded that people responded to the fear of crime of making 'subtle adjustments' rather than major shifts, though the elderly are most influenced by it (p. 225). From the macro victimization studies in the United Kingdom and America to the small-scale specific studies of women's experience of violence, fear of crime is found to affect daily freedom by curtailing social activity.

## Battered women seeking shelter

Studying women in refuges is often considered unorthodox and irrelevant. Yet women's experiences of violent assault have been variously studied since the 1960s. During research for the London Policing Study it became increasingly clear that it was important to gather information on women's own experiences of violence against them, and of police protection, so I approached a number of refuges in England, Wales and Scotland through the Women's Aid Federation. It was explained to me that since very few women in refuges had sought police assistance, they might not be able to provide the type of information I sought. But it was just this issue – women's lack of confidence in police protection – that I wished to explore. A questionnaire was devised in collaboration with women at a London refuge and with Manchester Women's Aid. A total of 70 were completed by January 1986, collected from women in Ealing and Islington, Manchester Women's Aid, York Women's Aid, Dewsbury Women's Aid, groups from Welsh Women's Aid in Rhondda, Newport and Torfaen, and groups in Midlothian and Grampian in Scotland. The women who responded were largely working class and poor, including white, Afro-Caribbean and Asian women, and women of other minority groups.

*Two experiences*

Amy's story is a tale of physical violence:

> I heard about Women's Aid through the TV. I decided that I could not stand the pressure. My boyfriend kept hitting, kicking and beating me and he would lock me up in the house for weeks on end. I left him! I have two kids! I tried to get into the refuge but they were all full up, so I went to a bed and breakfast but he soon found out which hotel I was in and I had to leave. Then I phoned up the number of Women's Aid and they got me in here, and I have been here ever since. Nearly six months. I could cope with that to start with, but then with my son being handicapped, it is really difficult. I could not stand it anymore. My boyfriend hit me in the past and I just could not take any more of it. He would go away for weeks and not leave me any money we were living on £13 a week. I don't want him to know where I am, in London, so if I go for custody, he is going to know where I am, and as for an injunction it is just a piece of paper, a piece of paper wouldn't stop him hitting me. Some injunctions have power of arrest, but the police don't like going to you and throwing him out or going round arresting him. Because they know it will happen all over again when he comes out. I called them out once, I don't think I'll call them out again. All they said was that if it is domestic we don't want anything to do with it. They said we can't do anything about domestics. He had come in in a bad mood and gave me a black eye. They just said it was domestic and left. The law is stupid. It is just the fact that the law in itself isn't very good. If the police come round, you have this piece of paper, you show it to them. They take him away and then he is going to come back again! If he comes out he'll go looking for you and beat you up the worse for it. The police can't do very much. Social services can be helpful sometimes. Most of the time all they are worried about are the kids. I mean if you are in bed and breakfast you say that you want help with social services, they are more liable to suggest that they take the kid into care; like temporary care. So that is the threat then, women would think twice before leaving a husband or the man they lived with, because of the problems of moving to temporary accommodation with kids. Sometimes the social services are not too happy about it because they think refuges are filthy. Kids that go in them get a lot of illnesses. Solicitors can be very useful at times. They do

> try to help you with injunctions, or custody. But there is not a lot that they can do really. It is all up to the judge.

Jane's story is a tale of sexual and mental abuse. She had two children, girls of six and three and a half years. She had been in the refuge for one week. She was accepted for emergency accommodation. On the day I met her, she was being moved to another refuge outside London, as she feared that her husband might discover her whereabouts. She had had no contact with the police or social services, the civil courts or the criminal law. She wanted to obtain a separation and then divorce and intended to seek the advice of a solicitor. She had been married seven years and throughout that time had suffered both physical and mental violence. 'If I stayed any longer, I'd end up hurting myself, I mean suicide. I couldn't do anything, I had to get away from him!' I asked her why she had not contacted the police and she said: 'It is no use contacting the police is it, they don't get involved, do they, they don't get involved between a man and his wife unless someone is half killing his wife.' She said she had left her husband after contacting the social services, who then found her a place quickly. They had referred to overnight accommodation provided by the housing authorities, and within two hours she had packed and left; the following day was placed in the refuge. Jane said that her husband was so possessive that he hit her; he cut her off from all contacts and all friends, and that he was overwhelmingly jealous.

> The arguments are always in the bedroom, he has a pleasure out of my misery, he makes me get out of bed and stand naked for hours on end, I'm actually freezing, but I can't get back into bed. If I try to get into bed he'd probably kill me, I don't know. He is totally overpowering. I mean you wouldn't believe it. I have to crawl to him, beg him to let me back into bed, I have to. You just don't understand, he has pleasure in seeing me grovel and seeing me in misery, he is totally overpowering. I suppose it is lack of self-confidence. He is insanely jealous and possessive. I suppose he must be a bit mad. I could give you other examples of how he is. He won't let me go out to socialise, take driving lessons, go to keep fit classes, he won't let me do anything, it leads to arguments. One day we went out together and he was dreadful, he just shouted at me in front of everybody and called me a slag, and he argued with me. He keeps saying that I am a slag and I am not fit to be the mother of my children. He tries to destroy my confidence, my pride and my dignity. I used to look after myself and I used to have a pride in my appearance, but now I mean look at me. It is because of what he has done to me, just because of what he has done . . .

### *The definition of violence*

Women victims of domestic assault were frequently beaten and strangled, but unless bones were broken beatings were rarely regarded seriously by the police or other authorities contacted. Mental torment and degradation does not seem to qualify as violence at all! Women in this study spoke of all kinds of violence. The definitive starting-point for all Women's Aid groups was stated by Barbara Street at a conference involving both Welsh Women's Aid and Welsh police in November 1986. She said: 'Fear, threats, mental torment and physical abuse are all recognized by women and Women's Aid.' But the legal framework has little place for mental violence. In divorce law scant regard is paid to threats from husbands, for example. Northern Ireland Women's Aid Federation, in their study *Police Response to Wife Assault* (Montgomery and Bell 1986) define wife-assault as 'the intentional physical abuse of a woman in a way that causes pain or injury or the threat of physical abuse by the male partner with whom she lives or has lived' (1986: 11). Yet the standard required by the courts is much more precise, emphasizing physical assault as the key indicator. In 1982 the Lord Chief Justice, Lord Lane, advising custodial sentence in rape cases, emphasized the importance to be given to rape cases involving physical violence. Rape was considered all the more serious when other factors were present (where a gun, knife or some other weapon had been used; where serious injury, mental or physical, had been sustained; where violence over and above the violence necessarily involved in the act itself had been used; where there were threats of a brutal kind; where the victim had been subjected to further sexual indignities or perversions; where the victim was very young or elderly; where the offender was in a position of trust; where the offender had intruded into the victim's home; where the victim had been deprived of her liberty for a time; where the rape or a succession of rapes had been carried out by a group of men; where the offender had committed a series of rapes on different women, or, indeed, the same woman). (Edwards 1984: 104; reference to guidelines in *Billam* ( [1986] 1 All ER 985).

Despite these worthy guidelines, legal practice contrives to recognize only physical violence. Both the criminal and the civil law require evidence of physical violence. The 1976 Domestic Violence and Matrimonial Proceedings Act provided for an injunction against a husband if there was evidence of 'molestation'. Molestation was intended to be interpreted more widely than physical violence, to include harassment and pestering. Yet, in practice, courts have required proof of physical violence if an injunction for non-molestation or exclusion is to be considered.

Women respondents in the refuge study saw violence against them as ranging from mental cruelty to physical violence. Experiences of violence were wide-ranging. In their own words: 'mental cruelty and smashing the house to bits'; 'my boyfriend was always battering me'; 'my husband was battering me causing serious injuries'; 'my husband

Table 5.1 *Forms of spousal violence experienced by women in UK refuges*

| | Experience of various forms of abuse | | | | |
|---|---|---|---|---|---|
| Form of violence | One form | Two or three forms | More than three forms | Total responses No. | % |
| With open hand | 1 | 18 | 19 | 38 | 54 |
| With clenched fist (punch) | 9 | 24 | 24 | 57 | 81 |
| With feet (kick or stamp) | nil | 16 | 22 | 38 | 54 |
| With objects (e.g. stick) | nil | 7 | 21 | 28 | 40 |
| With piece of furniture (e.g. chair) | nil | 6 | 21 | 27 | 38 |
| With knife | nil | nil | 13 | 13 | 18 |
| With bottle or other glass | nil | 3 | 12 | 15 | 21 |
| Other (sexual or mental) | 3 | 1 | 11 | 15 | 21 |
| Total responses | 13 | 75 | 143 | 231 | |
| Total respondents | 13 | 29 | 28 | 70 | |

*Source*: Data derived from interview/questionnaire study conducted by author, 1986.

was battering me and the child'; 'my husband intimidates and humiliates me, I feel I can't go on'; 'I am in a refuge now because of a death threat.'

### *The nature of the violence against women*

Eighty-four per cent of the respondents had experienced varying degrees of physical violence which extended over several years (see table 5.1). Fifty-seven respondents (81 per cent) had sustained extreme physical violence, involving several types of abuse. In most cases women suffered more than one form of violence, although 13 per cent of the sample experienced punching only (9 cases). Women's typical experience of violence, then, was being punched, kicked and beaten with an object. These findings are similar to the experiences of violence of Islington women reported in the Islington Crime Survey, in which MacLean, Jones and Young (1986: 5.16) found that 74.5 per cent were grabbed or punched, 92 per cent punched or slapped, 56.9 per cent kicked, a weapon was used in 19.7 per cent of cases, and 2.2 per cent were sexually assaulted. And as those authors found, 'In the cases where other forms of violence were reported, the interviewers recorded such things as strangulation, cigarette burns, punched and bitten, stabbed in the face with a cigarette, spat at, hair pulled and head butted.'

### *Why do women stay with violent men?*

Certain professionals, in their theories about why women stay with violent men, have produced some fantastic explanations. In both Britain and in America members of the medical and psychiatric professions have argued that women enjoy or come to enjoy and depend on physical violence. This representation of women as essentially masochistic is found in various forms throughout our culture. Whether in the romantic novel or in pornography, the theme is found constantly repeated. Women are presented not as they view themselves but as some men wish to view them. But despite the images, women's experience refutes these claims. Professionals should examine instead why men abuse women, why men enjoy seeing women abused and humiliated in film and photographs, why men are violent.

It is men who, in projecting their masochistic desires, construct for their convenience an image of female desire as one of masochistic longing. Psychoanalysts from Freud (1954: 11.258) and Deutsch (1944: 255) to Storr (1968: 64) have presented a vision of women as masochistic, desiring of violence and male domination. Curiously, Storr, despite his truly amazingly sexist and phallocentric writings, was asked to write the introduction to a book of essays on family violence (Eekelaar and Katz 1978)! James Kleckner, a clinical psychologist and marriage counsellor in Australia, wrote:

> I have never seen a chronically abused wife who truly objected to being abused. The chronically abused wife is one who permits her husband to beat her, refuses to take punitive action afterward, and remains in the same situation so that she may be beaten again . . . A woman who stays passive and allows herself to be beaten, is accepting the validity of beating as a method of communication, and interaction . . . Abused wives often explain that they have no place to go (not true), that they don't know where to go (anywhere), that they are afraid of losing their financial support (how much per beating?) or that they tolerate beatings for the sake of the children. Wife beating . . . can only be stopped through action by the victim or intended victims. It can only occur with the tacit permission of its victims. A wife who has been beaten for the first time may be a victim. A wife who is beaten again is a co-conspirator. (1978: 54–5)

Psychoanalysts such as Shainess (1979) and Blum (1982) in the USA are still using a 'blame the victim' theoretical and clinical model (see Walker 1985: 288; Jackson and Rushton 1982).

These and similar writings have attempted to identify aspects of the victim's behaviour which is seen as responsible or contributory to the violence which follows. In addition, the writings of Snell, Rosenwald and Robey (1964), Faulk (1974: 181) and Gayford (1975, 1979) lend support to the view that women who are battered are aggressive and provoke men – and thereby conclude that male violence is somehow justified.

Within one strand of victimology there has been a strong tradition of blaming the victim, a tradition revived by Erin Pizzey. She claims that some women are 'prone to violence' (Pizzey 1989; Pizzey and

Shapiro 1981, 1982). Her theory is that early childhood experiences can cement an association between pleasure and pain, with the result that some women become addicted to violence (Pizzey and Shapiro 1982). It was an encounter with 'Sarah' and other women that led Pizzey to this much criticized conclusion. Sarah had been pushed out of a window, and fallen 30 feet. Both her legs were broken in the fall. She wanted to return to her partner. Erin asked her, 'But why do you need to go back?', and Sarah replied: 'because we love each other'. Pizzey interprets this as follows:

> For her, the ultimate expression of love seemed to be a violent and painful death . . . she is powerfully addicted to amounts of violence in their relationship and cannot help going back to it. Having been reared on violence, she will only feel alive and satisfied in a situation of danger, so she often deliberately provokes a man to the point where he will hit her. (1981: 170–2)

The publication in the UK of *Prone to Violence* (1982), based on her findings, was met with resounding fury. Many in the feminist movement renounced the book as dangerous and reactionary. Liz Kelly had this to say of Pizzey's theory:

> We are back to the old idea of 'good' versus 'bad' families where violence has nothing to do with the structure of the family itself and the power men have in it. Other researchers or refuge groups have not found anything to support these views. The book is dangerous. It gives an excuse for further denial of the needs of the battered women. (1983: 11)

Eminent British sociologist Ronnie Frankenburg and writers, researchers and workers in the field of family violence Rebecca and Russell Dobash, Jan Pahl, Mervyn Munch, Jalna Hanmer and Fran Wasoff were among many who issued this statement to the press: 'We have found no evidence to support these views in our own work or in that done by the many researchers studying domestic violence' (Kelly 1983: 39). Similarly, research in the United States by Martin (1976) Walker (1979, 1985), Schechter (1982) and others found absolutely nothing to support Pizzey's ideas.

Sandra Horley, the current Director of Chiswick Family Rescue, argues that Pizzey is in part to blame for splintering the Women's Aid Movement in the UK.

> Erin Pizzey alienated feminist colleagues who wanted to combine the refuge movement and the women's movement to establish a national feminist organization, a move with which she totally disagreed. She wrote to local authorities and social services departments advising them to

> scrutinize all applications for grant aid from groups wishing to set up new refuges in case they propagated women's liberation ideals. (personal communication)

Talking to Women's Aid groups in England and Wales today, one finds that the scars have not healed. I spoke with Sandra Horley in October 1987 and put two questions to her.

> *Sue Edwards*: What is the policy of Chiswick Family Rescue today and why do women stay on or return to violent men?
>
> *Sandra Horley*: Women are trapped in violent relationships as a result of societal beliefs, lack of community support, poor access to resources and a personal feeling of helplessness. Wife-abuse is a crime, not social interaction gone wrong. At Chiswick we are aware of Erin Pizzey's 'prone to violence' theory, but at Chiswick we have found no evidence to support it. My five years' experience working in other refuges yielded no support for this theory and I know of no other empirical evidence to support this in the literature.
>
> *Sue Edwards*: If a similar questionnaire survey were conducted today, how would the findings compare with Pizzey's?
>
> *Sandra Horley*: I have known over the years many battered women, many stay on in violent relationships, many have been abused as children. Erin's interpretation is at fault and there is no basis whatsoever for her view that it is wives' addiction to violence which makes a husband beat them. It is his action not hers which produces the violence; he must be made responsible. (see Horley 1988)

The movement is also divided over the interpretation of aetiological factors in wife abuse. The evidence about the prevalence of childhood abuse in battered women's lives is not clear-cut. In work by Roy (1977), 66 per cent of the wives were found not to have experienced parental violence as children. And even in Gayford's (1975, 1979) study of 100 battered wives only 23 per cent had been exposed to violence as children. Theories on the cycle of violence or intergenerational transmission are promulgated by Pizzey and Shapiro (1982), among others. Being battered and battering others is not merely learned behaviour, but is also intermeshed with personal pathology. In the USA the 'battered woman syndrome' has dangerously gained the status of an official disease, recognized in the International Classification of Diseases (Ferraro 1981: 415). Walker (1987: 14), in criticizing the inclusion of 'Battered Woman Syndrome', records how the American Psychiatric Association in developing the 1987 revision to the *Diagnostic and Statistical Manual of Mental Disorders* (*DSM-III-R*) has approved of other 'new diagnostic categories which can be easily confused with post traumatic stress disorders'. Walker argues that these additional diagnostic categories could be used to misdiagnose battered women and other victims of violence. These categories are now named, e.g. 'Self-defeating Personality Disorder (masochism)', and many have provoked a storm of protest over the years.

At the 139th Annual Meeting of the American Psychiatric Association held in Washington, DC, in 1986, women protested over the way in which battered women are perceived as sick. As Nkenge Toure, Director of Community Education at the DC Rape Crisis Centre, said, 'These new diagnostic categories are an attempt at new weapons to be used against women. They encourage and perpetuate myths about women, so you blame her, victimize her, diagnose her as crazy and lock her up' (*Insight*, 26 May 1986: 20).

The *DSM-III-R* has identified and thereby pathologized male violence as a disease in the category of 'sadistic personality'. Such pathologization of male aggression and female dependency denies the social support and structures which perpetuate these behaviours.

In addition, the idea that pre-menstrual tension explains female aggression and female problems is a view widely promoted. For many it is pre-menstrual tension or the pre-menstrual syndrome that can explain family problems, women's crime and even men's violence toward women. The *Diagnostic and Statistical Manual of Mental Disorders* classifies symptoms of pre-menstrual syndrome as a disease. 'Pre-menstrual Dysphoric Mood Disorder'. Dalton in England believes that pre-menstrual syndrome can be held accountable for a wide range of family problems, from women's aggression and violence to male violence against women in the domestic context. One woman is cited as saying: 'Some cakes and biscuits disappeared on Sunday. It was all too much for me and I burst into tears. This in turn upset my husband, who went and found Mary in her bedroom and gave her a good thrashing' (Dalton 1978: 100–1). The move towards pathologizing women's behaviour is further seen in the recent alarming increase in the number of Duphaston prescriptions for synthetic progesterone dished out to female patients by general practitioners in England and Wales. In 1984 154,700 prescriptions were dispensed, and in 1986 154,500, compared with 50,000 in 1976 (figures supplied by Department of Health and Social Security).

By contrast male violence, while similarly pathologized in extreme cases, is usually exonerated. The category of morbid jealousy has been recognized and well documented (West 1961). It is often used in mitigation of sentence. In *Donnelly* ( [1983] 5 CAR(S): 70), a case that involved the attempted murder of a wife by the husband, who had hit her with a hammer, the light sentence was upheld on the basis that he was suffering from 'morbid jealousy'!

What alternative reasons can be found for women staying on or

Table 5.2 *Women in UK refuges' reasons for staying on with violent spouses*

| Reasons | One reason | Two or more | Total reasons |
|---|---|---|---|
| Nowhere to go | 23 | 24 | 47 |
| For the children | 3 | 16 | 19 |
| For the marriage | 3 | 12 | 15 |
| Financial reasons | 2 | 11 | 13 |
| Fear of further abuse | 7 | 16 | 23 |
| Fear of losing custody | 2 | 5 | 7 |
| Total individual respondents (65) | 40 | 25 | |

No response was given by 5 women in the sample.
*Source*: Interview/questionnaire study conducted by author, 1986.

returning, or permitting men to return? As we have seen earlier in the book, certain structural imperatives make leaving difficult, if not impossible. They include the impotence of civil and criminal legal remedies, the weakness of the police response, the lack of adequate statutory provision of shelter and accommodation (see chapter 2). In my study of women in refuges, they said they had stayed on because of fear of further violence to themselves and their children. Some women stayed on because they were going to 'give it another try' and some stayed on because it was not bad all the time. However, having nowhere else to go was the most frequently cited reason. The second most frequently cited reason was the fear of further abuse. Women cited 'for the children', 'for the marriage', and 'financial reasons' and 'fear of losing custody' in descending order of frequency (see table 5.2).

Walker (1979: 127), in her study of battered women, explored the less overt psychological factors which may underlie a women's decision to stay on in an abusive relationship. She argues that even middle-class women with economic resources feel that men control their money. Money or the lack of it traps women in relationships through fear of becoming poor: 'money is used as a coercive weapon. It is women's fear of being cut off with no money for the basic necessities of life that perpetuates this kind of psychological battering' (p. 130). Economic dependence is one of the several factors identified as part of the helplessness of so many battered women, and by extension part of the so-called 'battered woman syndrome'. The 'syndrome' describes a state of mind often induced in women who are the victims of abuse over a period of time. Walker (1985: 288) explains how, as victims of repeated abuse, women come to feel totally helpless, totally unable to control the situation or avoid further abuse. Given this feeling of helplessness, many women give up: 'Some women victims actually give up and want to die' (p. 291). Challenging the pathologizing of battered women, she argues that 'the observed hysteria of battered persons is more accurately described and labelled as terror responses' (p. 288).

Ferraro and Johnson (1983: 325), in a study of 120 women passing through shelters, looked at the interrelation of material and cultural conditions that contributed to women staying on, concluding that women themselves frequently rationalized and exonerated their partner's violence. But in making excuses for his behaviour, they eroded their own ability to escape from the abusive relationship. Fear of further abuse also kept women in the battering relationship. Martin (1976: 76) found that fear immobilized women, and ruled their actions, their decisions and their lives.

Why did the women finally leave men who had abused them? What was the deciding factor or the last straw? Women in the refuge study left for various reasons: 'the beating was bad', 'fear that the children were becoming aware and I didn't want them to live in such a place', 'advice from a social worker', 'advice from the hospital after they stitched me up', 'the doctor said I was on the verge of a nervous breakdown', 'the children were frightened', 'I couldn't take it any more', 'just had enough', 'my baby son was beginning to show signs of distress', 'either leave or go round the bend' (see table 5.3). Fear of further violence is not unfounded. Some women are pursued, battered and killed (Moore 1979; Jones 1980; Russell 1982).

*Women's reasons for his behaviour*

Medical professionals and practitioners have evolved some elaborate theories to explain male violent behaviour. Men are seen as addicted to drink, frustrated or under stress because of financial problems,

Table 5.3 *Women in UK refuges' reasons for leaving violent spouses*

| Reasons | No. |
|---|---|
| Effect of violence on mental state | 11 |
| Mental violence | 1 |
| 'Had enough' | 11 |
| Effect of violence on mental state of children | 9 |
| Severe physical violence | 15 |
| Safety of woman and child | 3 |
| Violence to child | 5 |
| Threats to kill | 2 |
| Advice from others | 3 |
| Don't know | 10 |
| Total respondents | 70 |
| Total sample | 70 |

*Source*: Interview/questionnaire study conducted by author, 1986.

work, or unemployment, or else, as we have already seen, it is women who have provoked them.

Dobash and Dobash (1984: 286) argue that violent episodes should be understood as constructed intentionally by the aggressor. Sandra Horley too makes a plea for making men responsible for their actions (*The Times*, 22 February 1989). My own study exposed such a wide diversity of women's rationalizations of male violence as to make any single explanation an erroneous reduction. The message is, as the women themselves expressed it, that 'men are violent', and although many women also utilize popular explanations, attributing their partner's violence to drink in 33 per cent of cases, 'anything' was cited as the next most frequent reason for violent outbursts (19 per cent of cases). Men were suspicious and jealous about wives' activities in 11 per cent of cases. In the final 25 per cent of cases a wide variety of petty matters were held to account for male violence (see table 5.4).

These perceptions of male violence are sustained in the wider social fabric of public and professional perceptions (see Dobash and Dobash 1985), and are incorporated in the language of mitigation in the judicial setting. In a recent study of police recruits I conducted at Hendon Training College in London I found that most trainees cited drink as the first choice in a list of possible causes of male violence. In this profile violence against wives is seen as the side-effect or unintended consequence; the real problems are external, in drink and drugs or in social factors which conspire to create loss of self-control, the result of an accumulation of anxiety and stress. Certainly social pressures are important and must be addressed, but as Straus (1977: 61) proposes: 'wife beating is not just a personal abnormality but rather has its roots in the very structure of society and the family;

Table 5.4 *Women in UK refuges' explanations of male violence*

| Explanations | No. | % |
|---|---|---|
| Anything | 13 | 19 |
| Male suspicions/jealousy | 8 | 11 |
| His infidelity | 2 | 3 |
| Refusal of sex | 3 | 4 |
| Drink-related | 23 | 33 |
| Children's noise | 1 | 1 |
| Over food | 1 | 1 |
| Money-related | 4 | 6 |
| Drugs-related | 2 | 3 |
| Minor argument | 11 | 16 |
| No response | 2 | 3 |
| Total | 70 | 100 |

*Source*: Interview/questionnaire study conducted by author, 1986.

that is, in the cultural norms and in the sexist organization of the society and the family' (1977: 61; Straus and Hotaling 1980; Straus, Gelles and Steinmetz 1980).

It is precisely this debate which split the UK women's movement in the early 1970s and led to the foundation in 1974 of the National Women's Aid Federation. Chiswick Family Rescue, run in 1975 by Erin Pizzey, argued for the recognition of individual personality factors in understanding the battered wife. Radical feminists working in other refuges argued that the structural relations of power within society and the family contributed to the problem.

## Women's experience of police protection

Women's experience of policing in UK and USA has on the whole been poor. Studies conducted in the United States and in Australia confirm that the battered women's perception and experience of police protection has not been happy. Bowker (1984: 84) sent out a questionnaire to a national sample of 1000 battered wives, after an earlier study of 142 women conducted in 1982. She found that the police were involved at least once in 53 per cent of the cases; 19 per cent of the battered women who had involved the police reported that services received from them were very effective, 20 per cent reported that they were moderately effective, 16 per cent found the police slightly effective and 26 per cent not effective at all. Nineteen per cent found that police intervention resulted in an escalation of violence. Brown (1984: 277) similarly sought information relating to women's experience of policing, and 84 women responded, of whom 48 reported their victimization to the police, and of those 71 per cent viewed the police as either concerned and helpful or concerned but not helpful (p. 283). Pahl (1978) found that as many as 63 per cent did not find the police useful. Binney et al. (1981: 14) found that as many as 64 per cent did not find the police useful.

Women who were interviewed in the Northern Ireland Women's Aid Survey (Montgomery and Bell 1986), and in the refuge survey described above, have consistently expressed little confidence in the police response to domestic assault. The Islington Crime Survey found that of those women who reported assault to the police, 42 per cent were highly satisfied, 24 per cent satisfied, 20 per cent dissatisfied and 13 per cent highly dissatisfied (MacLean, Jones and Young 1986: 5.16). Although in 66 per cent of cases women were satisfied with the police response, we must remember that not all women feel sufficiently confident about police response to report in the first place.

*Calling the police*

In my study, despite the obvious, gross and serious nature of the assaults, only 38 women (54 per cent) called the police, while 32 (46 per cent) did not. It cannot be assumed, however, that women who do not call the police are victims of minor or simple assault. They are often victims of severe violence. In 52 per cent of cases where the police were not called women were assaulted by kicking or with an object (knife, bottle, furniture). Hanmer and Saunders (1983) and J. Radford (1987) among others confirmed that women did not report to the police because they thought that they would be uninterested. Similar decisions not to call the police are recorded in many other studies (e.g. Schechter 1982: 157). Pagelow (1981) found that 57 per cent of women interviewed had contacted the police. Dobash and Dobash (1985) found that they contacted other agencies. Montgomery and Bell (1986) found that the police were contacted as a last resort. In the Islington Crime Survey only 27 per cent of declared victims said that they had contacted the police; similarly, in the National Crime Survey in the USA 48 per cent of victims did not contact the police. Table 5.5 shows the range of reasons given for not calling the police discovered in the Northern Ireland research by Montgomery and Bell (1986).

*Satisfaction with police response*

Of those women in the refuge study who called the police, many felt dissatisfied with the protection and service they received. Such a lack of confidence is widely documented. Binney, Harkell and Nixon (1981: 14–15) found that of those women who contacted the police 64 per cent had not found the police helpful. Of 59 women who had called the police, after the worst assault 8 per cent said that the police did not come, 51 per cent said that the police rendered no practical

Table 5.5 *Why women did not call the police when seriously assaulted*

| Reasons | No. |
|---|---|
| No confidence in the police | 32 |
| No phone | 5 |
| Prevented from calling and threatened by partner | 15 |
| Did not want anyone to know | 8 |
| Preferred to deal with it themselves | 9 |
| Lived in a politically sensitive area | 3 |
| Police not welcome | 5 |
| Don't know | 1 |
| Total | 78 |

*Source*: Montgomery and Bell 1986, p. 25, table 2.

help because they considered it a domestic matter, 20 per cent said the police referred the women to a refuge or ensured that the man was taken away for the night, and in 17 per cent of the cases the man was charged with assault or with breaking an injunction.

Jan Pahl (1985), in a Bristol study conducted in 1982, found that of those women who reported their victimization to the police, 63 per cent were dissatisfied with the protection and service offered. Dobash and Dobash (1984) also found a lack of confidence in the police. Borkowski, Murch and Walker (1983: 192) reported that battered women found police to be of little help. Many women in refuges said that the police were just not interested!

My own observation of police response in the London Policing Study was that 15 minutes was the maximum time recorded by the police in attending the call at the scene, but this was not the experience of women in the refuges (see table 5.6). J. Radford (1987) found a deep dissatisfaction with the police response. Hanmer and Saunders (1983, 1984) found that under half were satisfied. Police were slow to respond and were considered in the main unhelpful.

*The nature of police assistance*

Women in the refuge study were asked to describe the nature of the advice offered by police officers. According to them, police advised women to prosecute in 14 per cent of cases. In 7 per cent of cases they arrested the man concerned. In 17 per cent of cases women were

Table 5.6 *Police response to domestic violence calls as reported by women in UK refuges*

| Police response | No. |
|---|---|
| Total calls | 38 |
| *Speed of response* | |
| Didn't attend | 2 |
| Within 5 minutes | 4 |
| Within 2 hours | 28 |
| Later | 4 |
| *Number of officers* | |
| 1 | 8 |
| 2 | 23 |
| 3 | 4 |
| *Woman officer present?* | |
| Yes | 8 |
| No | 28 |

*Source*: Interview/questionnaire study conducted by author, 1986.

advised about civil remedies. In a further 17 per cent, women were given advice about other agencies, e.g. social services and Women's Aid. In under 5 per cent of cases men were informally cautioned. In 39 per cent of cases women reported no advice at all.

These findings from women in England and Wales compare with other findings on police response. The Northern Ireland study (Montgomery and Bell 1986: 30) found that in responding to wife-assault calls the police used four distinct strategies. In 47 per cent of the cases the police intervened, taking some form of action against the man. In 33 per cent of cases the police attempted to reconcile the couple, or otherwise refused to take any action against the man. In 11 per cent of cases, after everything else had failed, intervention was used as a last resort. In 9 per cent of cases the police took no action against the man but assisted the woman to leave the house.

## Why not fight back?

### *Socialization*

Women are battered, raped and murdered by men; they are mugged and robbed. They are harassed and intimidated on the street, on public transport and in the workplace. Women rarely fight back. Why? They have been socialized into silent submissiveness, because assertive behaviour is discouraged. Women learn from experience that girls who do defend themselves are circuitously portrayed as just the kind of girl who gets victimized in the first place. And the law places women on the horns of a dilemma: it refuses to protect them and is then condemning when women are forced to defend themselves.

Women are extremely vulnerable at the hands of violent and mentally tormenting men. Often physically smaller than their partners, they have been socialized from childhood not to fight, spar, box or 'land and punch'. Consequently, many have not learnt even the rudiments of self-defence. They have acquired instead the psychological accoutrements of and predisposition towards submission, and a consciousness of fear and helplessness. By contrast, boys have been taught to be assertive and have fashioned themselves in aggressive behaviour. Yet for Erin Pizzey this socialization of men and women is less important in predisposing sex differences than pathological factors. She has said that some women, battered women especially, respond to danger by playing 'possum'. This she explains is because of cortisone response to violence, which acts as a psychological inhibitor to action (1982: 173). Women in the refuge study vehemently challenged this pathological presentation and the view that certain women are 'prone to violence'. Clearly,

Pizzey vastly underestimates the force of their indoctrination: 'Girls should be girls'; 'Don't do that, it's not ladylike'; 'Marriage is something you stick at'; 'It's your fault if he beats you'. Leonore Walker also challenges this kind of pathological theorizing. She argues: 'Not only are men physically stronger than women, but also they are trained from early childhood how to fight. Women do not have this strength or training, so they are at an immediate disadvantage in a physical struggle' (1979: 78).

From early childhood women are socialized into passivity; from girlhood to adolescence to adulthood the female sex is rendered vulnerable. Throughout this vulnerability training programme, passive, docile, and submissive behaviour is not merely encouraged but positively rewarded. Similarly, assertive behaviour is negatively sanctioned, labelled aggressive, anti-social and boyish, frequently identified as symptomatic of a behavioural problem or a problem of sexual identity and nearly always penalized (see Heidensohn 1985; Tchaikovsky 1985). Such girls may find their way into children's homes and juvenile courts, and be defined as in 'need of care and attention' (Webb 1984). Anthropologists, sociologists and psychologists have documented the cultural acquisition of assertiveness by boys and the cultural denial of this behaviour to girls. Simone de Beauvoir writes:

> Against any insult, any attempt to reduce him to the status of an object, the male has recourse to his fists, to exposure of himself to blows . . . violence is the authentic proof of each one's loyalty to himself, to his passions, to his own will . . . The girl simply submits; the world is defined without reference to her, and its aspect is immutable as far as she is concerned. This lack of physical power leads to a more general timidity: she has no faith in force she has not experienced in her body. (1953: 330)

In the refuge study 38 per cent of abused women said that they had tried to defend themselves. However, as they explained, fighting back did not always have the desired effect. In fact in some situations it actually made the men more violent. One respondent explained, 'He sometimes would calm down when I hit him, but a few times he would become more violent.' Fifty-eight per cent of the women in the study did not defend themselves. Most explained that they were too frightened; some said 'he' would only get more violent. Some would try to escape, but mostly, as one woman explained: 'I'd cover my head with my arms and curl up so it would be over quicker.'

Dobash and Dobash (1984: 278) found that the 109 women interviewed responded to violence in the following ways: between 14 and 26 per cent withdrew from the situation (i.e. endured the attack without reacting externally); 5 tried to reason with the aggressor; 13 per cent tried to escape; 8 per cent tried to push the man away; and 8 per cent tried to protect themselves; while only 10 per cent actually hit back. Fear immobilized them, preventing women from really doing anything at all.

Research conducted in the United States by Hilberman and Munson (1978: 460) and Walker (1978: 525), among others, focuses specifically on this wider question of women's trained incapacity (in childhood and in adulthood) to defend themselves. Hilberman and Munson studied a sample of 60 women who had suffered serious and/or repeated physical injury. The researchers found a uniform psychological response to the violence and a learned helplessness. Women lived in terror, with the threat of the next assault ever-present. Walker concluded similarly, from a sample of 100 women, that they are trapped in violent relationships, unable to defend themselves because of psychological paralysis and learned helplessness. 'Even those women who had some form of self-defence training were unable to use their knowledge successfully to fend off a physical attack from their men' (Walker 1979: 78). Del Martin (1976: 148) and others argue that women are beginning to learn their own physical potential, and that this may be a vital aspect of their survival. This question of the need to defend and survive was also addressed in Jill Radford's study. The women interviewed took some precautions when they went out. Radford (1987: 33) explains the process of awareness as 'becoming street-wise'.

> That is being conscious of who else was in the street, walking close to other women, avoiding men, keeping to well lit streets, going the long way round if necessary, checking if they were being followed, being psychologically aware, wearing shoes and clothes they could run or fight back in . . . others carried . . . milk bottles, bricks, pepper and sprays.

The National Crime Survey in the USA, conducted between 1982 and 1984 (Timrots and Rand 1987: 6), found that about three out of four crime victims did something to protect themselves during the crime incident, and 'victims of a stranger crime were less likely to protect themselves than victims who knew the assailant.' Yet in only 16.6 per cent of assaults on women did the victim use physical force in self-defence (1987: 58).

### *Legal obstacles to self-defence*

Women who do defend themselves routinely encounter legal obstacles to their own protection. These have evolved through case law developments, which have rarely given much consideration to women who retaliate or react to extreme provocation. Consequently arguments in mitigation and exculpatory excuses have traditionally excluded women's reasons for violent or homicidal action directed at an abusing father or husband. Women who respond in this way find that their explanations are at variance with the case law orthodoxy, with the result that there is no legal precedent which acknowledges her predicament. Matza (1964: 61) explains how the criminal law invited the individual to neutralize his normative attachment to it. But this invitation in not extended to all, and the criminal law has never neutralized a women's normative attachment in situations where the battered or raped woman defends herself. Moreover, judges can be seen to overwhelmingly sympathize with the 'victim', however bullying or violent his behaviour. Consider for example the case of a young man who appeared before a judge at York Crown Court, on a charge of attempted murder. His victim was a girl, aged nineteen. She had been walking home late one night after stabling her pony, when she was viciously attacked by the man in question. Fortunately she managed to save her own life by defending herself with a sheath knife which she carried for cutting open bales of straw and hay. The man was given a suspended sentence. The judge commented, 'You have been punished enough' (Edwards 1984: 175).

Judges are arguably even more condemnatory in cases where daughters and wives kill or injure violent fathers or husbands. In 1980 Theresa Anne Land and Carol Young both pleaded guilty to wounding with intent, the 'victim' being Carol Young's husband. Both women were found guilty and sentenced to three and three-and-a-half years' imprisonment respectively. They had stabbed Young with a kitchen knife while he was sleeping. On 15 April 1981, they appealed against the sentence (*Land and Young* [1981] 3 CAR(S) 130). 'The first appellant claimed that she had been the subject of sexual advances by the victim, and the second appellant complained of violence and beatings' (p. 130). While many observers would agree that the offenders had been the repeated victims of harassment and violence inflicted by this man, the judge was far less sympathetic to their plight. He held that 'This was a potentially murderous attitude.' And later the appeal court judges went on to make plain their views on the appropriateness of such sentences, thereby dismissing the appeals against sentence: 'people must be actively discouraged from taking the law into their own hands in these circumstances' (p. 31). But this argument depends on the availability of effective legal remedies for the abused woman, which, as we have seen, are just not there.

In the case of *R.* v. *Tyler* (1986 Court of Appeal, Criminal Division, LEXIS Enggen) a youth custody sentence of four years was reduced to two. The defendant had been convicted for the manslaughter of a brutal and bullying father who had repeatedly abused his wife, daughter and son. On the night in question he had in the words of the appeal report 'become argumentative and feudalistic'. According to the law report:

> The father arrived home and threatened the son. He then grabbed the appellant by the collar, pushed her into a corner, slapped her face, and threw her on to the sofa. He called both the appellant and her mother a series of names: whores, lesbians, sluts and so on. Then, it seems, he ordered the mother to fetch some photographs, which apparently show the mother and father indulging in sexual practices together, and also some wooden penises which were concealed somewhere in the house. He then said to the appellant, 'I will prove that your mother is a whore', and put the photographs before her face so that she could see them, and threw the penises at her. He then asked her if she wanted a vinegar bottle put up her vagina.

Karen Tyler retaliated by stabbing him. The judge remarked: 'It is true that bullying fathers should not bully and deserve to be punished. On the other hand it must not be thought that society condones the killing of fathers by their children.' This condemnation of self-defensive retaliation was reflected in an earlier case against Annette and Charlene Maw, who were sentenced to three years in 1980 for the manslaughter of their father. Lord Justice Lawton in the Court of Appeal queried 'What should be the attitude of the law to those who unlawfully and with violence kill someone who has treated them badly? Can the law tolerate this kind of behaviour when there are ample remedies?' (*The Times*, 4 December 1980).

In cases of spousal homicide by wives the courts have been concerned to make it clear that a precedent for killing a husband should not be established, rather than stressing the need for greater protection of wives (see Edwards 1985c). Interestingly, there is no partial defence to homicide with accommodates a wife's fear of violence. Nor is there a partial defence which accommodates provocation of the wife in circumstances of continual violent abuse over years. All a wife can do in these circumstances is to plead guilty to murder, or say she was sick at the time. In almost all of the cases where wives have killed violent husbands judges have reiterated the common myth that there are other remedies open to a battered wife. In the case against Mabel Patterson in Scotland, tried for stabbing to death her brutal husband, Lord Wheatley in passing sentence remarked 'There are so many occasions when wives are subjected to the kind of rough treatment to which you were subjected. The difficulty is that I cannot establish a precedent to give a licence to wives who take the law into their own hands' (*The Times*, 27 July 1983). June Greig stabbed her brutal husband under similar circumstances. At her appeal in 1979 (*H.M. Advocate* v. *Greig*, May 1979), the appeal judge surmised: 'There were various expedients open to a woman regularly submitted to rough treatment by her husband, but a licence to kill was not one of them.' In the case against Valerie Flood, tried at the Central Criminal Court in London for the manslaughter of her husband, who regularly beat her with a hammer and burnt her, the judge in passing sentence said of battered wives: 'There are many other courses open to them ... they can leave, separate, take divorce proceedings or seek legal help' (*The Times*, 12 November 1986).

In *Hinton* ( [1988] 10 CAR(S) 49), a sentence of three years of imprisonment was upheld on a woman who attacked her husband with an axe. The husband had been violent towards her and had sexually abused their children. She told the police that she had bought the axe in order to kill her husband, and that she needed it for her own protection. Judge Hazan reiterated the principle in this and similar cases when he said: 'wives and women in the position of this appellant, in these circumstances have several other courses open to them both for the protection of themselves and of their children.' Women who defend themselves and their children against violent husbands often experience even more punitive treatment. In the case of *R.* v. *Begum* ( [1985] Court of Appeal, Criminal Division, 22 April, LEXIS Enggen), after a lengthy campaign it was recognized that there had been an appalling miscarriage of justice. A wife had been convicted of murder and sentenced to life imprisonment after pleading guilty to charges she was unable fully to understand. On 5 October 1981 at Birmingham Crown Court the appellant pleaded guilty to the murder of her husband and was sentenced to life imprisonment (mandatory sentence for murder). Mrs Begum had hit her husband on the head with an iron bar. Speaking in Punjabi through an interpreter, she said: 'I feel guilty myself, but I didn't know what I was doing. He wanted two of the children to be killed and I said "Don't let the children get killed." ' From the outset attempts to take instructions from Mrs Begum were fruitless, and the indictment presented in the court contained one charge - that of murder - to which she pleaded guilty. The Court of Appeal decided that the case was a nullity since she had not understood properly the distinction between murder and manslaughter and had not had the opportunity of proper representation, since no Punjabi interpreter had been made available to her.

In some cases in which women have retaliated in defence of their children, the courts have not always understood the degree and impact of the provocation involved. A mother who poured boiling water over the genitals of the young man who had raped her five-year-old daughter was sentenced to two-and-a-half years' imprisonment for grievous bodily harm at Exeter Crown Court by Judge Sir Jonathan Clarke. The sentence was met by a public outcry. With almost unprecedented speed, an appeal was lodged some twelve days later. Lord Chief Justice Lord Lane, in allowing the appeal, said that she had been 'grossly provoked', and that the raped child through no fault of her own had been 'doubly wounded' (*Guardian*, 28 January 1989).

In self-defence, then, some women have killed, and have invoked a criminal justice retribution which is unjust, as it denies the reality of their situation. Researchers have suggested (e.g. Browne 1984, 1987; Edwards 1985b, 1987a; Walker 1987, 1989) that women who kill in self-defence find that the legal defence of self-defence and the partial defence of provocation rarely extend to them, since defences to homicide have traditionally developed in a way which accommodates a gender-specific conceptualization of male self-defence and male provocation as the only 'reasonable' and justifiable kind. Defences to homicide are founded on particular versions of typical people and typical situations. These 'normal homicides' (to borrow Sudnow's (1965) characterization) are very much predicated on violent behaviour which men consider reasonable, and exclude women's definitions of motive. Defences to homicide according to the law in England and Wales include the legal categories of murder and manslaughter. Section 3 of the Homicide Act (1957) allows for the partial defence of provocation, while section 2 allows for the reduction of a murder charge to that of manslaughter on the basis of diminished responsibility. For the partial defence of provocation to succeed, three conditions must be satisfied. The things said or done must first of all constitute provocation; the action causing the death of another must be committed in the heat of the moment; and the retaliation to the provocation must be 'proportionate'. All these conditions must be satisfied, and each involves a subjective element in the first instance. Heavy reliance is made on case law, which undeniably is about males killing spouses or other males, and not about women killing spouses or others. As has been argued by Fiora-Gormally (1978), Rittenmeyer (1981) in the USA, and Bacon and Lansdowne (1982) in Australia, this highly subjective construction of what constitutes provocation in the USA, UK and Australian jurisdictions frequently precludes it as a partial defence to the wife who kills a violent spouse.

Provocation as a defence relies upon what particular things 'said or done' are considered to be provocative by the 'reasonable man'. And as Lord Simon of Glaisdale assures us, 'It is accepted that the phrase "reasonable man" really means "reasonable person", so as to extend to "reasonable woman" ' (*R.* v. *Camplin* [1978] AC 705). But how far, in legal practice, has an appreciation of the 'reasonable man' concept really embraced an understanding of the 'reasonable woman' and the 'reasonable battered woman'? We only have to turn to case law to find that what the reasonable person has considered to amount to provocation, in other words what behaviour has passed for provocation in the courts of law, has relied on a male-oriented vision of things 'said and done'. Precedent in the UK, USA, and Australia has mapped out precisely what situations and circumstances the courts consider to constitute justifiable provocation. At the top of the list in all these jurisdictions is the situation in which a husband kills his wife who has had another sexual relationship, or taunted him over his sexual prowess. In both situations the courts have agreed that the man who kills the unfaithful or goading wife does so under extreme provocation.

In the UK in cases where provocation is alleged arising in the domestic context the courts have accepted the husband's plea and sentences in such cases have ranged from non-custodial disposals to a maximum of eight years. In *Donachie* ( [1982] 4 CAR(S) 378), where an injunction was in force, a ten-year sentence was reduced to seven on appeal. The spouse had stabbed the victim 29 times because of her relationship with another man. In *Shaw* ( [1984] 6 CAR(S) 108), a sentence of eight years was upheld on a husband who was 'provoked' to kill because 'she taunted him with her sexual experience with other men.' In *Mellentin* ( [1985] 7 CAR(S) 9) a sentence of five years was reduced to four years, for a man who had strangled his wife after she taunted him with her sexual experience. Similarly, in *Taylor* ( [1987] 9 CAR(S) 175) the appellant took a kitchen knife from the kitchen drawer and stabbed her after she had told him that she was going out with another man. Extra-marital relationships by wives have understandably provoked husbands to the point of killing. Such examples are also mirrored in the American courts. But other kinds of female behaviour, both acts of commission and acts of omission, have been seen as amounting to provocation . In the USA there was the case of Clarence Burns, who received a two-and-a-half-year sentence for the murder of his estranged wife, whom he had been physically assaulting for 15 years. Judge Alvin Lichtenstein said that leniency was appropriate because Mrs Burns had engaged in 'highly provoking acts' before her death. These provoking acts included acting very lovingly towards him immediately before fleeing the marriage, and failing to leave a note explaining her departure (Waits 1985; Washington Law Review, LEXIS, US Law, Journal file).

This rationale has not been so readily extended to a wife who kills a husband because of his infidelity or goading, since although the situation is reversed, the 'reasonable man', 'reasonable person' or 'reasonable woman' is not thought to be gender-blind. It is thought that infidelity provokes men: that is their prerogative. The right to justifiable anger is not universal in our culture – men have the right under certain circumstances, but women have no right under any. This is reflected in the interpretation of the law and what things 'said and done' constitute provocation. But provocation is not simply about *being* provoked; it is also about the *right* to be provoked. Men have the right to react to provocation, while women do not. Women's response to similar situations is bound by gender expectations of women's appropriate response as one of patience, tolerance and acquiescence. When women try to present a defence of provocation, they rarely succeed. This cultural representation of male provocation is translated into specific legal attitudes which are gender-fixed and edge women out of an equal right to a provocation defence, either for the goading or adulterous husband or, more importantly, as is more often the case, the killing of a violent husband. In cases in which a husband has been violent, women lose out, since male violence extending over many years does not fit into the traditional idea of provocation, although Wasik (1982) suggests that it should be regarded as evidence of 'cumulative provocation'. But such a defence is obstructed by the second necessary ingredient of a provocation defence, which requires the retaliatory action to take place in the heat of the moment, i.e. immediately after the provocation.

Here the law has held the view that only 'heat of the moment' violence can be properly considered truly intentionless or less culpable than action which occurs some while after the provocation. This excludes from such a defence those acts of violence which have been committed after planning and with determined intent. The distinctions between these different kinds of homicide are sustained in popular culture and in pathological explanation by describing 'heat of the moment' killing as justifiable, and the actor as blameless, while planned killing, even after cumulative provocation, is seen as heinous and unjustified and the actor as scheming, cunning and wicked. These fixed polarities set the scene for the discussion on homicide. Neither scenario can adequately account for the battered woman who kills a spouse, but as long as these two images form the basis of the debate, women who kill their abusers will be misunderstood. For it is neither true that all 'heat of the moment' actions are blameless, nor that all actions committed after the provocative act has passed are scheming, evil and heinous crimes. The acceptance of 'heat of the moment' retaliation is based on the perceived credibility of the impulsive side of men, who, presented with certain stimuli, can do no other but act. It is rather like the model of uncontrollable male sexual urges, by which men, once aroused by a female, have no choice but to indulge in immediate phallic sex. Women who kill violent husbands rarely kill in the 'heat of the moment'; it is more usual for wives or daughters to wait until the husband or father is sleeping, not because they are any less provoked, or less eager to retaliate immediately, but because that is the only time when self-defensive action is likely to succeed.

The final ingredient of a provocation defence requires that the retaliation should be proportionate to the provocation received. This is based on some highly subjective formulae which deem certain behaviours to be equatable with certain forms and degrees of force in retaliation. But all this is very much about what men do and how. It is male retaliatory action, and male force, and male choice of weapons that has dictated the parameters of a cultural and legal understanding of force. It dates back to trial by combat and duelling, and it is also predicated on a notion of male physical strength.

What is female retaliation and female force, and what is the equivalent of male force in female conduct? Women who have used violence against violent fathers or husbands never use brute physical force in the form of beatings, and usually use a weapon (either a knife or a gun) to inflict harm. The use of a weapon in law is interesting, for a weapon has always been considered more serious than fists or feet; the presumption being that more harm can be inflicted with a weapon. It is assumed that one person with a weapon is more dangerous than another without one. But this presumption is not borne out strongly in homicide. In 1986, 50 per cent of homicides were caused by a sharp or blunt instrument, 8 per cent followed shooting and 32 per cent followed strangulation, hitting or kicking (*Criminal Statistics* 1986: table 4.3).

In addition, the possession of a weapon on the person is seen to indicate some degree of malice aforethought, in a way that the male fist, hands and feet, and their immediate potential to maim and kill, are not. Women, then, who use instruments or guns to inflict harm are judged less favourably because of the method used to inflict harm (the 'mode of resentment'). This is also bound up with prevailing constructions of intent, and attitudes to the means of committing a crime.

Clearly, in any attempt to provide protection for abused women we need to study in detail women's experiences of male violence, and the ways in which men learn to exonerate their actions. The ways in which certain exonerations are fixed in our culture, and mitigatory scripts exist in plenty for men, while few are available for women, need examination.

Studies that have sought to examine in depth the experience of violent assault have rarely been treated seriously. The intransigence of academic male criminology, both traditional and radical, continues. The recent focus on victimization surveys has done nothing to create a climate of awareness of or receptivity towards, spousal violence and its consequences for women. On the contrary, the victimization surveys have been dangerous in perpetuating the fallacy of the homogenized and invisible victim.

# 6
# Current Developments in the Policing and Prosecution of Violence against Women

## Introduction

This chapter considers the various developments taking place in law and policing policy towards violence against women in the home. In North America and in England and Wales changes in the substantive law and in police force policy have offered the opportunity for radical reform in the area of partner violence. It remains to be seen, however, how far changes will be implemented, and what impact they will ultimately have on protecting victims and deterring repeated abuse.

First, in the area of the statute law governing the rules of evidence and criminal procedure, spouses, in accordance with the Police and Criminal Evidence Act 1984 (s. 80, pt. 8), are now 'compellable' witnesses. This means that they can be compelled to give evidence against a spouse, thus reversing their previous immunity. Second, statute law enshrined in the Police and Criminal Evidence Act 1984 (s. 25) governing police powers confers on the police the power of arrest even when no criminal offence has been committed, if the police consider arrest necessary to ensure the protection of any person. Third, statute law governing the prosecution of offences in the Prosecution of Offences Act 1985 deems that a prosecution is not automatic on the police reporting cases, but that the decision rests ultimately with the Crown Prosecutor appointed for each area. In focusing on these pivotal strategies for change, the debate once again concentrates on the question of how far a greater degree of protection for women can be ensured through law and policing policy.

While the legal reforms in the policing of spousal violence and in the evidential status of spouses have been broadly endorsed, the success of these measures will also depend on the response of para-legal and non-legal agencies, people in the critical justice system and the Crown Prosecution Service. It is my view that a revision of the existing law and its application in regulating personal violence is appropriate. I argue for the criminalization of violence committed by men against women – but I recognize that such a change will not be effective until the seriousness of violence against women is realized generally in the community. Criminalizing violence will be at best ineffective and at worst place women at greater risk if the courts do not adequately sentence the violent offender and if the police do not remove *him* from the home, detain *him* in custody before trial, and after conviction, and inform the spouse of the outcome. In addition, the government and the local authority must make better provision for battered women and their dependants, including providing proper housing, or (more importantly) alternative accommodation for men so that they may be removed from the home. At present, when the court imposes a fine or a bind-over, the offender returns to the same address. His character is unchanged, and he continues in his violent behaviour.

In the short term the criminalization of violence and a new police response may lead to more violence against women by men who are charged with assault and released on bail, returning to abuse the woman. In the long term criminalization will serve to convey a powerful message, creating a public attitude of intolerance of and repugnance towards violence against women. While many in the police force are already radically challenging their own internal procedures, what is urgently required now is a similar rethinking of ways of solving the problem by Crown Prosecutors, magistrates and judges, local authorities and central government; otherwise the protection of victims may be an ideal beyond our reach.

While applauding new policing policy and recent changes in the evidential status of spouses I am dubious about the promised benefits of the Crown Prosecutor, and especially the criteria for prosecution, for the protection of the victim of spousal violence. Two problems emerge in considering the likely impact of these changes. The first is that the effectiveness of changes in police policy can only be truly assessed if other voluntary and statutory agencies are similarly moving towards reform on this issue. A chain is only as strong as its weakest link. For example, a police policy which emphasizes the importance of arrest and prosecution can only succeed if other agencies (the Crown Prosecutors and judges, for example) share the same sentiment. The second problem arises where reform in the area of criminal justice is actually contervailed by a contradictory reform elsewhere. Here, whatever police decide in spousal violence situations may reflect not considerations of law or policing policy but a response to the demands imposed by the Crown Prosecution Service. Such a contradiction can already be seen in new legal provisions.

## New directions in policing policy

During the 1980s the focus of attention has been on the police organization, their treatment of victims of rape and spousal violence, and the arrest and prosecution of rape and spousal assault suspects.

Feminist campaigners have had a tremendous impact and influence on the evolution of changes in policing policy and the implementation of new police training programmes designed to challenge sexist stereotyping and assumptions about women victims. In the USA, Canada, UK and Europe police policy-makers have sought the advice of both internal committees and outside statutory and voluntary organizations. The major policy proposals considered have focused on the need for the police to arrest and charge men who assault wives and cohabitees, rather than referring these cases to the civil justice system. These proposals have also resulted in the implementation of training programmes emphasizing that violence in private is as serious as violence in public. The new strategies also embrace a concern for crime prevention, especially prevention of repeated abuse and homicide.

### *North America and Australia*

When it comes to changing policing policy, developments in North America have taken the lead. In several states lawsuits have been brought against police departments for under-enforcement of the law. This endeavour has created a climate in which victims of spousal assault are redefining traditional concepts of them in their own terms, and this has had a significant impact on the response of the police and the criminal justice system. Though there is still persistent criticism of police discretion, women have nevertheless reaped the benefit of being able to bring lawsuits against the police for non-enforcement. The *Scott* v. *Hart* suit filed in 1976 in Oakland, California (see Gee 1983), which followed *Raguz* v. *Chandler* 1974 (see Tong 1984: 142), was a class action brought by four women (a married woman, a woman in the process of obtaining a divorce and two cohabiting women) against the Oakland Police Department for 'breach of statutory duty to arrest' (under California Penal Code section 836). The chief of police responded by denying any attempt to discriminate against women. The plaintiffs argued that discriminatory intent existed since there was a disproportionate impact on one particular class – women, as women are disproportionately the greatest number of domestic violence victims – and that in this case there was a departure from normal procedure since arrest was to be used 'as a last resort'. By November 1979, a comprehensive settlement was approved by the court, providing that no arrest avoidance policy was to be used. The court retained jurisdiction for three years in order to monitor the implementation of the new policy. This was followed by a series of class actions statewide including *Bruno* v. *Codd* 1977 (see Tong 1984: 142), and in Oregon in 1983, in the Nearing and Weaver case (Gee 1983), the Oregon police were sued for a similar failure to enforce the law.

The reality of spousal assault has been urged on the public in the hundreds of cases throughout the USA in which women have pleaded self-defence in murder trials after killing husbands who have repeatedly beaten and threatened to maim and/or kill them. The cases of Francine Hughes in 1977, Madelyn Diaz in 1985 and Damian Pizarro in 1988 have exposed the lack of alternatives for battered women in abusing relationships. Francine Hughes pleaded temporary insanity at her trial in Lansing, Michigan, on 4 November 1977, while on trial for the murder of her husband. She had poured kerosene around his bed and set it alight while he slept (*New York Times*, 10 March 1978). She had been a battered wife for many years and was acquitted of murder when the jury heard the details of her abuse. At that time acquittals were rare and women pleaded temporary insanity rather than provocation or self-defence.

During the late seventies and early eighties it was the women's movement's exposure of battering that led to greater public awareness about the plight of battered women, the lack of adequate police protection and the need to see the 'battered wife turned homicide defendant' in a new light. This was soon to have an impact in the courts, where an increasing number of women who had killed husbands started to claim provocation and self-defence, thereby challenging some of the traditional legal assumptions and precedents that have been established regarding homicide and self-defence. The challenge of those representing such battered women was to have significant impact on legal constructions regarding what is reasonable, what constitutes provocation, the psychological effects of battering on a woman over time, a battered woman's perception of imminent danger, how long is 'imminent', and under what circumstances is deadly force appropriate (*Ibn Tamas* v. *United States* 407, A 2d 626 (DC Ct App 19.9). In *State* v. *Wanrow* ( [1977] 88 Wash. 2d 221, 559 p. 2d 548) the Supreme Court declared that the key factor in determining whether or not a battered woman acted reasonably was the perception of the battered woman and not of the 'reasonable man'.

> The impression created – that a 5′ 4″ woman with a cast on her leg and using a crutch must, under the law, somehow repel an assault by a 6′ 2″ intoxicated man without employing weapons in her defense [was a mistatement of the law that was underlined by] the persistent use of the masculine gender leav[ing] the jury with the impression [that] the objective standard . . . is that applicable to an altercation between two men. (quoted in Tong 1984: 147)

During this time the introduction of expert witness testimony on the battered woman syndrome by psychologists to support the justification defence has been admitted in some cases (see Browne 1987; Sonkin 1987). However, the Supreme Court, faced with this question, has not yet ruled on such a case, although in *Moran* v. *Ohio* (Supreme Court of the United States 469 US 948, 29 October 1984, LEXIS Fedgen), where a wife had killed her brutal and bullying husband, the Supreme Court was asked to review the state appellate court's holding that the jury was properly instructed that she had the burden of proving self-defence. In this hearing there was substantial evidence at the trial that the deceased husband was an extremely violent man. In one incident the deceased 'had her by the neck, by the throat, and he was hitting' her with a gun. On the last occasion he threatened her that if she did not have the money for him by the time he woke up from a nap, he would 'blow [her] damn brains out'. The wife, realizing she had no way of securing any money, picked up a gun and fatally shot him. In her defence she stated that she was a victim of the battered woman syndrome. And the jury were instructed that the burden of proving the defence of self-defence was upon the defendant not the State, to which the defendant objected. At the Supreme Court, while the majority refused to grant certiorari, two Justices, Brennan and Marshall, dissented.

Like UK law, US law had been founded on a male perception of imminent danger, reasonableness, and when deadly force was appropriate. But in the States women were pleading self-defence while in the UK women were still trying to plead provocation. The prosecution lawyers, by contrast, in reply to these new initiatives, have tried to argue that the fact of being an abused wife/cohabitee over a period of time provides a motive for murder and therefore have examined intent, argued for a limitation of the interpretation of imminence and challenged the idea that battered women have a diminished perception of alternatives. In later cases women have pleaded justification in self-defence instead of temporary insanity, for example Madelyn Diaz in 1985, after she had murdered her brutal husband. She was charged with murder in the second degree in accordance with the Penal Code 125.25 and successfully managed to have admitted expert witness testimony on the effects of battering over time. The deceased was a police officer and on the night before the fatal shooting he threatened to kill the children and then kill her if she did not 'come over in bed the way he wanted'. Diaz shot her husband with his service revolver while he was asleep, and convinced the jury in the Bronx that she believed he meant to kill her and that her life was in imminent danger. She was found not guilty of all charges. Damian Pizarro on 20 August 1986 killed her husband in the street after he came after her, hit her, bashed her head against a lamp-post and threatened to kill her and bury her in the woods. She was arrested and charged with murder and held for twenty months in prison awaiting trial. She was a battered cohabitee who had made repeated attempts to escape from the deceased and repeated attempts to have him arrested for his assaults upon her. On one occasion, after she had run away from him, he found her, beat her and imprisoned her for several days. She reported to the police who charged him with rape, kidnap and assault. The case did not come to trial and was subsequently 'down-crimed' by the prosecutor (District Attorney) from a felony to a misdemeanour. At her trial the police officer who had been involved with the assault/rape/kidnap investigation testified for the defence, giving evidence about his brutality toward Pizarro. On 8 April 1988 Damian Pizarro was found not guilty on all charges (details from the programme 'I shot my husband and no one asked why', a Scarlet TV production for Channel 4 transmitted 20 June 1988).

In most cases where the battered woman turns defendant evidence of battering is suppressed, as in Diaz, since the prosecution will turn this evidence against the defendant by arguing that this provides the motive for murder. Since battered women usually kill husbands some time after the last beating and when the husband is asleep the courts have been required to review totally the concept of imminence – and review it in the light of the perception of imminence held by the battered woman rather than the 'reasonable man'.

Some cases have been less successful than those already cited, where evidence of battering and expert testimony to that effect has been excluded from the trial (see *Karen Anne Fennell a/k/a Ann Fennell* v. *Ann Goolsby, Warden, State Correctional Institution, Muncy, Pennsylvania and the Attorney General of the State of Pennsylvania* (District Attorney of Montgomery County No. 84–1351 United States District Court for the Eastern District of Pennsylvania 630 F. Supp. 451, 28 August 1985) and *United States of America, Plaintiff* v. *Lisa Gregory, Defendant* (No. 88 CR 295 United States District Court for the Northern District of Illinois, Eastern Division 988 US Dist LEXIS 10060 2 September 1988 Decided). In the Fennell case, the defendant/plaintiff filed a petition for habeas corpus on the ground that she had been denied the opportunity to present at her trial evidence of battering and expert testimony on the effects of the battered woman syndrome. Despite evidence of extreme battering by the deceased provided by the son, her petition was turned down. She was sentenced to 3½ to 10 years for voluntary manslaughter (provocation). In *Gregory*, the defendant pleaded the 'duress defence' in terms of the battered woman syndrome. She claimed she had been kept a prisoner by her husband

and abused over a period of years. In this case the battered woman's defence was not accepted.

Like the *Scott* v. *Hart* (1975) case, women in Bedford Hill Penitentiary (New York) are mounting a class action for clemency. They claim that there are similarities between them and those who killed in self-defence and were acquitted.

Over the last few years the police in the USA have been improving their training programmes and changing and reviewing their policy; in particular, arrest has been emphasized. Such policy reforms have emerged not only in response to the various pressures already outlined, but also in response to findings from studies commissioned by the American Police Foundation, among others. In some states the findings of these studies have significantly influenced local police decisions. In Oregon in 1977 a Bill was passed requiring the police to arrest if an assault had occurred or serious injury been threatened, unless the victim objected. This 'unless the victim objects' was deleted in a 1979 legislative amendment. Other states have passed similar laws. Research has subsequently examined the application and impact of such legislation on crime prevention and deterrence.

An American Police Foundation study (1976) established that men who seriously assaulted wives or cohabitees, or else were responsible for their murder, were often men who were already known to the police for violence against wives or cohabitees in the past. It was this major finding which provided the mandate for more rigorous police intervention at the outset. It was discovered that early intervention could interrupt the escalating chain of violence which the authors had uncovered as the norm in serious spousal assault and homicide. Following this and similar studies (e.g. Jolin 1983) it soon became generally accepted wisdom that early police intervention could significantly deter repeated abuse and homicide. But the American Police Foundation study was unable to discover whether one particular form of police response was more effective than any other.

It was to an analysis of this precise problem that Sherman and Berk turned in their study of the policing of spousal abuse in Minneapolis in 1981 (1984a). The research was designed to test three responses to simple domestic assaults: (a) arresting suspects; (b) ordering suspects to leave for eight hours; (c) providing information and advice to the people involved. The responses were randomly assigned, and their differential effectiveness evaluated by following up the behaviour of suspects in the sample for six months, and also by interviewing victims about any further violence. The broader questions the research team sought to address were: (a) Does calling the police in itself deter further violence, or does police presence aggravate the situation? (b) If calling the police deters repeated violence, is any one police response more effective in this endeavour than another? They found that of a sample of 252, those who had been arrested were the least likely to abuse again, compared to those who were ordered to leave the home and those who were merely advised. In only 10 per cent of these cases, where an arrest was made, was there a recurrence of violence, while violence recurred in 19 per cent of cases where the police had advised and 24 per cent where the police had told the suspect to leave.

Of course, as the researchers concede, the results of the experiment are to be treated with some caution in terms of policy implications, and certainly some aspects created ethical difficulties. First, the requirements of random assignment meant that the more serious cases were excluded. Someone had to decide the basis for exclusion, and therefore whether each case was one of simple assault or of a more serious nature. Further, patrol officers may have selectively excluded certain cases themselves by not reporting them. Second, as the researchers note (1984b: 264), most officers turned in only one or two cases, while three officers produced almost 28 per cent of all the cases in the study. Third, the deterrent impact of advice and information would vary considerably, depending entirely on the quality of the advice and the effort made by an individual officer. Of the 136 persons arrested in the Minneapolis study, only 3 were formally prosecuted. This is a small figure, but it does suggest that, as the authors point out, 'booking has a bite', i.e. the arrest alone is a deterrent to further violence. Since most of the suspects arrested were kept in custody overnight, the police cell was likely to have had the most salutary effect. Sherman and Berk found that where a suspect was released shortly after arrest, the deterrent effect might be reduced.

One of the most widely reported police monitoring studies has been the Ontario experiment in Canada. In May 1981 the London Police Force in Ontario instituted a policy that directed officers to lay criminal charges in cases of wife-assault. After the evaluation studies conducted by Sherman and Berk (1984a, 1984b) and Berk and Newton (1985) in Minneapolis, Jaffe, Wolfe, Telford and Austin (1986) monitored the impact of the new Ontario policy on the reporting of domestic violence by victims, neighbours and bystanders. The researchers reported a 2,500 per cent increase in charges laid by the police in 1983, the third year of the policy. They laid charges in 298 of the 443 reported cases of wife-assault, while spouses laid charges in a further 22 cases. Figures for 1979, one year prior to the implementation of the new policy, show that police laid charges in only 12 cases, and wives in 92 cases, resulting in a total of 104 prosecutions arising out of 444 reported cases. Although the overall reporting rate had not increased between those years (444 in 1979 and 443 in 1983), the overall proportion of cases prosecuted rose from 23 per cent of reported cases in 1979 to 72 per cent in 1983. This increase, while not as dramatic as the researchers would have us believe when using a comparison of spouse-laid charges to police-laid charges (where police bring charges when the complainant may be reluctant), is nevertheless highly significant, constituting a 208 per cent increase in the total number of cases prosecuted. The researchers chose to focus on the shift from the previous predominance of the spouse laying charges to the majority of charges being laid by the police after the directive, thus taking the responsibility and burden of prosecution away from the spouse altogether. They also found a shift in the mode of trial and place of hearing, from the Family Division where cases were regarded as civil matters heard before family judges, to the Criminal Division, a forum where spousal assaults were regarded as criminal matters, heard alongside other assaults occurring outside the home.

Another important aspect of the Ontario experiment is the fact that although the police laid charges where both the officer and the victim agreed on the appropriateness, they also did so in cases where the victim was reluctant to proceed with an allegation of assault. In 9 per cent of cases the police officer wanted to charge but the victim was reluctant, and in accordance with the Evidence Act (1970, s. 4), under which wives are compellable witnesses, the police decided to charge notwithstanding their reluctance. Later analysis showed that when the police, rather than the victim, laid charges, victims reported a reduction in or termination of the violence. And even in cases in which victims were reluctant to prosecute and police, regardless of their wishes, preferred charges, a reduction in repeated violence was reported. Although the sample size is small, the Ontario experiment's findings suggest that independent police intervention is effective, and encouraging officers to arrest and prosecute is important in the long-term protection of the victim. Yet the studies of Sherman and Berk (1984a, 1984b), Berk and Newton (1985), and Jaffe et al. (1986) left one question unanswered, since they were not able to establish whether women who did not call the police fared better or worse than those who did. Put simply, is it better to call the police or to try and deal with the violence without their intervention?

A US national victim survey went some way towards addressing this question. The accepted wisdom that calling the police, however good or bad their response, deters repeated violence, was borne out in findings from the National Crime Survey. From 1978 to 1982 a total of 2.1 million were estimated to be victims of spousal violence. Of those, about 1.1 million (52 per cent) were 'callers'. That is to say that either they or neighbours or bystanders contacted the police. During the six-month period after the initial victimization, 180,000 (16 per cent) of the 1.1 million 'callers' reported further victimization. Of the 700,000 'non-callers', approximately 165,000 (23 per cent) reported subsequent victimization (Langan and Innes 1986: 4). These findings indicate that calling the police in itself acts as a deterrent to repeated abuse. No similar study has been conducted elsewhere.

In Australia similar policy initiatives reflect a commitment and concern to provide victims of spousal assault with more protection (Fisher 1981; Baker 1984; Cornish 1985; Hatty and Sutton 1985). As in the USA, each state has its own independent jurisdiction. In March 1981 the Report of the New South Wales Task Force examined the law, the police response and the role of other statutory and voluntary agencies in remedying domestic assault, and made a series of recommendations, including providing the police with powers of entry and encouraging arrest where assault had occurred. It suggested that a 'peace bond' be instituted, involving the detention in police custody of the aggressor for a period of 12 hours. The Task Force further recommended that section 407(a) of the South Wales Crime Act should be amended so that a spouse would be a compellable witness.

Law reforms have recently amended provisions relating to breach of the peace, in order to make them more applicable to situations involving spousal assault. In Queensland, the Peace and Good Behaviour Act 1982 has been introduced, while in New South Wales the Crimes (Domestic Violence) Amendment Act 1982 and s. 547AA as amended in 1983 and the Periodic Detention of Prisoners (Domestic Violence) Amendment Act 1982 have been passed. The Peace and Good Behaviour Act provides for the prosecution of an aggressor if he is in breach of an order to keep the peace. If convicted, he is liable to a fine of 1000 Australian dollars, or a one-year prison sentence. In New South Wales the legislation has resulted in making spouses compellable.

After the introduction of this new legislation, research studies have attempted to evaluate the impact of the new law on policing, prosecution and the protection of the victims. Baker (1984), in a study conducted in Victoria in 1982, very shortly after the new legislation came into force, shows the impact of the law on police dispositions to have been minimal. In 601 domestic disputes and domestic assault cases, a study of police recording practices revealed that in 547 cases no offence had been 'officially' committed. Of the 547 cases for which no offence was recorded, civil action was advised in 93 cases (17 per cent), no action at all being advised in the remaining 400 cases. In the remaining 54 cases arrests were made (9 per cent of the total sample). But although the complaints made were in respect of domestic violence assault, only 50 per cent of arrests made were for assault; the other 50 per cent recorded an arrest for street offences. Police action in Baker's study showed a continued reluctance on the part of the police to arrest for spousal assault, either because of a privately held reluctance to arrest a man for an assault on his wife, or else because evidence was insufficient, although there might have been sufficient moral justification for the arrest.

The research findings of Hatty and Sutton (1985) further reflect the problem of police reluctance to act even in the presence of clear policy directives. In their study, based at Campbelltown police station in 1985, they examined the impact of both current training programmes and police policy on deterring repeated violence. In an examination of police dispositions, client satisfaction, the use of referral, and police attitudes, the researchers found that after the implementation of a new policy about arrest and prosecution, while officers followed the directives, this did not indicate any change in their own privately held sexist views and prejudices. Officers in the study continued to hold negative attitudes towards this area of work. New policy directives had some effect because of the mandatory requirement of implementing force policy. How far 'service delivery' was improved, and whether some cases dropped out because these attitudes continued to affect officers' discretion is not known. It does seem likely, however, that wherever traditional police attitudes remain uncontested, although policy directives give the appearance of change, real change will only occur in dealing with the more serious cases.

While these various studies show that police policy directives about spousal assault can have an impact on police practice, and ultimately on the prevention of further abuse and homicide, as Jaffe et al. (1986) and Hatty and Sutton (1985) found, in the short term such changes make little impact on police culture and police attitudes to violence against wives. Evidence submitted to the New South Wales Task Force on Domestic Violence (1985) supports this finding. First, arrests by the police in spousal violence cases have not shown a marked increase (p. 20). Second, the compellability provision of 1982 is not being implemented (p. 31). Australian feminists (Kelly 1984; Scutt 1986) see the main obstacle to the success of the recent legislation in the intransigence of police attitudes.

*The European Commission*

In Europe, too, there have been initiatives to combat violence against women in the home. On 12 June 1986 the European Parliament adopted a resolution about violence against women. This followed the submission of evidence by Hedy d'Ancona, a Dutch socialist member, who demanded the provision of shelters for battered wives and urgent support for those women. D'Ancona argues that the present lack of consideration for victims of violence in Europe is incongruous and in breach of articles 100 and 235 of the EEC Treaty of Rome (1957), and also abrogates the Universal Declaration of Human Rights. The resolution was adopted by 197 votes to 66, with 50 abstentions. It called for (a) better training of police officers to deal with violence; (b) detailed statistical records of all crimes of violence against women; (c) refuges to be made available to women. Unfortunately the resolution has so far made little impact on this problem in Europe.

*Changes in police responses in London*

Many police forces in England and Wales have been reviewing their policies and procedures in dealing with domestic violence, and policing priorities differ in each of the 43 police forces in England and Wales, each force being bound by different force instructions - or having no such instructions. Bourlet (1988: 143) found that only nine forces had any specific policy. After the American initiatives in 1984, the Metropolitan Police set up their own internal working party to look into the problems of domestic violence. It was composed of seven officers from the Metropolitan Police and five outsiders (three representatives from Islington Social Services Department and two from COPE (a training consultancy for social workers in community group skills). One might immediately suppose that the preponderance of police officers in the group might have led to a pro-police report, but that was not so. The group's mandate was to make contact with individuals and organizations with the aim of examining their differing perspectives on the question of police response to domestic violence. The recommendations of the working party reflect the recommendations of the Women's National Commission Report (1985), Women's Aid groups and various other voluntary organizations.

The report (1986) indicated the need to consider a series of changes with regard to (a) statistics; (b) policy; (c) training; (d) victim support; (e) information. It found that the main classifications of domestic cases (05 (Disturbance); 06 (Assault) and 07 (Criminal Damage) ) did not indicate the seriousness or nature of the incidents. The disturbance category seemed to be liberally used to identify any incident, including those involving abuse or violence between partners. The report also indicated the need for more detail on the relationship of the victim to suspect to be given in crime reports, together with a system for more effective retrieval of other police records relating to the same incident, including incident report books and injunctions.

Although not a matter directly addressed in the report, or indeed in the force order which followed it, the indications from informal discussions are that the use of 'no criming' (challenged in chapter 4 of this book) is to be reviewed, in order that statistical sources be more accurate. With regard to police policy, the working party recommended that consideration be given to the conveyance of victims to a place of safety, and that guidelines should be drafted on the implementation of the new legislation and on conducting a prosecution even if the witness is hostile. An emphasis, too, was placed on training, with a view to challenging entrenched attitudes. This is to be conducted at all levels, for recruits, inspectors and management. With regard to victim support, the report stressed that efforts should be made to establish a multi-agency approach, effectively facilitated by single referral points between police and supporting agencies. Finally, internal publicity should be given to promote the importance of dealing with domestic violence as an area of police work, in order to enhance its status. It is easy to criticize police work in this area and harder to praise, but it must be conceded that the Metropolitan Police report offered a radical and new approach for future policing of domestic violence in London. It showed the commitment of senior police officers and police policy-makers to the improved handling of these cases. Two crucial questions remain, though: how much of this report will be implemented, and how far can service delivery to victims be improved and prosecutions increased, given the prevailing constraints of law, the CPS and police culture?

There are some indications that police culture is changing. By February 1989 women officers represented 11.55 per cent of force strength (28,078 officers) (table 6.1). The Metropolitan Police is

Table 6.1 *Women officers in Metropolitan Police Force, 1989*

| Women officers | Uniform | CID | Total | % of force |
|---|---|---|---|---|
| Commander | 2 | | 2 | 4.76 |
| Chief Superintendent | 3 | | 3 | 1.76 |
| Superintendent | 2 | 3 | 5 | 1.98 |
| Chief Inspector | 5 | 3 | 8 | 1.59 |
| Inspector | 27 | 3 | 30 | 2.10 |
| Sergeant | 198(E1) | 33 | 231(E1) | 5.41 |
| Constable | 2,792(E82) | 171(E5) | 2,963(E87) | 13.85 |
| Total | 3,029(E83) | 213(E5) | 3,242(E88) | 11.55 |

E = ethnic minorities.

*Source*: Figures supplied by kind permission of the Equal Opportunities Unit of the Metropolitan Police, London.

committed to being an Equal Opportunities Employer, and racist or sexist behaviour or language towards colleagues or members of the public is a serious offence against the discipline code in accordance with special police order 10/87. In July 1988 the Metropolitan Police issued Equal Opportunities Guidelines for police managers. Apart from genuine occupational qualifications, such as allowing only male officers to conduct searches on male prisoners, and allowing female victims of rape a choice of whether a male or a female officer conducts the interview, the document takes some positive steps towards eradicating discrimination in the occupational structure. The guidelines emphasize that both the quota system and the limits set on the squad are unlawful (p. 9), and point to the need for positive action in favour of recruiting, keeping and promoting more women and more black officers.

In January 1987 the Metropolitan Police issued a 'Strategy Statement' for the year. Already, the change in emphasis with regard to the policing of domestic assaults was beginning to emerge. The statement read:

> Domestic safety: The home is not secure for all women or for all children. Police action cannot unravel the complexities of the emotional, psychological and financial dependencies between women and men in a shared household. What the Force can do is to respond more positively at times of crisis and give real help to victims of domestic violence. Item (c) of the Force Goal will be expanded to read 'the enhanced support, care and concern for victims of crime including the victims of domestic violence'. (p. 5)

On 24 June 1987, the Metropolitan Police announced new guidelines to London's police on how to handle incidents involving domestic violence and disputes. Commander Walter Boreham of the Community Relations Branch said: 'Nothing is more invidious than the circumstances of a woman subjected to violence in the place where she expects to be safe – her own home. We have been carefully looking at the issue for some time now, and our new policy is designed to tackle the problem.' The guidelines extended the working definition of violence to include threats and attempts. 'A domestic dispute is defined as any quarrel including violence between family or members of the same household. Domestic violence occurs when a person or persons causes, attempts to cause, or threatens to cause physical harm to another family or household member' (Metropolitan Police press notice 199/87).

New instructions were issued to police officers in the form of a force order. The fundamental principle guiding the four-page order is that 'an assault which occurs in the home is as much a criminal act as one which may occur in the street.' The force order emphasizes the need to improve training procedures, reporting procedures, arrests and support to victims. Officers are required to write up such incidents either in a crime report book or else in an incident book. They are encouraged to use their powers of arrest in accordance with section 25(g) of the Police and Criminal Evidence Act 1984, which states that where 'there is evidence that a non-arrestable offence has been committed, an arrest may be necessary to protect a child or a vulnerable person.' In considering the appropriate criminal charge, officers are encouraged to use section 47 of the Offences Against the Person Act 1861, and where the victim may be reluctant to substantiate the charge police are encouraged to prosecute in accordance with section 80 of the Police and Criminal Evidence Act 1984, which makes the wife a compellable witness. The force order emphasizes the need to improve support to victims of crime and to work closely with other agencies such as Women's Aid and Victim Support schemes. Consideration should also be given to 'follow up' calls to the victim, to ensure that the victim is well or to offer advice, or warn the victim when the suspect may be released from custody.

The police definition of domestic violence, which now includes attempts and threats, is to be welcomed, but it does not go far enough. Evidence from the London Policing Study in 1988 indicated that in 29 per cent of the cases crimed the parties were not living together. Divorced and separated women, female ex-cohabitees, ex-girlfriends and current girlfriends are at risk from partner violence. Moreover, a breakdown of spousal homicide figures for England and Wales for 1986 and 1987 revealed that of all the incidents in which male spouses killed female spouses, in 76 cases (69 per cent) and 59 (71 per cent) the suspect was residing with the victim and in 33 cases (31 per cent) and 24 (29 per cent) suspect and victim were no longer living together.

It is appropriate to classify an incident as either 'domestic' or 'spousal' or 'partner', principally according to the relationship of victim to suspect. Included here are incidents between spouses (legal or common law cohabitees), girlfriend/boyfriend, ex-spouses, ex-cohabitees, ex-girlfriend/boyfriend. Such incidents are characterized by violence; the potential for violence including threats and harassment; intimidation, arguments; evidence of criminal damage; and any other situation - sexual, mental or any other - which does harm to the victim through engendering fear. In theory, the new policing policy holds out a promise of radically changing the police response to domestic violence. First, we would expect an increase in arrests and the number of recorded incidents of domestic violence against women; second, a wider use of other agencies; third, a greater demand on the courts; and fourth, a greater demand for sheltered accommodation and housing.

After the issuing of the force order many stations throughout London adopted improving the police reaction to spousal violence as part of their divisional goal. At Holloway supervising officers were called upon to report such cases fully, and have a tagged computer-aided dispatch (CAD) record made of each case (Instruction, 25 June 1987). A further instruction was issued on 25 September, indicating that where arrests were not made women should be conveyed to a place of safety, and that Beat officers should follow up these cases as recommended in the force order. Similarly at Hounslow the aim of improving the police response to domestic violence was identified as the divisional goal for 1988, accompanied by a similar tagging initiative and by follow-up visits to victims. Here, two women police officers took on the task of monitoring all calls. Similar initiatives are to be found in many other London police stations, e.g. Ealing, Croydon and Tottenham.

Since the 1984–5 London Policing Study described in detail in earlier chapters, the Metropolitan Police have undergone some reorganization. First, the use of station message books has been replaced in many although not all stations by a system of computer-aided dispatch (CAD), whereby information on calls received is translated into codes and logged centrally. The opportunities for 'cuffing' described in chapter 4 are not available using this system. All calls are attended, and each call is given a code according to a series of predefined codes indicating the nature of the incident, (05) disturbance, (06) assault and (07) criminal damage, etc., and a 'result code' including 'all quiet on arrival', 'no call for police action', 'advice given', whether a crime report has been made, a suspect detained or an incident report book classification made.

The follow-up study (see Introduction) set out to evaluate the impact of the new force order on domestic violence on public victim/witness reporting, service delivery, police recording practice, arrest, charging and prosecution. All relevant records at Holloway and Hounslow police stations were examined between March and August 1988.

*Holloway* At Holloway during the six-month period a total of 732 domestic incident calls were made by the public to the police (see table 6.2). One hundred and eighty of these calls, a total of 25 per cent, were further recorded as crimes. And arrests, including 'at the scene' arrests, and arrests resulting from inquiries, were executed in a total of 14 per cent of all reported incidents. Sixty-three direct arrests were made; in these cases charges were usually preferred later and

Table 6.2 *Evaluating police policy on domestic incidents: Holloway, 1984–1985 and 1988*

| | 1984–1985 (Aug.–Jan.) | 1988 (Mar.–Aug.) |
|---|---|---|
| No. of incidents | 449 | 732 |
| *Crimes* | | |
| No. | 57 | 180 |
| As % of incidents | 13 | 25 |
| *Arrests* | | |
| No. | 11 | 104[a] |
| As % of incidents | 2 | 14 |
| *Cases reported for prosecution*[b] | | |
| No. | 11 | 24 |
| As % of crimes initially recorded | 19 | 13 |
| *'No crimes'* | | |
| No. | 46 | 118 |
| As % of initial crimes | 81 | 65 |
| IRB entries | 40 | 119 |

[a]41 as result of inquiries; 63 direct arrests.
[b]By police before Prosecution of Offences Act 1985; by crown prosecutor after that.
*Source*: author's research for six-month period.

were made in respect of breach of the peace, drunkenness or related behaviours. Very few indeed involved direct arrests for assault on a wife, although some were made for assault or obstructing the police. A further 41 arrests were made as a result of inquiries after the opening of a crime report. In 23 per cent of crimed cases an arrest followed. A total of 24 crimed cases were finally reported for prosecution. This meant that 59 per cent of crimes where a result of inquiry arrest was made led to a prosecution. Prosecutions, however, constituted only 13 per cent of all cases initially crimed. And, finally, 65 per cent of all cases initially crimed resulted in a 'no crime' classification.

*Hounslow* At Hounslow during the same six-month period a total of 633 domestic incident calls were made (table 6.3). Of these calls, 103 (a total of 16 per cent) were further recorded as crimes. And arrests, including 'at the scene' arrests and arrests resulting from inquiries, were executed in a total of 22 per cent of all reported incidents. Ninety-nine direct arrests were made in cases initially complained of and coded as involving some domestic disturbance/assault. In most of these cases arrests were followed by charges relating to breach of the peace, drunkenness and related

Table 6.3 *Evaluating police policy on domestic incidents: Hounslow, 1984 and 1988*

| | 1984 (June–Dec.) | 1988 (Mar.–Aug.) |
|---|---|---|
| No. of incidents | 324 | 633 |
| *Crimes* | | |
| No. | 36 | 103 |
| As % of incidents | 11 | 16 |
| *Arrests* | | |
| No. | 5 | 131[a] |
| As % of incidents | 2 | 22 |
| *Cases reported for prosecution*[b] | | |
| No. | 5 | 22 |
| As % of crimes initially recorded | 14 | 21 |
| *'No crimes'* | | |
| No. | 31 | 63 |
| As % of initial crimes | 86 | 61 |
| IRB entries | 33 | 177 |

[a] 32 as result of inquiries; 99 direct arrests.
[b] By police before Prosecution of Offences Act 1985; by crown prosecutor after that.
*Source*: author's research for six-month period.

behaviours. In some cases arrestees were released without charge or cautioned. There were 32 arrests made where crime reports were instigated, constituting 31 per cent of all cases crimed. A total of 22 crimed cases were finally reported for prosecution. This meant that 69 per cent of the crimed cases where a result of inquiry arrest was made led to a prosecution. Prosecutions, however, constituted only 21 per cent of all cases initially crimed. And, finally, 63 per cent of all cases crimed resulted in a 'no crime' classification.

A more detailed analysis of Holloway police station records for the month of March 1988 is given in figure 6.1. A total of 109 calls were made to the police. Of these calls, 45 per cent were dealt with at the scene. A further 55 per cent of calls were considered by officers to require further recording. A total of 24 incident reports were made out and by definition involved no further action. A total of 24 crime reports were made out on assault and criminal damage cases arising from spousal/domestic disputes, and 11 arrests were made. Three were released some time later, 'no charge', and one was charged and transferred. Four men were given bail and three kept in custody. So, out of a total of 24 crimed cases, only three were detained pending court appearances, while seven were prosecuted. Altogether 67 per cent of the 24 crimed cases were later 'no crimed' because the complainant was unwilling to press charges. However, it must be

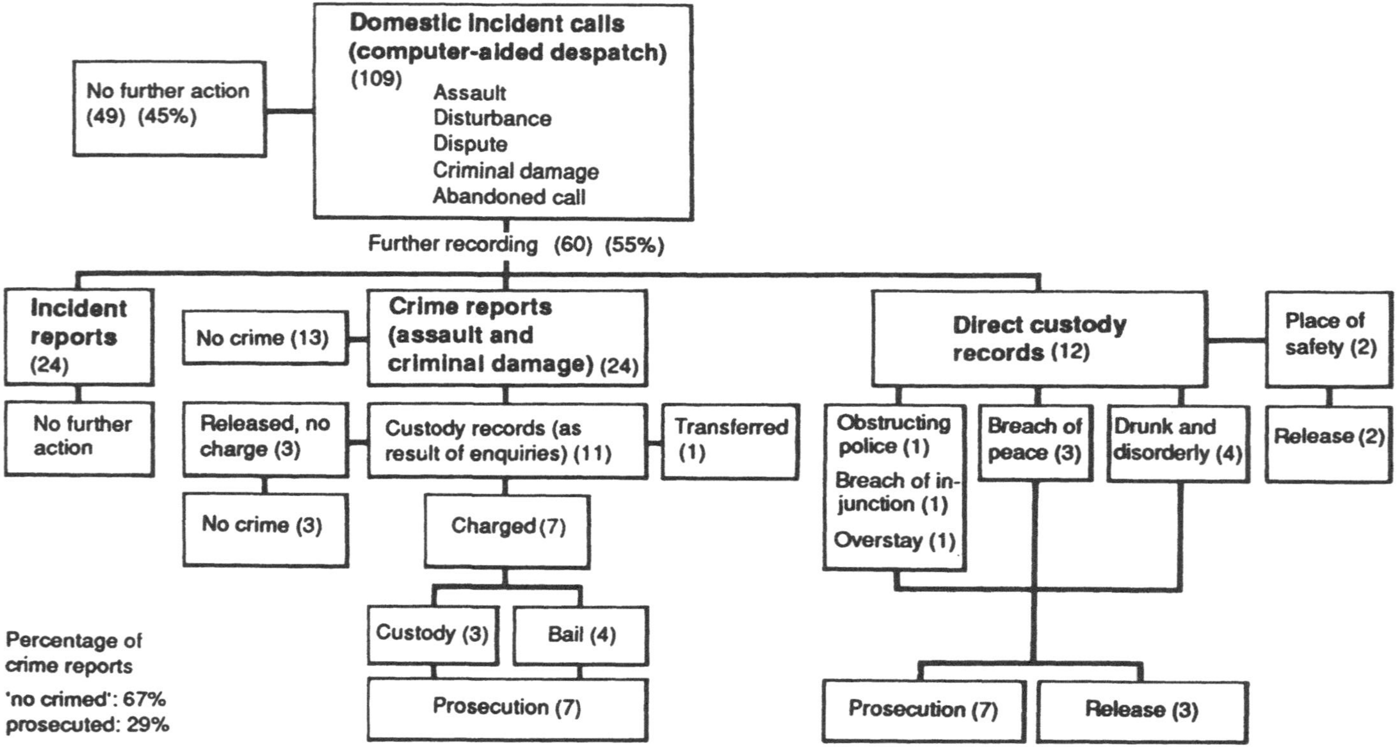


Figure 6.1 *Records of domestic incident calls at Holloway, March 1988*

noted that the 'no criming' process for some followed after the offender has been detained in custody and was subsequently released 'no charge' and 'no crimed'.

A total of 12 persons were kept in custody momentarily or for a longer period of time following incidents arising from domestic disputes. In two cases the detention was necessary to allow the police to make immediate inquiries with relatives and social services with a view to making a place of safety order. These two were immediately released when appropriate provision had been made. In the remaining 10 cases, although all arose out of physical assault, the men were variously charged: four with being drunk, three with breach of the peace, one for obstructing the police, one for breaching an injunction, and one for overstaying. In all these cases the use of 'alternative' charges can be seen as clear examples of 'resource charging' (see p. 106). Three of the drunks were subsequently released after a period of drying out (between three and four hours). One was detained until his court appearance, along with the three breach of the peace defendants. The 'overstay' was particularly a case of resource charging, since the suspect had been initially arrested in respect of assault on his wife.

It can be seen that although calls to the police have increased, together with recording, at the end of the day a total of 23 custody reports resulted in the prosecution of 14 (60 per cent), and of these 50 per cent were prosecuted for assault and criminal damage and 50 per cent for breach of the peace or related offences. Whatever the reported changes, the problem is that service delivery is only as good as the supervising officers and the attitudes of officers at the crime desk and those attending calls. Comparisons of public reporting and policing practice between 1984–5 and 1988 (table 6.4) indicate a dramatic increase in public reporting, the number of criminal cases initially recorded by the police, the number of arrests for common law offences, e.g. breach of the peace, and the number of arrests arising out of criminal assault allegations. Cases reported by the police for prosecution as a percentage of all crimes initially recorded by them remain roughly the same in 1988 as in 1984–5.

There were key differences between the two stations studied. First, there was a significant difference in the number of arrests made. At Hounslow more men were arrested in connection with a crime (31 per cent, compared with 23 per cent at Holloway). Second, more men were arrested at the scene (direct arrest) for breach of the peace arising out of domestic incidents (at Hounslow 19 per cent and at Holloway 11 per cent). At Hounslow more incident reports were made, at 33 per cent of all incidents remaining after excluding the cases crimed, compared with 21 per cent at Holloway. And cases

Table 6.4 *Domestic violence reported and recorded in the Metropolitan Police District, 1984–1985 and 1988 (estimate only, for a year)*

| | 1984–1985 | 1988 |
|---|---|---|
| No. of incidents | 54,110 | 95,550 |
| *Crimes* | | |
| No. | 6,510 | 19,810 |
| As % of incidents | 12 | 21 |
| *Crime arrests* | | |
| No. | 1,120 | 5,110 |
| As % of crimes | 17 | 26 |
| *Direct and crime arrests* | | |
| No. | n.k. | 16,450 |
| As % of incidents | n.k. | 17 |
| *Cases reported for prosecution*[a] | | |
| No. | 1,120 | 3,220 |
| As % of crimes initially recorded | 17 | 16 |
| *'No crimes'* | | |
| No. | 5,390 | 12,670 |
| As % of initial crimes | 83 | 64 |
| IRB entries | 5,110 | 20,720 |

n.k. = not known.

[a]By police before Prosecution of Offences Act 1985; by crown prosecutor after that.

*Source*: Estimated figures projected from actual figures for Holloway and Hounslow, 1984–5 and 1988 (six-month periods). (There are 76 stations in all; estimated as projection × 70.)

reported to the Crown Prosecution Service amounted to 21 per cent of crimes at Hounslow and 13 per cent at Holloway.

While Hounslow showed a lower criming of cases than Holloway, when Hounslow crimed there was a greater likelihood of some action, either arrest, arrest and charge, or arrest, charge and report for prosecution. Why did the profile differ in these important respects? Although both stations showed a commitment to remedying the problem of spouse abuse, for example Holloway produced more police orders, and senior officers liaised with local consultative committees at both localities, Holloway had less on-the-ground back-up, which meant that management policy could not so readily be translated into policing practice. Hounslow, by contrast, had a Domestic Unit staffed by two full-time officers, the presence of which served continually to remind all officers of their commitment to responding positively to the problem of domestic violence.

Significantly, at Tottenham, where a Domestic Unit has also been set up, the impact of the unit (two women police officers) shows what can be achieved with regard to prosecution, criming and service delivery. In the month of March 1988 in Tottenham 36 cases were crimed. Of those 36, 29 cases have been reported to the CPS and are being pursued. Officers have got the message: domestic violence is, as the force order states, as much a crime of violence as any other violent crime on the street. It seems that in Tottenham, an area of London which has had many police–community relations difficulties, this problem at least is being tackled vigorously, sensitively and seriously. Women are not given the option to continue with a prosecution or to drop it, and while they are often unwilling to testify against a husband, the woman police officers in the unit have adopted advocacy tactics, encouraging them to see other options in their lives and to perceive the charging of the violent husband as one of these options. It remains to be seen whether corroborative evidence (witness and medical statements) will remove the necessity for women to appear in the witness box, which is something they are extremely loth to do. Changes are afoot, but at the end of the day the success of charges depends on what the CPS and the court may or may not accept. In short the new policing policy in London is making a significant impact on (a) service delivery, (b) police recording, and (c) police support to victims. The Metropolitan Police officially reported having recorded 354 cases of domestic violence in 1986; by 1987 this had increased to 1,194 (Metropolitan Police figures). Yet there are numerous obstacles ahead within the legal framework itself. It is to a consideration of these legal and procedural fetters that we now turn.

## Legislative measures

First, there is the difficulty that the reforms proposed so far are piecemeal and inconsistent. Without the comprehensive revision of policy and practice by statutory and voluntary agencies (from victim support to council accommodation and the court itself), police reform, however committed, cannot be effective. Second, already within the criminal justice system three legal reforms – the widening of arrest powers, the impact of the new compellability provision, and the new criteria for prosecution – have created a new situation for the police. The Crown Prosecution Service will very much influence what police do with regard to arresting and charging and the reporting of cases.

### *Arrest and charge*

As we have seen earlier, in cases in which physical assault has taken place the police have always possessed the power of arrest, but in the domestic context arrest is rarely automatic. The situation is sometimes complicated by a victim who refuses police entry to the premises on arrival and denies that the visible injuries were sustained during an assault on the person. In addition, the arrest of the suspect is thwarted when the offender has left the premises before the police arrive. These difficulties have been translated into police culture as typifying the domestic assault situation, and they have responded by evolving specific styles of policing, offering advice and arbitration and tending to adopt a 'rule of thumb' policy of non-arrest.

The advent of the Police and Criminal Evidence Act 1984 provides at least in theory for the protection of women, even though no assault or crime is proven to have occurred. In accordance with section 17(1)(e) an officer may enter any premises without a search warrant or arrest warrant for the purpose of 'saving life or limb' or 'preventing serious damage to property'. The position before the 1984 Act was unclear and ambiguous. In *Bailey* v. *Wilson* ([1968] CLR 617) a police officer had gone to investigate a domestic disturbance. He heard the woman screaming as he approached the front door of the house, and entered. He was subsequently asked to leave by the male occupier, who attacked him when he refused. The court held that the officer had reasonable cause to suspect that an arrestable offence was being committed, distinguishing assault (s. 47), an arrestable offence, from common assault (s. 42). But it was held that the officer could not rely on section 6 of the Criminal Law Act (1967), which allowed him to enter the premise.

By contrast, in *McGowan* v. *Chief Constable of Kingston upon Hull* ([1967] CLR 34) the divisional court held that police officers *were* entitled to enter and remain in a private house where they feared that there would be a breach of the peace arising out of a domestic quarrel. Police right of entry remained unclear until the 1984 Act, and, as these cases show, if an officer had reasonable cause to suspect that an arrestable offence assault (s. 47) was likely to be committed he had no right of entry. If he thought a breach of the peace might be committed, he could enter.

However, it is unlikely that powers of entry under section 17(1)(e) have been exercised where the call for assistance relates to domestic violence on a spouse. The general arrest conditions under the Police and Criminal Evidence Act (1984) have particular application in spousal violence cases. An arrest can be executed when 'the constable has reasonable grounds for believing that an arrest is necessary to prevent the relevant person (i) causing physical injury to himself or any other person; (iii) causing loss of or damage to property' (s. 25 (3) (d) (i) and (iii) ). Emphasis here is placed on the role of arrest in preventative or proactive policing, where the future protection of the would-be victim is prioritized. This proactive move is further enshrined in section 25 (3)(e), when an arrest can be executed where 'the constable has reasonable grounds for believing that arrest is necessary to protect a child or other vulnerable person from the relevant person.' In this case the protection of another person is prioritized without the offending behaviour being specified, which then allows the police to arrest in situations where violent behaviour or the threat of violence is absent. In London, force policy is in line with this. If both provision in substantive law and police policy guidelines are heeded, an arrest should take place in the majority of domestic incidents in which there is an assault and in some instances where an assault is likely.

*Compelling a spouse*

*Spousal immunity in the UK* As we have seen, the treatment of violence against wives as a purely private matter was particularly well represented in the rules governing evidence up until the introduction of the Police and Criminal Evidence Act 1984 (see Edwards 1985a). Edwards (1986b) found that in 80 per cent of crimed cases women withdrew their allegations. Sanders (1988b) found that women also withdrew charges at the later prosecution stage. Neither study, however, could shed any light on the process of withdrawal and how far such a decision was variously instigated, supported, facilitated or resisted by investigating officers, although in one London station (not part of the London Policing Study), in which the police have rigorously adopted a pro-prosecution policy since 1988, women victims show a very low rate of complainer withdrawal (20 per cent). This strongly suggests that withdrawal of allegations by women complainants is not exclusively related to their fear of retaliation, etc., as previously thought, but may be intimately bound up with police service the prosecution process and continuing support.

Prosecutions for assault in the absence of the chief and often only prosecution witness have not proceeded. The Prosecution of Offences Act 1985, in accordance with earlier Attorney General's guidelines, makes it clear that in the absence of a credible witness, since a conviction is unlikely, case ought not to proceed. Arguably provisions in the Police and Criminal Evidence Act 1984 may change this. Until 1984, the wife's position with regard to evidence was a peculiar and unique one, and differed from that of girlfriend or cohabitee. The wife was competent but not compellable so far as giving evidence against a husband under section 4 of the Criminal Evidence Act 1978 was concerned. This immunity flowed from a wealth of feeling summed up by Lord Wilberforce in *Hoskyn* v.

*Commissioner of Police for the Metropolis* ( [1978] 2 All ER 136 HL), when he said:

> A wife is in principle not a competent witness on a criminal charge against her husband. This is because of the identity of interest between husband and wife and because to allow her to give evidence would give rise to discord and to perjury and would be, to ordinary people, repugnant. (p. 142)

This position was also reflected in the common law, where the wife was considered 'incompetent', based on the doctrine of the unity of husband and wife. From Hale (1736: 1.301) and Blackstone (1857: 556) onwards this unity is assumed.

> And it would be very hard that a wife should be allowed as Evidence against her own husband when she cannot attest him: such a law would occasion implacable divisions and quarrels, and destroy the very legal policy of marriage that has so contrived it, that their interests should be but one; which it could never be if wives were admitted to destroy the interests of their husbands, and the Peace of Families could not easily be maintained if the law admitted any attestation against the husband. (Gilbert 1769: 136)

It was with reference to these and other legal authorities that Lord Wilberforce reached his decision that the wife should be held non-compellable. Viscount Dilhorne, in consideration of this same problem in the case of *Hoskyn* v. *Metropolitan Police Commissioner*, reflected on the case of Lord Audley in 1631 (3 State Tr 401 at 414), who was tried by his peers for the rape of his wife; in this case it was decided that a wife could give evidence, but the precedent was not followed. Dilhorne also cited the case of *R.* v. *Lapworth* ( [1931] 1 KB 117), in which the wife was reluctant to give evidence against a husband who had assaulted her, but was ordered to do so, resulting in the husband's conviction. On appeal, the ruling was overturned. Agreeing with this decision, Dilhorne concluded that 'Mrs Hoskyn should not have been compelled to give evidence' (*Hoskyn*, p. 148). Lord Salmon supported the view that it was repugnant to make a wife a compellable witness, rejecting the argument in Lord Audley's case and the original ruling in *Lapworth*. In his concluding remarks Salmon said:

> Imagine also a case of incest in which a father has compelled his two daughters aged ten and twelve to have sexual intercourse with him. Surely that is a case far more serious than a husband's physical violence against a wife, and one in which the public weal, to say nothing of the weal of those young children, might reasonably be considered to require any competent witness to such a crime to be a compellable witness. . . . Nevertheless when parliament made a wife competent to give evidence against her husband charged with incest, it did not make her a compellable witness. This, in my

> view, was because parliament did not see fit, even in such a case, to depart from the common law rule that a wife should not, in any circumstances, be compelled to give evidence against her husband. (p. 152)

Lord Edmund-Davies, in his dissentient view, rejected the doctrine of unity of a man and wife in the face of appalling violence against her, and invoked the concept of citizenship rights.

> The criminal law serves a dual purpose; to render aid to citizens who themselves seek its protection, and itself to take active steps to protect those other citizens who, though grievously in need of protection, for one reason or another do not themselves set the law in motion. (p. 154)

Edmund-Davies went on to argue that the prosecution of such cases is likely to advance the public good, citing in support of his argument the notorious case of *DPP* v. *Morgan* ( [1975] 2 All ER 347). Here the husband encouraged and procured three other men to rape his wife. He was indicted on a charge of aiding and abetting, since he could not be indicted with rape on his own wife. The three accused claimed in their defence that they believed she was in fact consenting. Edmund-Davies noted: 'it surely creates a revulsion going far beyond "repugnance" if the wronged wife at the last moment declined to testify against her husband and, in consequence he and the four other accused were acquitted' (*Hoskyn*, p. 159), thus making a plea for the prosecution of serious cases of physical maltreatment even when the injured spouse is a reluctant and hostile witness. He concluded:

> Such cases are too grave to depend simply on whether the injured spouse is, or is not willing to testify against the attacker. Reluctance may spring from a variety of reasons and does not by any means necessarily denote that domestic harmony has been restored. A wife who has been subject to a 'carve up' may well have more reasons than one for being an unwilling witness against her husband. (*Hoskyn* v. *Metropolitan Police Commissioner*, p. 159)

These contrasting ideologies about family obligations were revealed in the case against Edward Hoskyn. One evening in September 1975 Janis Scrimshaw was in a public house with her mother when her ex-boyfriend Edward Hoskyn called her outside. Some while later she fell through the door 'screaming and covered with blood'. She was found to have sustained two stab-wounds in the chest penetrating the lung each side; a 9-centimetre cut extending from the temple to her right ear; smaller cuts to her right lip and chin; and a 4½-centimetre cut on the left forearm. On Saturday 2 October 1976, Edward Hoskyn married Janis Scrimshaw, apparently (it was rumoured), after legal advice. On the following Tuesday, now as his wife, she was called to testify for the prosecution as a hostile witness, but as the defendant's wife her evidential status was technically (and by three days) one of non-compellability. She was nevertheless compelled to give evidence against her husband which resulted in a conviction and a sentence of two years' imprisonment. Hoskyn appealed to the Court of Appeal on 8 July 1977 on the grounds that the court had incorrectly compelled her. The Court of Appeal dismissed his appeal. He later appealed to the House of Lords, and the presiding view there concurred with his grounds for appeal. As a result the conviction against Hoskyn was quashed in April 1978 ( [1978] 2 All ER HL).

*Spousal immunity in the USA* In the USA the doctrine of spousal immunity has similarly led to the protection from prosecution of husbands who beat wives (see Straus 1977: 64). The 'law of marital privilege' provides first for the 'adverse testimony privilege' and secondly for the 'confidential communications privilege'. The 'adverse testimony privilege' permits spouses to refuse to testify against one another. Wigmore (1970) explains that it arose from a sixteenth-century belief that a wife or servant who harmed the head of the household could be tried for petit treason. This disqualification rule, while abolished in certain states after the Federal Court decision in *Funk* v. *United States* (290 US 371 (1933) ), still pertains in some jurisdictions. Waits (1985: nb 30) points out that fourteen states empower a party to prevent his or her spouse from giving adverse testimony. In Illinois in *Moran* v. *Beyer* (734 F. 2d 1245 (7th Cir. 1984) ), spousal immunity was declared unconstitutional in a suit brought by a battered wife against her ex-husband for injuries inflicted during the course of their marriage. In this case the courts declared that immunity was not rationally related to the alleged purpose of maintaining family harmony.

*Compellability* By 1984 the UK parliament in the Police and Criminal Evidence Act (s. 80, pt. 8) took the view that a spouse in a prosecution against the other spouse could be compelled to give evidence. Section 80 (1) states: 'In any proceedings the wife or husband of the accused shall be competent to give evidence (a) subject to subsection (4) below, for the prosecution; and (b) on behalf of the accused or any person jointly charged.' Section 80 (2) states that 'In any proceedings the wife or husband of the accused shall, subject to subsection (4) below be compelled to give evidence on behalf of the accused.' The section was introduced primarily to allow the courts in cases of armed robbery to compel a spouse to give evidence. It was not until the Act had been introduced that the relevance of compellability in domestic violence cases was fully considered.

Bevan and Lidstone (1985), in remarking on this new provision and its impact on domestic violence cases, reflect once again on the conflict of opinion over the question of public or private interest in such cases. They write: 'it represents a balance between a public interest in prosecuting violent crime and the social policy preserving the integrity of marriage' (p. 305). The main problem is getting the right balance between deciding for wives (sometimes against their interest), or else letting wives decide for themselves and thus decline a prosecution out of fear of retaliation. The new provision has received a very mixed reception. Feminist idealists regard it as yet another example of the unrelinquishing efforts of the present government to extend the arm of state control into family life, thereby restricting individual freedom to decide – extracting information from wives by compelling them to give evidence. Feminist realists argue that the previous immunity of wives from giving evidence represents the traditional non-interventionist stance taken by the state in matters of family life, even where the life and limb of women is being threatened. However, feminist organizations and Women's Aid groups remain sceptical about how far the compellability provision will be put to the test unless police arrest violent or potentially violent men and report all cases of physical assault to the Crown Prosecutor.

There is certainly some evidence, prior to the 1984 Act, that hostile witnesses have not received sympathetic treatment from the police, the prosecution, the court or the judiciary or magistracy. The appellant in this case was sentenced to five years' imprisonment (*R.* v. *Thompson* [1977] 64 CAR 96–7) for incest and indecent assault. His sixteen-year-old daughter was reluctant to give evidence and received bludgeon-like treatment from the judge.

> *Witness*: I'm not saying anything. I'm not going to give evidence.
> *Judge*: Oh yes you are.
> *Witness*: I'm not.
> *Judge*: Unless you want to spend some time in prison yourself, don't you?
> *Witness*: No.
> *Judge*: You won't like it in Holloway I assure you. You answer these questions and behave yourself.

As a rule prosecution witnesses in criminal prosecutions who are reluctant to give evidence can be dealt with for being in contempt (cf *R.* v. *K.* [1983] 78 CAR (1984) 82), but this would happen very rarely. It is much more likely that where the victim is the prosecution witness the proceedings would be dropped and the case dismissed without any investigation into why the complainant had changed her mind at the last moment.

Are the fears of left-wing feminist realists borne out? Will this new compellability provision actually place women in a more difficult position than before? Will they be forced to give evidence, or, if they refuse, imprisoned for contempt? In answering these questions the probable impact of the compellability provision must be assessed in the light of the advent of the Crown Prosecution Service. The criteria guiding CPS decision-making in a case where a wife does not wish to give evidence and retains this objection throughout are such that it is likely that the Crown Prosecutors will turn the case down (discontinue proceedings) unless the violence is serious (these are considered in detail later in the chapter). The compellability provision is therefore unlikely to make any impact on the police reporting of cases and/or the prosecution of cases in which the assault is considered trivial. Compellability is likely to affect only those cases in which the violence is considered exceptional. Here the police may be encouraged to report cases to the CPS regardless of the wishes of the victim, and the CPS may be inclined to prosecute in such cases notwithstanding the reluctance of the victim to give evidence in court. Certainly in cases of serious violence a prosecution is in the interests of the victim and also in the public interest. The real tragedy, in my view, is that for the majority of spousal assault victims the compellability provision will make no impact at all. The application of this provision will depend on the interpretation and attitude of the judiciary, the CPS and the police. This will result in regional variations, in the absence of a national policy on the weight to be given to the various criteria to be considered. As yet there has been no systematic study of this issue; I can only point out the difficulties from personal observation. A woman superintendent with the South Wales Police gave me an example of the type of problems she had encountered:

> In a recent case where the complainant did not wish to prosecute, we (the police) continued with the proceedings (in accordance with the compellability provision) but the court (the judge) was not satisfied. The victim who was sitting with her head bandaged at the back of the court was asked (by the judge) if she wanted the prosecution to continue. She said she did not, and the case was dropped!

In another more recent case from the Metropolitan Police District the reluctance of the woman to proceed with a prosecution resulted in the CPS dropping the charges. In 1987 I asked a branch Crown Prosecutor for one of the three London areas about the attitude of the CPS to such cases.

> *Sue Edwards*: In the case of an assault against a wife where the complainant was reluctant to give evidence notwithstanding the compellability provision in the Police and Criminal Evidence Act, what would be the view of the CPS?
>
> *Crown Prosecutor*: We will follow on serious assaults subject to other considerations. If injuries are not that serious, as in a bruise or a small cut, and the complainant does not wish to give evidence, we would probably say that it was not in the public interest to prosecute.

In a regional news item for Independent Television Network on 27 February 1989 Stephen Wooler of the Crown Prosecution Service in London reiterated what appears to be the main problem presented by such cases. He said: 'The primary source of difficulty is the willingness of the victim to support the prosecution once it gets to court. Only too often I'm afraid there are proceedings started with the support of a victim who subsequently withdraws that support.'

Despite this overall view some local initiatives are already developing between the Crown Prosecution Service and local police stations. Two such local initiatives in North and South London have begun. In these initiatives, where a spouse wants a case dropped, the CPS try to to ensure that such cases are dropped because of a genuine desire on the part of the victim for reconciliation, rather than a victim being threatened by a spouse or the spouse's family and withdrawing out of fear.

While it may well be that some Crown Prosecutors weed out cases in which the victim is a reluctant witness despite the compellability provision, others may not adopt this approach, and decisions are based on individual discretion. Certainly if judges direct the prosecution to drop charges where the prosecuting witness is hostile, and direct that the police pay costs, the police will proceed cautiously in further cases.

The compellability provision, even if used fully, can only improve the situation in cases of prosecutions brought on behalf of wives against husbands. In cases of violence inflicted by ex-husbands, boyfriends, ex-boyfriends and male cohabitees, victim/witnesses have always been compellable. In these cases there is little evidence that women victims are being or indeed have ever been compelled, or that the police are pressing charges where the victim is a hostile witness. In cases where partners are not legally married (my data suggest this accounts for roughly 50 per cent of all cases I studied), experience has shown that compellability has made no difference at all. The prosecution of boyfriends by girlfriends has been as absent from the daily court lists as the prosecution of husbands by wives bound in marriage. Girlfriends have often been effectively denied protection because of a presumption on the part of the police that they will be hostile witnesses. Where the cohabitee is a hostile witness, unless the violence is very serious prosecutions have been exceedingly rare. This suggests that it is not the legal rules about compellability of a spouse *per se* that have constituted the main obstacle to prosecution. And this suggests that compellability alone will be insufficient to bring about a change in police and/or prosecutors' attitudes towards this kind of case.

There is one final problem with compellability. As the committal to prison in March 1989 of Michelle Renshaw, for contempt of court in refusing to give evidence against her boyfriend attacker, shows, while the compellability provision can compel a witness to stand up in court, it cannot make the witness testify against the accused. Ms Renshaw was a hostile witness for the prosecution, and when she refused to give evidence Judge James Pickles at Leeds Crown Court committed her to prison for contempt, treating her in the same way as other hostile witnesses have been dealt with when they have refused to give evidence. Michelle Renshaw was to have given evidence against her boyfriend, who was charged with wounding her. She decided not to give evidence because she had received telephone threats and had been followed. It remains to be seen whether further cases will be treated in this way, and what impact such outcomes will have on victims' willingness to report cases to the police and prosecute.

Other jurisdictions have taken the view that making a spouse a compellable witness, and enforcing the compellability provision where relevant, is an essential step towards the protection of the victim and is a move that must be supported at all stages of the criminal justice process. The Report of the New South Wales Task Force on Domestic Violence (1981: 55), in recommending compellability, argued that 'the placing of a choice in the hands of the woman herself is almost an act of legal cruelty.' In 1982 the introduction of the Crimes (Domestic Violence) Amendment Act (s. 407AA) stressed the importance of compellability. Yet evidence submitted to the New South Wales Report on Domestic Violence (1985: 31) indicated that compellability as provided for in the 1982 Act was not being enforced.

The Law Reform Commission of Australia in its report on domestic violence (1986) also received such submissions. The Commission did not, however, give mandatory compellability its full support. While they advised that the spouse should be compellable, at the same time they recognized that upon application from the spouse some cases might more properly be excluded. In 1986, The Crimes (Domestic Violence) Ordinance 1986, s. 17, made further provision for compellability: 'in a prosecution for a prescribed offence, a person shall not be taken not to be compellable to give evidence by reason only that the person is the spouse of a defendant' (see Law Reform Commission 1986: 76).

In the United States various steps towards ensuring victim protection including compellability are currently being taken. The Attorney General's Task Force on Family Violence (1984) made a series of recommendations in this respect. First, victims of domestic violence should not be required to testify at a preliminary hearing where hearsay evidence should be sufficient. Since 1981 some programmes have attempted to make the case with other evidence such as medical reports, photographic evidence, or a full preliminary statement. In other areas prosecutors spend some considerable time persuading the victim that a prosecution will help her family. And finally, in some jurisdictions, compellability or 'no drop' policies are strictly enforced, where victims are held in contempt of court if they fail to testify (McGuigan and Pascale 1986: 115–17). The US Attorney General's Task Force on Family Violence (1984: 30) endorsed 'no drop' policies, provided that they do not penalize the victim. One Assistant District Attorney said to the Task Force: 'I have seen relief on a woman's face when I've said, I'm sorry I am not waiving a prosecution' (see also McGuigan and Pascale 1986: 126).

Although the impact of the compellability provision in the UK is also compromised, it will nevertheless carry important symbolic functions (see Arnold (1969) on the symbolic function of law). First, treating wives as compellable witnesses against husbands removes their differential treatment in all cases including domestic assault. This not only changes their evidential status at a trial but has repercussions throughout the investigation and pre-trial process. In the event of a wife dropping charges against her husband police have traditionally taken the wife's perspective as the mandate for not proceeding, with the consequence that serious occasions of violence go unprosecuted and as indicated earlier unrecorded. One end result of evidential immunity, among other things, has been to convey to police officers the unimportance of domestic violence. Second, the compellability provision puts the commission of the crime first, rather than giving first place to the relationship of victim to suspect. In so doing the provision facilitates the breaking down of the divide between public and private maintained in evidential procedure. But its success depends upon police making the decision to report cases, instead of placing such decisions on the shoulders of wives or girlfriends. It also acknowledges that where violence has occurred the sentiment which emphasizes family privacy is abhorrent, since it is already demonstrated that a loving relationship has broken down. In short, the compellability provision and its full implementation is a necessary step toward, but will not of itself revolutionize the situation.

In Canada, while at a case-law and policy level compellability is supported, and hostile witnesses jailed for contempt, the reluctant spouse still determines the prosecution process. In Canada, in Yukon, in *R.* v. *McGinty* ([1986] 52 Criminal Reports Third Series, p. 161), the appeal court upheld the ruling of the territorial court inter alia: that spouses should be compellable witnesses. J.A. McLachlin held, 'the interest of society in securing proper prosecution of persons who commit crimes of violence against their spouses is vital. Such crimes are common and consequences frequently grave. Because they tend to be committed in the privacy of the home, it is often impossible to prosecute the aggressor unless the victim-spouse testifies. A rule which leaves the husband or wife the choice of testifying is more likely to be productive of family discord than to prevent it.' Thereby he reaffirmed the position held in two earlier cases *R.* v. *Lonsdale* ([1974] 2 WWR 157) in Alberta, *R.* v. *Sillars* ([1979] 1 WWR 743). In 1984, new prosecutorial policy was introduced in Saskatchewan, as in other provinces, with a view to reducing police and prosecutorial discretion. In the words of Kenneth McKay, the Director of Public Prosecutions for Saskatchewan, 'Police were instructed not to put the onus on the complainant, but to lay charges as they would in any other case, that is, where the evidence supported the charges; prosecutors were instructed not to discontinue cases if the only reason for doing so was the reluctance of the complainant' (McGillivray 1987: 30).

In addition, courts have supported the compellability decisions pre-*McGinty* in imposing sentences on witnesses who refuse to testify. In 1984 in Canada, Karen Mitchell was sent to prison for three months for contempt in refusing to testify against a cohabitee who had assaulted her. Criticism and public outcry followed in this case, as in the case in Leeds in March 1989, where Judge Pickles imprisoned a spousal violence victim for refusing to testify. The National Action Committee on Women said that three months in prison for contempt (freed after three days) was too harsh, but did not condemn the contempt finding: 'to permit the woman, as witness, to decide whether or not to testify, leaves her subject to intimidation' (McGillivray 1987: 37).

Yet, notwithstanding these provisions an evaluation of the 'no drop' policy in 1985 by the Saskatchewan Spouse Abuse Project found that in 35 per cent of 233 reported cases during an eight-month period, the victim requested that charges be dropped. In addition, in 25 per cent of cases the victim actively hindered prosecution. The prosecutor responded by withdrawing or staying prosecution in 17 per cent of cases (McGillivray 1987: 32).

*Prosecuting domestic violence*

How will the Crown Prosecution Service, brought into being by the Prosecution of Offences Act 1985, help to protect victims? Will the criteria for prosecution facilitate the diversion away from the criminal process of many domestic assault cases? One of the main criticisms of police dispositions in England and Wales has arisen over their absolute discretion in the decision to prosecute. Optimists have argued that the introduction of the Crown Prosecution Service does away with that omnipotence, since prosecutors promise to be independent. Lord Gardiner, when Lord Chancellor, described the police as 'the most powerful and least accountable of any in Western Europe; nowhere else do they have the power to prosecute without any independent evaluation' (Whitaker 1982: 283). The Crown Prosecutor now acts as the final arbiter in the decision to prosecute, and the system is designed to remove from the police the decision to continue with a case or to drop charges. But the police still remain as the 'gatekeepers' of the prosecution process, responsible for feeding cases in. Some argue that the Crown Prosecution Service cannot be independent of the police, while others maintain that it may seriously frustrate and obstruct what the police may be trying to achieve.

Sanders (1986) represents the first view. He argues that instead of being an independent service, the CPS is likely to be independent neither from the police nor from the courts. He points out that both here and in the United States it is usual to screen cases. In England and Wales Crown Prosecutors may advise the police to prosecute or they may 'discontinue' proceedings before the police send the charge sheet to court. Sanders writes: 'The power of discontinuance can be used only if the police refer charged cases to Crown Prosecutors prior to sending off the charge sheets. Similarly, Crown Prosecutors can only advise the police about cases which the police have first decided to show them' (1986: 16). During the twelve-month period ending 31 March 1988 a total of 57,760 cases were referred by the police to the CPS for advice prior to any charges being made. In a significant proportion of these cases the CPS advised that no action should be taken (Hansard, 27 May 1988).

Proceedings may be discontinued at the outset; a case may be withdrawn or the prosecution may decide to offer no evidence. Even once proceedings are under way, the discretion to discontinue is still available. During the twelve-month period ending in March 1988 a total of 109,580 defendants had the cases against them wholly discontinued by the CPS, either under the formal provisions of section 23 (whereby proceedings may be discontinued at an early stage by written notice to the court) or by no evidence being offered at court. Of these 108,750 cases a total of 17,852 were cases discontinued by the three CPS areas serving London (Hansard, 27 May 1988).

The second argument is that not only will Crown Prosecutors be independent, but they will have an impact on the exercise of police powers in decisions to arrest and charge, and will seriously encroach on police freedom and discretion. If the police have been accused of identifying with the offending spouse, of letting subjective judgements of blameworthiness of the victim influence discretion to arrest and charge, will Crown Prosecutors be any less influenced by their own private predilections? By introducing another pivotal element into the decision-making process we may simply be replacing one level of subjectivism with another. Adler (1987: 41), for example, tells us that the legal profession is dominated by men. Out of 339 circuit judges only 10 are women. Women currently number 3 out of 77 High Court judges, and no woman has ever sat on the judicial committee of the House of Lords. Moreover, the overwhelming majority of barristers are male. We have already seen (chapter 2) a similar sex ratio in policing. Will there be a larger proportion of women in the CPS, and will their presence have any more impact than is the case elsewhere in the criminal justice system?

It is clear that the CPS provides another selective mesh through which cases have to pass in order to reach prosecution. The CPS view on racial incidents is clear, and prosecutions are always brought with regard to public interest criteria. But it is not at all certain that there is any similar climate with regard to domestic assault. And the CPS have the absolute authority to proceed or to mark cases 'no proceedings'. As at other pivotal points in the criminal justive process, another level of discretion will interfere with justice. Will this leave women more or less protected?

There is too the problem of how to interpret what exactly is the public interest. What does it mean? Has the public been consulted? Is it an impression founded on consolidated research, or is it the educated gut reaction of a particular section of society, i.e. prosecutors? In the execution of their task the Crown Prosecutors, as managers of the prosecution system, are required to consider four main criteria in the bringing of cases: whether there is a sufficiency of evidence in a given case; the prospects of conviction; whether a prosecution is in the public interest; and the credibility of the witness or victim. No indication has been given as to how much weight should be given to any one criterion, whether more weight should be given to one than another, or whether the weight given to any one factor is related to the particular type of offence under consideration. Nor are there guidelines as to how these criteria should be applied in particular cases. Indeed, while one might argue that most prosecutions serve the public interest, it is this criterion that gives the CPS maximum discretion, and it is this criterion that is astonishingly vague. It abandons systematic consistent justice to idiosyncracy and sophistry. In cases of spousal assault and racial attack one could argue that the public interest is always served in a prosecution, and therefore that this criterion should be put first whatever the likely outcome, regardless of the sufficiency of evidence and the prospect of conviction. Yet the CPS may take the view that there is no public interest to be defended in bringing a prosecution.

*Sufficiency of evidence* The first criterion to be considered by the CPS when assessing whether or not to prosecute is whether there is a sufficiency of evidence. Here there must be a more than 50 per cent chance of a conviction. The imposition of this criterion was a response to the inefficiency of the old prosecution service, a concern that number of acquittals as the result of directions by the judge was on the increase. (This constituted 47 per cent of all acquittals in 1983, and was significantly reduced by the advent of the CPS, to 32 per cent in 1987). It was intended to make the system more efficient and cost-effective by weeding out weak cases.

*Likelihood of conviction* The second consideration for the CPS is to assess the likelihood of a conviction. Here the *Code for Crown Prosecutors* (1986) states 'The Crown Prosecution Service does not support the proposition that a bare *prima-facie* case is enough, but rather will apply the test of whether there is a realistic prospect of conviction.' The application of the 'reasonable or realistic prospect of conviction' test is particularly problematic where assaults of a violent or sexual nature are concerned. It requires the CPS to consider both the evidence and other extraneous matters - the likely impact witnesses will have on jurors, and jurors' likely predisposition to the type of case under consideration.

Essentially the CPS has to guess at the likely outcome, and base part of their decision to prosecute on what jurors might make of the case and their likely verdict. And in cases involving domestic assault and minor sexual assault jurors are likely to acquit. They are also likely to reflect the prevailing sexist and cultural assumptions about family violence, and to hold the views that women who do not conform provoke violence and that in circumstances like this a man has every right to hit. Jurors, in assessing guilt or innocence, do not simply consider their 'verdict according to the evidence', but weigh in the balance the likely motivation of the offender and the consequences for the offender if they convict (Kalven and Zeisel 1971). Jurors also tend to be influenced in reaching a decision in this kind of case by the demeanour of the victim and her credibility: does she conform to the 'typical' stereotype of the genuine battered wife, or does she look like a wife who flaunts convention or is perhaps too sure of herself? The CPS will assess all these possibilities in considering the prospect of conviction. 'Reasonable' or 'realistic' is vague, and depends on the interpretation of particular individuals in their assessment of particular cases.

*The public interest* Clearly, cases brought 'in the public interest' will involve those incidents in which some wider public norm has been broken, where the public good has been offended or the public indiscriminately offended! The factors to be considered by the CPS give priority to the offender's perspective, over the interest of the victim. The guidelines give little consideration to whether protecting victims is a matter 'in the public interest'. They outline instead the staleness of the case and certain characteristics of the offender, such as youth, old age, mental illness or stress. The only references to victims are unfortunately prejudicial ones:

> I sometimes get cases in which it is abundantly clear that a girl of 15 has persistently seduced a number of men considerably older than herself. In such circumstances I may either take no proceedings or prosecute only those men who are of such maturity that it can reasonably be said that they should have resisted the temptation.' (Attorney General's Guidelines appendix 25, Royal Commission on Criminal Procedure 1981: 214)

However, if the men are considerably older, they should legally be expected to take full responsibility for their action. The attitude quoted is part of the perpetual condemnation of the victim and exoneration of the offender. A second reference to victims, this time victims of violence in the family, carries the implication that women who want to prosecute husbands do so vengefully, 'in the heat of the moment'.

> In some cases, I think it is proper to have regard to the attitude of a complainant who may have gone to the police in the heat of the moment – as in many husband/wife assault cases – but later expresses a wish that no action be taken. Usually in such circumstances, I would not prosecute unless there was suspicion that the change of heart was actuated by fear or the offence was of some gravity. (Crown Prosecution Service 1986: 6)

This broad misunderstanding of women's motivation for complaint in the first instance and later withdrawal was given further ratification in a Home Office Circular (26/1983) on police prosecution, in which it was stated that 'Although in some cases it may subsequently be established that *a complaint is without foundation*, the need for tact and understanding remains at all stages of the investigation' (my emphasis).

The understanding of 'public interest' reflects the preponderance of an attitude which perceives violence within the family as a private matter. For instance, where a victim is hostile and reluctant to give evidence, yet the public interest would be served in bringing a prosecution, what view will the CPS take? Will the public interest element outweigh the credibility of a victim, or will the latter prevail and the case be marked 'no proceedings'?

Yet it is just this public interest argument which allows for the prosecution of prostitute women. It is, as Box argues (1987: 153), a powerful cloak which justifies a whole range of police activity, but has always left certain groups, such as battered women, out in the cold.

*Witness credibility* In cases of spousal violence the witness may not always appear credible. Even though there may be sufficient evidence, her character and demeanour may have an impact not only on how the prosecutor sees her but on how he/she anticipates the court and the jury will view her. Cases might then be dropped because her credibility seems open to question. Vennard (1985), in her observation of screening policies and practices in the United States, found that the two factors most strongly related to case dismissal at this point were the prior relationship between the defendant and the victim, and the defendant's criminal history. In over half the cases where the defendant had no prior criminal record, cases were dismissed. This assessment is influenced by discretionary thinking as much as by legal criteria.

**The likely impact of prosecution policy**

I would argue that the public is under seige or threat when any one of its members is in danger of victimization. Spousal violence affects particular members of society - wives, girlfriends, female cohabitees - and has never been viewed as a public threat. Spousal or domestic assault has always been regarded as private wrong; and this construction of the public/private divide will affect the assessment of whether a domestic assault prosecution is in the public interest. Case law itself reflects this divide. Returning to *Hoskyn*, in that case Lord Edmund-Davies challenged the accepted wisdom of the boundaries between public and private and argued that certain cases 'ought not to be regarded as having no importance extending beyond the domestic hearth. Their investigation and, where sufficiently weighty, their prosecution is a duty which the agencies of law enforcement cannot properly neglect' (p. 759).

How will the prosecution criteria be applied? Will all prosecutors have a uniform response to the adjudication of these cases? Let us look at the experience of other jurisdictions. Moody and Tombs (1982) in Scotland found that in assessing domestic assault cases prosecutors (in Scotland called Procurator Fiscals) considered not only the legal criteria but also the offenders' possible motivation and thus the 'appropriateness' of prosecution in a criminal court. Prosecutors often marked domestic assault cases as 'not to be proceeded with' because they anticipated problems in obtaining convictions, further aggravated by the presence of often hostile witnesses. Prosecutors see their role in such cases not so much as prosecutors, but rather as mediators between husband and wife: 'we regularly interview wives, exercise discretion and decide whether or not to drop the charges . . . I would be, as a rule, prepared to concede to a request by a wife not to proceed provided I had seen the wife and seen the husband in the presence of the wife' (p. 68). Some prosecutors also regarded assault in the domestic context as a matter largely irrelevant to the criminal courts: 'why prosecute . . . when . . . it is a drinking problem?' (p. 68). Some prosecutors felt that the woman herself had provoked the assault, and was therefore to blame: 'there have been cases where I felt the husband acted in a way you would expect a normal person to react . . . perhaps finding his wife with another man . . .' (p. 69).

Wasoff (1982, 1987) also examined the role of the Procurator Fiscal in Scotland: 'The prosecutor is the main transitional figure who transforms the crude realities of violent offences to the form suitable for court scrutiny.' In the exercise of discretion, both moral and legal considerations were brought to bear. She writes: 'Their discretion, like that of the police, is shaped not only by the strict requirements of the written or common law, but also by the demands of efficiency, limitations of resources and time, and ideologies of the family' (p. 190). In the prosecution of domestic assault the discretion of prosecuters is acted upon by family ideologies and notions of privacy in much the same way as police officers' discretion is affected at earlier stages. Consider the following case which was marked 'no proceedings'.

> About 6.15 pm on Sunday . . . the now accused arrived at the dwelling house where he resides with his wife. The accused, who had been drinking heavily, came into the living room where his wife was sitting, reading a newspaper, carrying a pot of stew. He said: 'Is this what you call dinner, you bastard? It's like bloody water.' Whereupon he threw the bowl on her.

He then struck his son, kicked his wife, and threw her on to the ground. She was subsequently admitted into hospital. The accused was sent for trial. Before the trial the wife wrote to the Prosecutor Fiscal explaining that she wanted to drop the charge because her husband was now behaving himself. The Procurator Fiscal responded by simply dropping the proceedings.

Had the same cases involved strangers, the reluctance of the victim to prosecute would not have had the same impact. Arguably the Procurator Fiscal in question may have felt the case should not have been started in the first place, and a hostile witness provided just the ratification needed to mark it 'no proceedings'. However, in the cases studied by Wasoff, by the time cases had got to the stage of being adjudicated by the Procurator Fiscal, in only 2 per cent did the wife want to drop the prosecution. When cases were not proceeded with at this stage, this was usually the result of a decision made by the Procurator Fiscal alone.

Moody and Tombs (1982) found evidence that some Procurators did support the prosecution of domestic cases notwithstanding the reluctance of the victim: 'domestic assault must be taken seriously . . . there are a considerable number of cases where the wife does not wish us to continue . . . very seldom do we let that influence us . . . the wife is not necessarily her own best adviser'; 'every wife beater, in my view, is a potential murderer' (p. 69). Nevertheless, if Wasoff's findings of a 2 per cent victim withdrawal at this stage is right the latter expression of support for prosecution in cases where the victim is reluctant must be very rare indeed.

Procurator Fiscals not only exercised discretion in whether cases were to proceed, but also made decisions about the mode of trial. Wasoff (1987) observed that there was a clear preference for referring domestic violence cases to the lower courts. Having interviewed Procurator Fiscals she concluded that three considerations are relevant in the decision: first, whether a weapon is used, and the nature of the weapon; second, the method of inflicting injuries, and their seriousness; and, third, whether the accused had any previous convictions. She quoted one Procurator Fiscal as saying

> If it were a knife or something of that kind, then I think we would be taking it, all things being equal, in the High Court. If on the other hand, it was a severe injury by the use of fists or perhaps a glass or household utensils, then I think we would be looking in terms of Sheriff and jury on indictment, particularly if it's a domestic matter. (1987: 5)

The intervention of a moral perspective or extra-judicial considerations also influenced prosecutors in their decisions not to proceed with rape cases. Chambers and Millar (1986), again in a Scottish study, found that in 33 per cent of rape cases prosecutors decided not to proceed (table 3.1, p. 31). In most cases of non-procedure, this was the result of legal considerations such as lack of corroboration, medical evidence or identification, but in some cases the quasi-legal or extra-legal factors also intervened, which were not in themselves constituent components of the legal definition. The researchers observed: 'This particular conception of the incident allows moral blame to be awarded to the complainer, thus arriving at a "presumption against rape"' (p. 43). Prosecutors were also strongly influenced in their decision-making by the prospect of conviction. The Crown Prosecutor in this case reveals its intrinsic 'moral' weakness.

> It will emerge from the complainer's evidence that the complainer is an unmarried mother with a young child, that she was having regular sexual intercourse with her boyfriend, who at the time of the alleged incident was in prison, and who had, even before the event, complained of having a chance sexual encounter with an ex-boyfriend. It will also emerge that on the day in question, she and a friend spent the entire afternoon and the early part of the evening in a public house where they consumed a considerable amount of Super Lager and Vodka and that she and her friend took the initiative and joined the accused and his friend when they came into the public house. It would also appear that the complainer quite willingly left the public house in the company of the accused. All things considered, there is much grist for the defence-mill. (p. 44)

In the USA, as in the UK, the prosecutors' decision to proceed is pivotal. As Ellis argues, in the USA: 'A prosecutor who consistently refuses to initiate a prosecution following an arrest will communicate to police that these events are not to be treated as crimes and accordingly, are not worth valuable time and effort' (1984: 58). While there are 43 police forces in England and Wales, these forces are served by 31 Crown Prosecution Service field areas or divisions (see Crown Prosecution Service Annual Report 1986–7: 8), with their own policies. At both the police and prosecutorial level the need for a national policy becomes obvious.

To sum up, the success of the recent revision in policing policy in London regarding criminalization of domestic assault depends in part on the response of prosecutors and the courts. As I have shown above, the police may decide not to report the cases; when they do report, the CPS may decline a prosecution; when cases are marked for prosecution they may nevertheless still fail at the court stage either through the prosecution withdrawing the case on the advice of the judge, whereby an acquittal is recorded; or by the judge directing the jury to acquit, which leads to the same record. Even when convictions are secured, the nominality of the sentences affects the decisions made earlier in the process in similar cases.

### Alternatives to prosecution

Alternatives to prosecution have been tried both in the USA and in the UK. Traditionally these diversion procedures were widely practised because on the whole prosecution was considered to be inappropriate in cases of family violence. In the past such programmes were simply viewed as a way of avoiding criminalizing the violence. Newman (1966: 161) and Holmes (1982), noted that the misdemeanour complaint bureau of the Detroit Police Department attempts to settle by 'peace bond' the bulk of family and neighbourhood cases in Kansas. Charges are dismissed if the offender agrees to probation. In the USA since the late 1970s many pre-trial diversion programmes have been established for abusers, with a view to discovering the most effective means of deterring repeated abusive behaviour. Such programmes aim to break the continuation of violence. Here prosecution is deferred while the abuser takes part in a counselling programme. If he completes the programme the prosecution is dropped; if he fails then the prosecution continues. In a scheme in Johnson County established in 1982 about 80 per cent of husbands charged participated. But, as Gottlieb and Johnson (1983: 549) note with caution, reliance by the courts on such diversion programmes may be unjustifiable if the programmes are ineffective, that is to say if men continue to use violence in their relationships. A central concern of feminists and women's refuge workers in the USA and UK is that such programmes should not place victims in any further danger (see Walker 1987; Horley, *Guardian*, Letters, 8 March 1989).

Diversion from the criminal justice process is currently used in the UK for dealing with juveniles, where offenders are dealt with by means of an informal (warning) caution, or a formal (recorded) caution. The use of cautioning has been extended to some crimes committed by adult offenders. In the UK, in Scotland for example, diversion from the criminal justice process is considered by MacKay (1985) as a viable alternative to prosecution for crimes of domestic violence. But it is the introduction of an alternative to prosecution that worries feminists. Sanders (1988b: 528) argues that diversion might be appropriate in cases of domestic violence if the use of informal and formal cautions could be extended. Some police forces in the UK are already considering such measures: Streatham in south London has already started a pilot scheme, investigating the feasibility of such a measure. Sanders (p. 529) quite rightly points out that post-trial diversion, such as the increased use of probation and counselling, is more likely to be welcomed in the UK, where feminists have struggled for some time to criminalize domestic violence.

## Sentencing

Sentencing in all criminal cases is affected by a variety of considerations. Sentencing is the product of a collectivity of intentions, reflecting public disapproval of the offence, punishment, and the provision of some measure of reparation to the offender. Historically, sentencing has reflected broader movements within society which have been either predominantly retributive or restitutive. All societies have used some measure of both punishment and welfare considerations. Probation orders, treatment programmes, community service projects and intermediate treatment programmes are broadly considered to be restitutive, set against the retributive measures of prison and monetary penalties. The UK sentencing system has developed along tariff lines, in which offences are assessed according to their seriousness, graded, and given a tariff, and within the range considerable judicial discretion may be exercised. More recently, sentencing has reflected the concern to bring the victim in, and the 'punishment model' and 'welfare model' have existed alongside an attempt to introduce greater reparation.

The debate over sentencing includes political and ideological elements, and over recent years the pendulum has swung backwards, with demands for stiffer penalties, more sanctions and more retribution. This has been particularly the case in calls for stiffer penalties for juveniles, and for other particular categories of offender. A major prison-building programme and continual increases in the number of prisoners have been the result.

By contrast, the Left have consistently argued for a relaxation in the current regime and for decarceration for many offenders currently serving prison sentences. A wide variety of groups have argued for alternatives to imprisonment. The problem of sentencing the spousal violence offender has not only become implicated in the broader sentencing debate, but also generates particular problems of its own.

In the USA post-trial diversion is frequently used for spouse abusers where, after a prosecution, judges can impose probationary sentences which can include a requirement of therapy or counselling. Probationers may then receive similar counselling services to those received by defendants in pre-trial diversion programmes (Gottlieb and Johnson 1983: 550). Probation for spouse abuse is not available in the UK, although proposals are being considered along these lines by magistrates and judges, and those who work with victims and offenders.

Both left-wing feminist idealists and realists have agreed that sentences meted out to the domestic violence offender have been always too lenient. Perpetrators of domestic assault convicted under section 47 of the Offences Against the Person Act 1861 generally receive a fine; where the charge is common assault or breach of the peace then a bind-over in the sum of £50 to keep the peace is considered appropriate. Very rarely is a suspended term of imprisonment imposed by the court, and a term of immediate imprisonment is rarer still. The use of the bind-over in domestic incidents is perhaps the most controversial of all forms of court disposal, although it is provided for in a number of statutes. In section 115 (1) of the Magistrates' Courts Act 1980, the power to bind over is explicit. 'The power of the Magistrates' court on the complaint of any person to enter into recognition with or without sureties, to keep the peace or to be of good behaviour towards the complainant shall be exercised by order of complainant.' A bind-over may also be used where a breach of the peace is likely to be occasioned, and in the case of people convicted of common assault a bind-over may be imposed in addition to other penalties. The bind-over has traditionally been used as a means of disposing of cases involving disputes and violence between spouses, and the fact that one is imposed in any case does not indicate that the case was trivial, as the Law Commission's Working Paper (1987 no. 103: 38) makes clear: 'While most of the examples are apparently of a relatively low degree of seriousness, a few are not and presumably in the cases attracted a bind-over rather than a heavier penalty in the light of the special circumstances of the parties involved.' The bind-over was used in sentencing 116 offenders of a total of 1,772 offenders proceeded against for common assault in the magistrates' courts in 1985, and it was used in 794 cases of breach of the peace in 1985. It has been argued that the use of the bind-over can be seen in the domestic context as a preventative measure. But clearly the guiding belief behind this is that in domestic disputes the fault is 50 per cent with one and half with the other, i.e. there is really no aggressor and no victim, just a domestic situation that has got out of hand.

The new policy introduced by the Metropolitan Police in June 1987 may have resulted in more domestic violence aggressors being arrested. Yet it may well be that such aggressors are more likely to be charged with breach of the peace and in consequence simply bound over to keep the peace.

Turning to those cases of violent assault which are prosecuted in accordance with section 47 (assault) or section 18 or section 20 of the Offences Against the Person Act 1861, for these, sentences are invariably more lenient than in any other instances of violence except violent assault between other family members (L. Radford 1987). If the offender pleads guilty to an assault on his wife, judicial discretion can then be worked on, through the opportunity of mitigation on his behalf. As we have seen earlier in the chapter, arguments accepted in mitigation resoundingly echo familialistic ideologies about gender role, wherein typically the batterer is exonerated and the victim deemed responsible.

Appeals against sentences also reflect these attitudes to victim and offender. Counsel for the appellant frequently invoke gender-based ideologies as rationales for explaining and excusing male violence. Counsel also try to minimize the criminality and dangerousness of the crime by referring to the crime as one bound by the domestic situation. Domestic offenders are presented to the court as less violent and dangerous than non-domestic offenders, their crimes being one-off mistakes rather than examples of repeated criminal behaviour. For instance, in an appeal against sentence Lord Justice May said of the appellant: 'he was not a man addicted to the use of violence at all' (*Reilly* [1982] 4 CAR(S) 288). In another appeal the appellant's counsel said on his behalf: 'he is not a person from whom society has to be protected.' The appellant had nevertheless struck his wife on the head and face with a hammer, blinding her (*Ghuman* [1985] 6 CAR(S) 114). In reply to Lord May in *Reilly*, one could argue that while he was not addicted to the use of violence against a non-specific other, he *was* particularly addicted to the use of violence against his wife. In reply to the counsel in the second case one could argue that he is just the sort of husband from whom wives must be protected.

A typical profile of current sentencing practice in domestic violence cases can be gleaned by looking at the outcome of those few cases prosecuted in the 1984–5 London Policing Study. A total of 16 cases, 2 per cent of all calls (773), and 12.5 per cent of recorded cases of violence (128) were put up for prosecution (see figure 6.2). Of these 16, only 9 were finally formally sentenced, with 6 of the 9 cases being heard before magistrates.

Taking the cases dealt with by magistrates first: in case 2 a husband was fined £50 after beating his wife. In case 3 an ex-husband was sentenced to 2 months' imprisonment, suspended for 12 months, for breaking a vase over his wife's head and causing multiple lacerations. In case 7 the defendent had punched and kicked his wife to the floor, for which he received a £75 fine. In case 12 the defendant, a boyfriend, had kicked and thrown his victim to the floor; he was fined £50. Offender 13 was fined £75 for assaulting his wife. The case against 15 started out as a malicious wounding of a common law wife, involving a wound requiring several stitches. The defendant pleaded guilty and received a fine of £40.

Three cases were heard at the Crown court. In one, 16, the victim was pushed through a glass door after being punched on the back of the head by a man with whom she was having a drink. He wanted sex; she did not. The man was sentenced to nine months' imprisonment. In another case the defendant pleaded not guilty, and he was acquitted. Finally, in case 10 the defendant was sentenced to 9 months' imprisonment, suspended for 18 months, after throwing a wooden cabinet at his wife, causing a wound that needed 16 stitches and multiple lacerations and bruising.

Sentences in spousal assault cases may influence the decisions taken at earlier pivotal points in the system in two ways. First, trivial sentences in domestic assault cases serve an ideological and

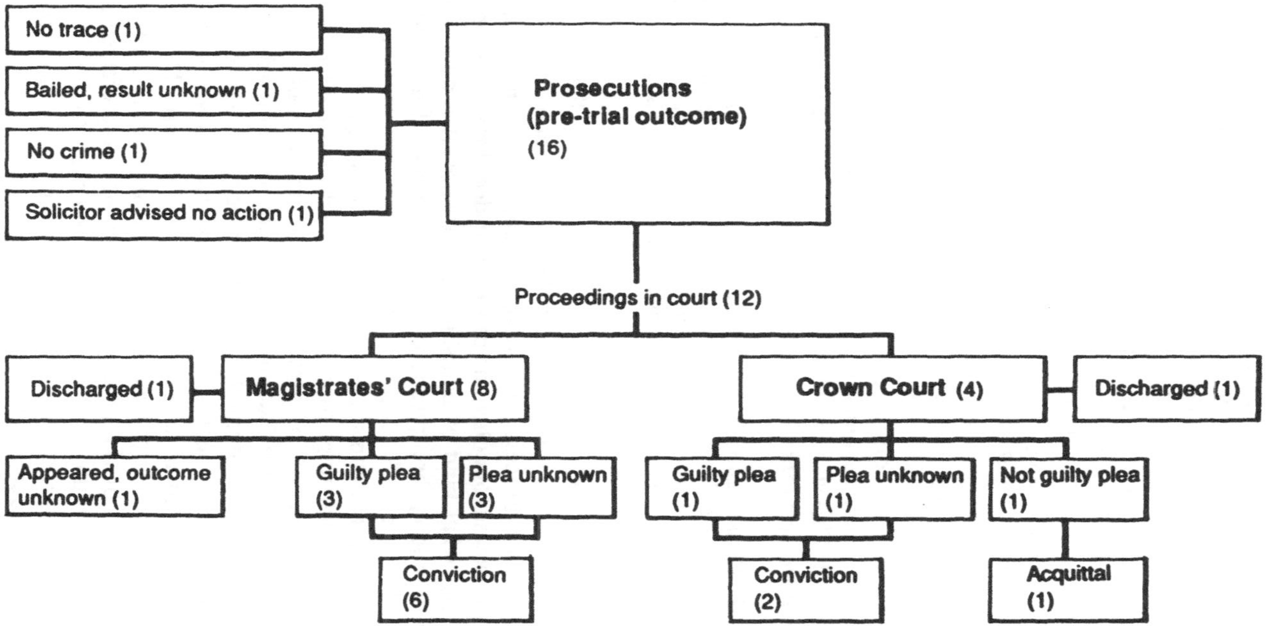


Figure 6.2 *Prosecutions for assault on wives, cohabitees and girlfriends, Holloway and Hounslow, 1984–1985*

reproductive function. Second, trivial sentences result in diverting cases out of the criminal justice system. Rather than criminalizing violence, they encourage the use of the civil courts to deal with it, and discourage prosecutions in favour of other measures, such as the use of a caution. Trivial sentences serve to confirm the widely held belief that domestic assaults, excepting homicides, are in the main trifling and non-criminal. The traditional use of a bind-over in section 42 (common assault) cases, and a fine in section 47 (assault) cases reinforces this view.

The fact remains that the majority of spousal assaults are classified by the police as assault (s. 42 or s. 47) and dealt with as civil offences, although in fact they may be more serious, and no pronouncement about treating these less serious cases on a par with other assault cases has been made. Any judgment made in a more serious case is not likely to influence the treatment of less serious cases. Sentencing in criminal cases is often regarded as a barometer of disapproval, whereas such sentencing in domestic assault cases remains uncommitted. This view circulates back into police culture. The *Code for Crown Prosecutors* 1986 states:

> When the circumstances of an offence are not particularly serious and a Court would be likely to impose a purely nominal penalty, Crown Prosecutors should carefully consider whether the public interest would be better served by a prosecution or some other form of disposal, such as where appropriate a caution.

The success, then, of the force order of the Metropolitan Police in London depends on other decisions taken at pivotal stages in the criminal justice process, including sentencing. Trivial sentences provide the excuse for police and prosecution decisions not to proceed further. But what kind of punishment or treatment *is* appropriate, and for how long, are questions which have provided a very real dilemma for the Left. Not surprisingly, few left-wing feminists actually believe that punishment can reform or change the individual offender, although imprisonment of the violent offender protects women for the period of detention and more generally serves to convey a wider message that violence will not be condoned.

If the seriousness of domestic assault is to be realized, and if recent changes in policing policy are to have any effect at all, sentencers must also review their approach in this type of case. Despite the evidence of the success of breach of the peace measures in Australia, the use of breach of the peace action must not be preferred as an alternative to assault, and likewise a bind-over to be of good behaviour and keep the peace is totally inappropriate when aggressors are convicted of common assault.

**Victim support and crime prevention**

The problem of marital assault requires not only a radical improvement in policing, prosecution and sentencing, but the whole-hearted commitment of statutory and voluntary agencies. Criminalizing marital violence, in my view, is the way forward in the long term, but it is not the way forward for the victims who, without adequate back-up and support to sustain prosecution against violent men, may be exposed to further danger. The need for police to follow up calls to women who have decided both for and against prosecution, a more adequate system of referral, together with consultation meetings of the various agencies and organizations so that help may be co-ordinated, are all crucial elements in the fight against marital violence. The Metropolitan Police force order has stressed the need for follow-up calls and effective referral, but the police cannot effectively act on their own, and here the role of victim support is crucial. Indications from my study of the impact of the force order in 1988 (referred to earlier in the chapter) suggest that cases *are* being followed up. The truth is that in the past referring cases of domestic violence to other agencies has often been seen as a means of getting rid of them, merely passing the problem on to other agencies. Police officers knew little of the statutory or voluntary agencies that could be of assistance with housing, finance or safety. In addition, the whole idea of getting too deeply embroiled in these problems conflicted with officers' expectations about police work and the police role.

During the last decade the multi-agency approach has been at the centre of police thinking about many of the problems they deal with. In the field of juvenile crime, domestic violence, rape and prostitution the police have looked for a new way of dealing with crime and its victims, and looked to working with other agencies as a means of evolving a more sensitive, informed and relevant approach to the problem of crime and victims.

*Victim support*

This multi-agency endeavour in the USA, for example, arose as a direct result of victim pressure groups and victims' legislation. By 1981 the plight of victims was recognized at federal level. The National Victims' Advisory Committee defined a set of priority issues. In 1982 the President's Task Force on Victims of Crime made 68 recommendations, which led to the setting up of the later Attorney General's Task Force on Family Violence (1984). In 1982 the Victims and Witnesses Assistance Act was passed, followed in 1984 by the Victims of Crime Act. The legislation has led to the setting up of victim/witness programmes involving over 200 prosecuting attorney officers, and a vast amount of funding for victim compensation. One of these victim/witness advocate schemes is in operation in Orange County, Florida. The service is available 24 hours a day, provides crisis intervention, including counselling and assistance to victims and their families, explaining what to expect of the trial process and criminal injuries compensation.

In Canada since 1981 there has been a similar 'justice for victims of crime' initiative, which recognizes the double victimization of the victim which results from the insensitivity of the criminal justice system (Rock 1986: 1). In 1986 the Ministry of Justice and Attorney General of Canada published a booklet *After Sexual Assault - Your Guide to the Criminal Justice System*, designed to help victims.

Victims' initiatives have taken place in England and Wales (see Shapland et al. 1985), where the work of the National Association of Victim Support Schemes has been considerably extended. However, the UK is still without a victim/witness agency which provides, as of right, advice and support to victims and their immediate families.

The police in the UK have encouraged a police-public partnership (Commissioner of the Police of the Metropolis 1986: 4), with a view to preventing crime and providing a better police service to crime victims. Sir Kenneth Newman, in this annual report, stressed the philosophy behind the approach: 'crime is a problem for society as a whole; it is too important to be left to the police alone.' The building blocks of this partnership include crime prevention panels and victim support schemes. The police have recognized that victims of crime have been the Cinderella of the criminal justice system for too long. These new initiatives introduce procedures for keeping victims informed of the progress of their case. In the London area alone there are currently 42 victim support schemes. In addition, the Metropolitan Police have produced leaflets to explain to victims the relevant court and police procedures and to provide additional information about clinics for sexual diseases, criminal injuries compensation and victim support counselling. Following on from the force order on domestic violence in the Metropolitan Police area, Tottenham and Hounslow police in London have developed a system of recording every single incident and following up each incident with a letter. The Tottenham police have developed excellent links with a wide variety of local agencies. It is too soon, however, to asses the success of their initiative. Other police forces in the UK are adopting similar policies. In the South Wales police, wherever there is a women's refuge there is also a policewoman liaison officer.

*Crime prevention*

Part of this wider movement towards rendering support to victims of crime is the effort to prevent the initial victimization. Crime prevention depends on education, on the implementation of the law and on protecting the victim, by arresting and punishing the offender. Crime prevention schemes in the UK and elsewhere, have instead focused on reducing an individual's risk of becoming a victim by concentrating on victims' behaviour. Reduction of risk has also depended on the correct identification of the high risk groups. This identification is made on the basis of official returns on victimization as well as official crime figures. Since the official profile of high risk victims in both victimization surveys and crime statistics largely excludes battered and sexually assaulted women, the risk to women intimately associated with their aggressors is masked and remains hidden. Understandably, therefore, crime prevention schemes have focused on preventing known crimes, i.e. street crime, theft, etc.

A disturbing aspect of such schemes is the way they encourage a sense of individual responsibility for one's own protection. This can result in increasing fear and limiting freedom of action. Crime prevention strategies, in setting out 'do's' and 'don'ts', function as a mechanism of social control. Crime prevention schemes frequently impose a curfew on women, an echo of the medieval way of coping with crime, and similar to that of many third world countries. Even under the apparently politically neutral efforts of crime prevention schemes is found an implicit bias towards the social control of women on the streets, while victimization in the home is not recognized. Some even make their bias explicit. In Bremen, for example, the State Bureau of Crime Investigation produced a leaflet for women on crime prevention which included a series of questions. One question clearly reflects the presence of a victim-blaming model: 'Do you and your daughter dress and behave so that a man doesn't feel he's being given a green light?'

In the UK crime prevention strategies have yet to address the problem of violence against women in the home, or to address the problem of sexual and spousal assault for Afro-Caribbean and Asian women (Hanmer and Stanko 1985). The booklet *Positive Steps*, produced by the Metropolitan Police to promote safety for women, says very little about victims of domestic or spousal violence. The police are particularly eager to reduce the homicide rate, yet so far, although nearly 20 per cent of all homicides are committed against wives, the need to deter repeated and escalating abuse has not been considered to have a necessary part in a crime prevention strategy. But at Streatham in south London police have developed a booklet designed to guide and support victims of domestic violence.

As part of crime prevention efforts in the USA and the UK batterers' programmes are being set up. The Attorney General's Task Force on Victims of Family Violence (1984: 49) heard from a variety of batterers' programmes, including EMERGE (New York) and Family Violence Diversion Network (Austin, Texas). Such programmes are becoming more widely available.

## Conclusion

The success of the new spousal violence initiatives in London and in other police force areas does not depend on the criminal law and the exercise of police discretion alone. If criminalization of marital violence is the way forward, an arrest and prosecution policy unaccompanied by measures to protect victims from repeated violence will have disastrous consequences. In 1975 the Select Committee on Violence in Marriage recommended action and provision of resources by the government to promote shelter and housing nationwide. The sentiments of the Select Committee have been echoed in the Women's National Commission Report (1985), in Hedy d'Ancona's Report to the EEC on Violence against Women (1986), and in the Commonwealth Secretariat Report (1987). We do not need more committees, but we do need action. Shelters and emergency accommodation are required, together with a greater degree of communication between the police and support agencies, such as has been achieved between Welsh Women's Aid and the police in South Wales, and Chiswick Family Rescue and the police in London. There is a need for improvement in police training. Already police training centres in England and Wales are putting considerable emphasis on training recruits as well as junior and senior police managers. Certainly, the police force's efforts in this direction have the support of Sir Peter Imbert, the Metropolitan Police Commissioner. On 24 January 1989, in his strategy statement (1989: 3) he said:

> The rise in the number of recorded sexual offences and domestic violence may be due, in part, to changes in police policy and procedure. We have sought to encourage victims to report these types of offences. In the past many such crimes were not notified to the police, and therefore have remained undetected. It is a reflection of the growing confidence in the police that victims are now coming forward and enabling us to take appropriate action and make more arrests than in the past.

Bourlet (1988: 148), on the other hand, found that only 16 forces claimed to give any specific advice or instruction in this area of policing. He also found that such training programmes as existed concentrated on the lower ranks. There is also a real need for training of those working in the Crown Prosecution Service who are now responsible for deciding the fate of these cases. In addition the CPS should be issued with guidelines emphasizing that the prosecution of spousal assault is in the public interest, and guidelines regarding the application of the 'credibility of victim' criteria where the complainant is reluctant to give evidence. Otherwise the aim of the compellability clause in the Police and Criminal Evidence Act will be annulled.

In the light of the present lack of government commitment in the UK at central and local level and a lack of communication between agencies, police policy may fail, since they may refer women to agencies still under-resourced and unable to deal with an increasing caseload, and may arrest and lay charges that prosecutors turn down.

This book has identified the past and present legal form, the present administration of justice, the present methods of policing and patriarchal attitudes in law and society as the key obstacles to the protection of women from violence in the home. The law can be used both to subordinate women's needs and to protect them. But we need not concentrate exclusively on law and policing. Women's interests need to be evaluated within the political arena through labour and union struggles, party politics, and at European Community and United Nations levels. The protection of women can only be ensured when women make demands on governments and nation states, and when the state and its institutions take proper account of women. Policing policy is a first base, but other institutions must follow. The danger is that, as has occurred in the past, once certain concessions have been won many consider the struggle over. The struggle for accountability to women in legal and policing matters has only just begun.

While the protection of women is an objective shared by all women at various points on the political spectrum, deep divisions are evident as to how it is best achieved. A similar divide characterizes the debates on pornography, rape, prostitution and child sexual abuse. Left-wing feminist idealists totally reject the notion that reforms in policing policy and practice can have any real effect on providing protection from violence, since the state and its institutions (including the law and police) are oppressive and coercive. Indeed, some regard attempts to reform policing as fundamentally dangerous, a tampering which works to help the state and its police in providing them with legitimation while coercion continues as before. The left-wing feminist realist position, while not endorsing the state and its police, recognizes that the law and police are here to stay. The problem, then, is to strike a balance between controlling the excesses of male violence without opening the door to further excesses of state power, surveillance and control.

This exploration has been principally concerned with the problem of spousal violence, which has provided an occasion to examine women's engagement with the law and the police. The book makes a plea for the reform of law and policing policy in the direction of controlling male violence against women in the 'privacy' of the family. Inevitably such a stance demands the criminalization of the wife-beater. Protection from violent men also requires an understanding of why men batter, and undoubtedly the prerogative to assault within the home is sustained in the legal system and in cultural and social ideologies which permit this behaviour by exonerating men when they strike. Violence is not going to be deterred simply by criminalization and harsher legal sanctions while societal values, perpetuated by the media and other institutions, continue to present this behaviour as both acceptable and normal. The fact that violent and sexual assault continue to remain immune from legal condemnation or sanction and social disapproval, merely because a victim has at some time shared a degree of intimacy with the offender, is absurd, perverse and obscene.

# References


Adams, T.F. (1963) Field Interrogation. *Police* March–April: 28

Adler, Z. (1987) *Rape on Trial*: London: Routledge and Kegan Paul

Althusser, L. (1971) Ideology and Ideological State Apparatuses. pp. 127–88 in *Lenin and Philosophy and Other Essays*. New York and London: Monthly Review Press

Amir, M. (1971) *Patterns in Forcible Rape*. Chicago, Ill.: University of Chicago Press

Anderton, J. (1981) Towards a Progressive Police Force. Address to the West Pennine Branch of the British Institute of Management

Andrews, B. (1987) Violence in Normal Homes. Bedford College Medical Research Unit paper presented to the Marriage Research Centre Conference on Family Violence, 15 April 1987

Andrews, B. and Brown, G.W. (1988) Marital Violence in the Community. *British Journal of Psychiatry* 53: 305–12

Arnold, T.V. (1969) Law as Symbolism. p. 46 in V. Aubert (ed.) *The Sociology Law*. Harmondsworth: Penguin

Atkins, S. and Hoggett, B. (1984) *Women and the Law*. Oxford: Basil Blackwell

Attorney General (Canada) (1985) *Report of the Special Committee on Pornography and Prostitution*. Canadian Government Publishing Centre. Vols 1 and 2

Attorney General (UK) *Guidelines on Prosecution* (1983). London: Crown Prosecution Service

Attorney General (US) (1984) *Task Force on Family Violence*. Washington, DC: US Department of Justice

Attorney General (US) (1986) *Report on Pornography and Prostitution* (Meese Report). Washington, DC: US Department of Justice

Bacon, W. and Landsdowne, R. (1982) Women Who Kill Husbands: The Battered Wife on Trial. pp. 67–93 in C. O'Donnell and J. Craney (eds), *Family Violence in Australia*. Melbourne: Penguin

Baker, R. (1984) Domestic Violence: Legal Considerations. *Criminal Law Journal* 8 (1): 33–40

Banton, M. (1964) *The Policeman in the Community*. London: Tavistock

Barry, K. (1984) *Female Sexual Slavery*. New York: New York University Press

Becker, H.S. (1967) Whose Side Are We On? *Social Problems* 14 (3): 239–47

Bedfordshire Police (1976) *Report on Acts of Domestic Violence Committed in the County between 1 February and 31 July*. Bedford

Begin, P. (1987) Rape Law Reform in Canada: Evaluation Impact. Paper presented at the Fourth International Institute on Victimology, NATO Advanced Research Workshop, Tuscany, Italy, 9–15 August

Bell, D.J. (1984a) The Police Response to Domestic Violence: An Exploratory Study. *Police Studies* 7 (3): 23–30

Bell, D.J. (1984b) The Police Response to Domestic Violence: A Replication Study. *Police Studies* 7 (3): 136–44

Bell, D.J. (1985a) A Multi-Year Study of Ohio Urban, Suburban, and Rural Police Dispositions of Domestic Disputes. *Victimology* 10 (1–4): 301–10

Bell, D.J. (1985b) The Police Response to Domestic Violence: A Multi-Year Study. *Police Studies* 8 (1): 58–64

Benn, M. (1985) Policing Women. pp. 124–39 in J. Baxter and L. Koffman (eds), *Police: The Constitution and the Community*. London: Professional Books

Berk, R.A., Berk, S.F., Newton, P.J. and Loseke, D.R. (1984) Cops on Call: Summoning the Police to the Scene of Spousal Violence. *Law and Society Review* 18 (3): 479–98

Berk, R.A. and Newton, P.J. (1985) Does Arrest Really Deter Wife Battering? An Effort to Replicate the Findings of the Minneapolis Spouse Abuse Experiment. *American Sociological Review* 50 (April): 253–62

Berk, S.F. and Loseke, D.R. (1981) Handling Family Violence: Situational Determinants of Police Arrest in Domestic Disturbances. *Law and Society Review* 15 (2): 315–46

Bevan, V. and Lidstone, K. (1985) *A Guide to the Police and Criminal Evidence Act 1984*. London: Butterworth

Binney, V., Harkell, G. and Nixon, J. (1981) *Leaving Violent Men*. Women's Aid Federation

Blackstone, W. (ed.) (1857) *Commentaries on the Laws of England* Vol. 1 London: John Murray

Blair, I. (1985) *Investigating Rape: A New Approach for Police*. Croom Helm and Police Foundation

Bland, L. (1985) In the Name of Protection: The Policing of Women in the First World War. pp 23–49 in J. Brophy and C. Smart (eds), *Women-in-Law*. London: Routledge and Kegan Paul

Bloch, P. and Anderson, D. (1974) *Policewomen on Patrol: Final Report*. Washington DC: Police Foundation

Blom-Cooper, L. and Drabble, R. (1982) Police Perception of Crime: Brixton and the Operational Response. *British Journal of Criminology* 22: 184–7

Blum, H.P. (1982) Psychoanalytic Reflections on the 'Beaten Wife Syndrome'. pp. 263–7 in M. Kirkpatrick (ed.), *Women's Sexual Experiences*. New York: Plenum

Borkowski, M., Murch, M. and Walker, V. (1983) *Marital Violence: The Community Response*. London: Tavistock

Bourlet, A. (1988) Police Intervention in Marital Violence. University of Kent M. Phil. Dissertation

Bowker, L. (1984) Battered Wives and The Police: A National Study of Usage and Effectiveness. *Police Studies* 7 (2): 84–93

Bowles, P. (1986) Modifying Police to Domestic Disturbance Calls. University of Texas M. Sc. Dissertation

Box, S. (1971) *Deviance, Reality and Society*. London: Holt, Reinhart and Winston

Box, S. (1987) *Recession Crime and Punishment*. London: Macmillan

Brady, N. (1632) *The Lawes Resolution of Women's Rights*. London

Brants, C. and Kok, E. (1986) Penal Sanctions as a Feminist Strategy: A Contradiction in Terms. Pornography and Criminal Law in the Netherlands. *International Journal of the Sociology of Law* 14 (3–14:) 269–86

Breci, M.G. and Simons, R.L. (1987) An Examination of Organizational and Individual Factors that Influence Police Response to Domestic Disturbances. *Journal of Police Science and Administration* 15 (2): 93–104

Brogden, M. (1985) Stopping the People – Crime Control v. Social Control. pp. 91–110 in J. Baxter and L. Koffman, *Police, the Constitution and the Community*. London: Professional Books

Brown, B. (1986) Book Review. *Journal of Law and Society* 13 (3): 433–9

Brown, S.E. (1984) Police Response to Wife Beating: Neglect of a Crime of Violence. *Journal of Criminal Justice* 12: 277–88

Browne, A. (1984) Assault and Homicide at Home: When Battered Women Kill. Paper presented at the Second National Conference for Family Violence, Durham, New Hampshire, 7–10 August

Browne, A. (1987) *When Battered Women Kill*. New York: Free Press/Macmillan

Brownmiller, S. (1975) *Against Our Will*. Harmondsworth: Penguin

Bryan, M. (1984) A Question of Housing. *Journal of Social Welfare Law*. July: 195–207

Bunyan, T. (1985) From Saltley to Orgreave via Brixton. *Journal of Law and Society* 12 (3): 293–304

Burrows, J. (1986) *Burglary: Police Actions and Victims' Views*. Home Office Research and Planning Unit Paper 37. London: Home Office

Burrows, J. and Tarling, R. (1985) Clearing up Crime. pp. 79–93 in K. Heal, R. Tarling and J. Burrows (eds) *Policing Today*. London: HMSO, Home Office Research and Planning Unit

Cain, M. (1973) *Society and the Policeman's Role*. London: Routledge and Kegan Paul

Cain, M. (1986) Realism, Feminism, Methodology and Law. *International Journal of the Society of Law* 14 (314): 255–67

Campbell, A. (1984) *The Girls in the Gang: A Report from New York City*. Oxford: Basil Blackwell

Caputi, J. (1987) *The Age of Sex Crime*. London: Women's Press

Carlen, P. (1983) *Women's Imprisonment* London: Routledge and Kegan Paul

Carlen, P. and Collison, M. (1980) *Radical Issues in Criminology*. Oxford: Martin Robertson

Chambers, G. and Millar, A. (1983) *Investigating Sexual Assault*. Edinburgh: HMSO, Scottish Home and Health Department

Chambers, G. and Millar, A. (1986) *Prosecuting Sexual Assault*. Edinburgh: HMSO, Scottish Home and Health Department

Chatterton, M. (1976) Police in Social Control. pp. 104–22 in Joan King (ed.), *Control Without Custody*. Cambridge: University of Cambridge Institute of Criminology

Chatterton, M. (1983) Police Work and Assault Charges. pp. 194–220 in M. Punch (ed.) *Control in the Police Organisation*. Cambridge, Mass: MIT Press

Christian, L. (1983) *Policing by Coercion*. London: GLC Police Committee Support Unit

Cleveland, A.R. (1896) *Women Under English Law*. London: Hurst and Blackett

Cohen, S. (1979) The Punitive City: Notes on the Dispersal of Social Control. *Contemporary Crises* 3: 339–63

Cohen, S. (1985) *Visions of Social Control*. Oxford: Polity

Cohen, S. (1986) Community Control: To Demystify or to Reaffirm? in H. Bianchi and R. van Swaaningen (eds), *Abolitionism: Towards a Non-Repressive Approach to Crime*. Amsterdam: Free University Press

Coleman, C. and Bottomley, A.K. (1976) Police Conceptions of Crime and 'No Crime'. *Criminal Law Review* 344–60

Collins, H. (1984) *Marxism and the Law*. Oxford: Oxford University Press

Commissioner of the Police of the Metropolis (1981) *Written Submissions to the Scarman Inquiry into the Brixton Disorder of April 1981 and Appendices*. London: Metropolitan Police

Commissioner of the Police of the Metropolis
1984: *Report*. Cmnd 9541. London: HMSO

1985: *Report*. Cmnd 9790. London: HMSO
1986: *Report*. Cm 158. London: HMSO
1987: *Report*. Cm 389. London: HMSO

Commonwealth Secretariat (1987) *Confronting Violence*. London.

Cornish, P. (1985) The South Australia Police Department's Restraint Order System: 'Three Years Later'. Paper presented to the National Conference on Domestic Violence, Canberra, 11-15 November

Cousins, M. (1980) *Men's Rea*: A Note on Sexual Difference, Criminology and the Law. pp. 109-22 in P. Carlen and M. Collison (eds), *Radical Issues in Criminology*. Oxford: Martin Robertson

Coward, R. (1982) Sexual Violence and Sexuality. *Feminist Review* 11: 9-22

Cowell, D., Jones, T. and Young, J. (eds) (1982) *Policing the Riots*. London: Junction Books

Cox, B., Shirley, J. and Short, M. (1977) *The Fall of Scotland Yard*. London: Penguin

Criminal Law Revision Committee (1980a) *Working Paper on Sexual Offences*. London: HMSO

Criminal Law Revision Committee (1980b) *Fourteenth Report: Offences Against The Person*. Cmnd 7844. London: HMSO

Criminal Law Revision Committee (1984a) *Fifteenth Report: Sexual Offences*. Cmnd 9213. London: HMSO

Criminal Law Revision Committee (1984b) *Sixteenth Report: Prostitution in the Street*. Cmnd 9329. London: HMSO

Criminal Law Revision Committee (1985) *Seventeenth Report: Prostitution and Allied Offences*. Cmnd 9688. London: HMSO

*Criminal Statistics, England and Wales*
1982: Cmnd 9048. London: HMSO
1983: Cmnd 9349. London: HMSO
1984: Cmnd 9621. London: HMSO
1985: Cm 10. London: HMSO
1986: Cm 233. London: HMSO
1987: Cm 498. London: HMSO

Crown Prosecution Service (1986) *Code for Crown Prosecutors*. London: HMSO

Crown Prosecution Service (1987) *Annual Report 1986-87*. London: HMSO

Dalton, K. (1978) *The Pre-Menstrual Syndrome*. Harmondsworth: Penguin

d'Ancona, H. (1986) Violence Against Women. Report to EEC. Mimeo

Davis, A. (1982) *Women, Race and Class*. London: Women's Press

Deane, G.D. (1987) Cross National Comparison of Homicide: Age/Sex-Adjusted Rates using the 1980 U.S. Homicide Experience as a Standard. *Journal of Quantitative Criminology* 3 (3): 215-27

de Beauvoir, S. (1953) *The Second Sex*. London: Jonathan Cape

De Haan, N. (1987) Fuzzy Morals and Flakey Politics: 'The Coming Out of Critical Criminology'. *Journal of Law and Society* 14 (3): 321-33

Desborough Committee (1920) *Report of the Royal Commission on the Police Service*. Cmd 874. London: HMSO

Deutsch, H. (1944) *The Psychology of Women*. London: Grune and Stratton

Dicey, A.V. (1969) Law and Public Opinion in England. pp. 71-9 in V. Aubert (ed.), *The Sociology of Law*. Harmondsworth: Penguin

Ditchfield, J.A. (1976) *Police Cautioning in England and Wales*. Home Office Research Study 37, London: HMSO

Dobash, R. and Dobash, R.E. (1980) *Violence Against Wives*. Shepton Mallet: Open Books

Dobash, R. and Dobash R.E. (1984) The Nature and Antecedents of Violent Events. *British Journal of Criminology* 24 (3): 269–88

Dobash, R. and Dobash, R.E. (1985) The Contact Between Battered Women and Social and Medical Agencies. pp. 142–65 in J. Pahl, *Private Violence and Public Policy*. London: Routledge and Kegan Paul

Doerner, W.G. (1975) A Regional Analysis of Homicide Rates in the United States. *Criminology* 13 (1): 90–101

Doig, A. (1984) *Corruption and Misconduct in Contemporary British Politics*. Harmondsworth: Penguin

Donaldson, Iain (1987) Is Obscenity Obsolescent? *Police Journal* 60 (2): 112–17

Dunhill, C. (ed.) (1989) *The Boys in Blue: Women's Challenge to the Police*. London: Virago

Dworkin, A. (1981) *Pornography: Men Possessing Women*. London: Women's Press

Dworkin, A. (1982) Interview with Elizabeth Wilson. *Feminist Review* 11: 23–9

Eaton, M. (1986) *Justice for Women*. Milton Keynes: Open University Press

Eckersley, R. (1987) Whither the Feminist Campaign? An Evaluation of Feminist Critiques of Pornography. *International Journal of the Sociology of Law* 15: 159–78

Edwards, S.S.M. (1981) *Female Sexuality and the Law*. Oxford: Martin Robertson

Edwards, S.S.M. (1984) *Women on Trial*. Manchester: Manchester University Press and New Hampshire: Dover

Edwards, S.S.M. (1985a) Compelling a Reluctant Spouse: Policing and the Prosecution Process. *New Law Journal* (November): 1076–8

Edwards, S.S.M. (1985b) A Socio-Legal Evaluation of Gender Ideologies in Domestic Violence, Assault and Spousal Homicide. *Victimology*, Proceedings of the Lisbon Institute. 10 (1–4): 186–205

Edwards, S.S.M. (1985c) Male Violence Against Women: Excusatory and Explanatory Ideologies in Law and Society. pp. 183–213 in S. Edwards (ed.), *Gender, Sex and the Law*. Beckenham: Croom Helm

Edwards, S.S.M. (1985d) Gender 'Justice'? Defending Defendants and Mitigating Sentence. pp. 129–58 in S. Edwards (ed.) *Gender, Sex and the Law*. Beckenham: Croom Helm

Edwards, S.S.M. (1986a) Neither Bad nor Mad: The Female Violent Offender Re-assessed. *Women's Studies International Forum* 9 (1): 79–87.

Edwards, S.S.M. (1986b) Police Attitudes and Dispositions in Domestic Disputes: The London Study. *Police Journal*. July: 230–41.

Edwards, S.S.M. (1986c) The Real Risks of Violence Behind Closed Doors. *New Law Journal* (12 December): 136 (6284): 1191–3

Edwards, S.S.M. (1987a) Provoking Her Own Demise: From Common Assault to Homicide. pp. 152–68 in J. Hanmer and M. Maynard (eds), *Women, Violence and Social Control*. London: Macmillan

Edwards, S.S.M (1987b) Prostitutes: Victim of Law, Social Policing and Organised Crime. pp. 43–57 in P. Carlen and A. Worrall (eds), *Gender, Crime and Justice*. Milton Keynes: Open University

Edwards, S.S.M. (1987c) Prostitutes and Allied Offences: The Over-enforcement and Under-enforcement of Unjust Law: The UK Experience. Paper presented at the Fourth International Institute of Victimology, NATO Advanced Research Workshop, Tuscany, Italy, 9–15 August

Edwards, S.S.M. (1988) Mad, Bad or Pre-Menstrual. *New Law Journal* 138 (6363): 456–8

Edwards, S.S.M. and Armstrong, G.A. (1988) Policing Prostitution: A Profile of the

SOS. *Police Journal* (July-September): 209-19
Edwards, S.S.M. and Halpern, A. (1988) Conflicting Interests: Protecting Children or Protecting Title to Property. *Journal of Social Welfare Law* (April): 110-24
Eekelaar, J.M. and Katz, S.N. (1978) *Family Violence*. London: Butterworth
Ekblom, P. and Heal, K. (1985) Police Response to Calls from the Public. pp. 65-78 in K. Heal, R. Tarling and J. Burrows (eds), *Policing Today*. London: HMSO
Ellis, J. (1984) Prosecutorial Discretion to Charge in Cases of Spousal Assault: A Dialogue. *Journal of Criminal Law and Criminology* 75 (1): 56-102
*Employment Gazette* (1987) 95 (5). London: HMSO
*Employment Gazette* (1988) 96 (5). London: HMSO
English, J. and Houghton, R. (1981) *Police Training Manual*. McGraw Hill
Fagan, J., Stewart, D.K. and Hansen, K.V. (1983) Violent Men or Violent Husbands? Background Factors and Situational Correlates. pp. 49-68 in D. Finkelhor, R. Gelles, G. Hotaling and M.A. Straus (eds), *The Dark Side of Families*. London and Beverly Hills: Sage
Fagan, J. and Wexler, S. (1987) Crime at Home and in the Streets: The Relationship between Family and Stranger Violence. *Violence and Victim* 2 (1): 5-23
Fairweather, E. (1982) The Law of the Jungle in King's Cross. *New Society*, 2 December: 375-7
Faragher, T. (1985) The Police Response to Violence Against Women in the Home. pp. 110-24 in J. Pahl (ed.), *Private Violence and Public Policy*. London: Routledge and Kegan Paul
Farrington, D.P. and Bennett, T. (1981) Police Cautioning of Juveniles in London. *British Journal of Criminology* 21: 123-35.
Farrington, D. and Morris, A. (1983) Sex, Sentencing and Reconviction. *British Journal of Criminology* 23: 229-48
Faulk, M. (1974) Men Who Assault Their Wives. *Medicine, Science and the Law* 14 (3): 180-3
Ferraro, K.G. (1981) Processing Battered Women. *Journal of Family Issues* 2 (4): 415-38
Ferraro, K.J. and Johnson, J.M. (1983) How Women Experience Battering: The Process of Victimization. *Social Problems* 30 (3): 325-39
Fine, B. (1984) *Democracy and the Rule of Law*. London: Pluto
Fiora-Gormally, N. (1978) Battered Wives Who Kill. *Law and Human Behaviour* 2 (2): 133-65
Fisher, C.J. and Mawby, R.I. (1982) Juvenile Delinquency and Police Discretion in an Inner City Area. *British Journal of Criminology* 22: 63-75
Fisher, R.G. (1981) Domestic Violence. *Australian Police Journal* 35 (4): 203-17
Flynn, J.P. (1977) Recent Findings Related to Wife Abuse. *Social Casework* 58: 13-20
Foot, P. (1969) *The Rise of Enoch Powell*. Harmondsworth: Penguin
Freeman, M.D.A. (1980) Violence Against Women: Does the Legal System Provide Solutions or Itself Constitute the Problem? *British Journal of Law and Society* 7: 215-41
Freud, S. (1954) *Collected Papers*. vol. 2. Oxford: Hogarth Press
Gayford, J.J. (1975) Wife Battering: A Preliminary Survey of 100 Cases. *British Medical Journal* 1 (January): 194-7
Gayford, J.J. (1979) Aetiology of Wife Beating. *Medicine, Science and Law* 19 (1): 19-24
Gee, P.W. (1983) Ensuring Police Protection for Battered Women: The *Scott v Hart* Suit. *Signs* 8 (3): 554-67
Gelles, R. (1972) *The Violent Home*. Beverly Hills, CA: Sage

Gelsthorpe, L.R. (1986) Towards a Sceptical Look at Sexism. *International Journal of the Sociology of Law* 14: 125–52

Gelsthorpe, L. and Morris, A. (1988) Feminism and Criminology in Britain. *British Journal of Criminology* 28 (2): 93–110

Gibson, E. and Klein, S. (1961) *Murder: A Home Office Research Report*. London: HMSO

Gibson, E. and Klein, S. (1969) *Murder 1957 to 1968*. Home Office Research Study 3. London: HMSO

Gifford, A.M. (1985) *The Broadwater Farm Inquiry: Report of the Independent Inquiry into Disturbances of October 1985 at the Broadwater Farm Estate, Tottenham*. London: Karia Press

Gilbert, Justice (1769) *The Law of Evidence*. London

Giller, H. and Tutt, N. (1987) Police Cautioning of Juveniles: The Continuing Practice of Diversity. *Criminal Law Review* pp. 367–74

Golden, K. (1981) Women as Patrol Officers: A Study of Attitudes. *Police Studies* 4 (3): 29–33

Gottfredson, M. (1984) *Victims of Crime: The Dimensions of Risk*. Home Office Research Study 81. London: HMSO

Gottlieb, D.J. and Johnson, L.E. (1983) Reform in Kansas Domestic Violence Legislation. *Kansas Law Review* 31: 527–78

Gramsci, A. (1971) *Prison Notebooks*. London: Lawrence and Wishart

Grassie, R.C., Sweeney, T.H., Bussi, E.A., Crowe, T.D., Evans, J.V. and Wallace, W.D. (1978) *The Role of Communications in Managing Patrol Operations*. Washington, DC: LEAA Department of Justice

Greater London Council, *Policing London*. Monthly publication, 1982–5

Green, E., Hebron, S. and Woodward, D. (1987) Women, Leisure and Social Control. pp. 152–68 in J. Hanmer and M. Maynard (eds), *Women, Violence and Social Control*. London: Macmillan

Griffin, S. (1971) Rape: The All American Crime. *Ramparts* (10 September): 25–35

Griffin, S. (1981) *Pornography and Silence*. London: Women's Press

Grimshaw, R. and Jefferson, T. (1987) *Interpreting Police Work*. London: George Allen and Unwin.

Hale, W. (1736) *History of the Pleas of the Crown*. London

Hamilton, R. (1984) Has the House of Lords Abolished the Domestic Violence Act for Married Women? *Legal Action Bulletin* (March): 25–7

Hammersmith and Fulham Survey (1986) London: Hammersmith and Fulham Council

Hanmer, J. (1977) Community Action, Women's Aid and the Women's Liberation Movement. in M. Mayo (ed.), *Women in the Community*. London: Routledge and Kegan Paul

Hanmer, J. and Maynard, M. (eds) (1987) *Women, Violence and Social Control*. London: Macmillan

Hanmer, J. and Saunders, S. (1983) Blowing the Cover of the Protective Male: A Community Study of Violence to Women. pp. 28–46 in E. Gamarnikow, D. Morgan, J. Purvis and D. Taylorson (eds), *The Public and the Private*. London: Heinemann

Hanmer, J. and Saunders, S. (1984) *Well Founded Fear: A Community Study of Violence to Women*. London: Hutchison

Hanmer, J. and Stanko, E. (1985) Stripping Away the Rhetoric of Protection: Violence to Women, Law and the State in Britain and the USA. *International Journal of the Sociology of Law* 13 (4): 357–74

Hatty, S.E. and Sutton, J. (1985) Policing Violence Against Women. Paper presented

to the National Conference on Domestic Violence, Canberra, 11-15 November
Heal, K. and Laycock, G. (1986) *Situational Crime Prevention*. Home Office Research and Planning Unit, London: HMSO
Heal, K., Tarling, R. and Burrows, J. (eds) (1985) *Policing Today*. Home Office Research and Planning Unit. London: HMSO
Heidensohn, F. (1985) *Women and Crime*. London: Macmillan
Hilberman, E. and Munson, K. (1978) Sixty Battered Women. *Victimology* 2 (3–4): 460–71
Hilton, J. (1976) Women in the Police Service. *Police Journal*, pp. 93–103
Hindelang, M., Gottfredson, M. and Garofalo, J. (1978) *The Victims of Personal Crime*. Cambridge, MA: Ballinger
Hindman, R.E. (1975) A Survey Related to Use of Female Law Enforcement Officers. *Police Chief* 42: 58–9
Hirst, P. (1980) Law, Socialism and Rights. pp. 58–105 in P. Carlen and M. Collison (eds), *Radical Issues in Criminology*. Oxford: Martin Robertson
Holmes, S. (1982) A Detroit Model for Police-Social Work Co-operation. *Social Casework* 64: 220–6
Homant, R.J. and Kennedy, D.B. (1985) Police Perceptions of Spouse Abuse: A Comparison of Male and Female Officers. *Journal of Criminal Justice* 13: 29–47
Home Office (1978) *Cautioning*. Circular 70/1978. London: Home Office
Home Office (1984) *Cautioning by the Police*. London: Home Office
Home Office (1986) *Violence Against Women*. Circular 69/1986. London: Home Office
*Home Office Statistical Bulletin* (1986) 29/86 *Violent Crime: Characteristics of Victims and Circumstances of Recorded Offences*. 25 September. London: Home Office
*Home Office Statistical Bulletin* (1989) 4/89 *Statistics on Offences of Rape 1977–87*, 21 February. London: Home Office
Homer, M., Leonard, A.E. and Taylor, M.P. (1984) *Private Violence: Public Shame*. Middlesborough: Cleveland Refuge and Aid for Women and Children (CRAWC)
Horley, S. (1988) *Love and Pain*. London: Bedford Square Press
Horne, P. (1979) Policewomen: 2000 AD. *Police Journal* 70 (4): 344–56
Hough, J.M. and Mayhew, P.M. (1983) *The British Crime Survey: First Report*. Home Office Research Study 76. London: HMSO
Hough, J.M. and Mayhew, P.M. (1985) *Taking Account of Crime: Key Findings from the 1984 British Crime Survey*. Home Office Research Study 85. London: HMSO
Humphreys, J.C. and Humphreys, W.O. (1985) Mandatory Arrest: A Means of Primary and Secondary Prevention of Abuse of Female Partners. *Victimology* 10 (1–4): 267–80
Jackson, S. and Rushton, P. (1982) Victims and Villains: Images of Women in Accounts of Family Violence. *Women's Studies International Forum* 5 (1): 17–28
Jacobs, J. (1961) *The Death and Life of Great American Cities*. New York: Vintage Books
Jaffe, P., Wolfe, D.A., Telford, A. and Austin, G. (1986) The Impact of Police Laying Charges in Incidents of Wife-Abuse. *Journal of Family Violence* 1: 37–49
Jamieson, K. and Flanagan, T. (eds) (1983) *Source Book of Criminal Justice Statistics*. Washington, DC: US Government Printing Office
Jefferson, T. and Grimshaw, J.R. (1984) *Controlling the Constable: Police Accountability in England and Wales*. London: Muller/Cobden Trust
Jeffreys, S. and Radford, J. (1984) Contributory Negligence or Being a Woman: The Car Rapist Case. pp. 154–83 in P. Scraton and P. Gordon (eds), *Causes for Concern*. Harmondsworth: Pelican

Jolin, A. (1983) Domestic Violence Legislation: An Impact Assessment. *Journal of Police Science and Administration* 11: 451–6

Jones, A. (1980) *Women Who Kill*. New York: Holt, Rinehart and Winston

Jones, S. (1986) *Policewomen and Equality*. London: Macmillan

Judicial Statistics, Annual Reports:
1983: Cmnd 9370. London: HMSO
1984: Cmnd 9599. London: HMSO
1985: Cmnd 9864. London: HMSO
1986: Cm 173. London: HMSO
1987: Cm 428. London: HMSO

Kalven, H. and Zeisel, H. (1971) *The American Jury*. Chicago, Ill.: University of Chicago Press

Kelly, J.E. (1984) Patriarchy, Domestic Violence and the State: The Crimes (Domestic Violence) Act No. 116, Macquarie University LL B Dissertation

Kelly, L. (1983) Who Needs Enemies with Friends like Erin Pizzey? *Spare Rib*, February, p. 39

Kinsey, R. (1985) *Merseyside Crime Survey and Police Survey: Final Report*. Liverpool: Police Committee Support Unit

Kinsey, R., Lea, J. and Young, J. (1986) *Losing the Fight Against Crime*. Oxford: Basil Blackwell

Kinsley, P. and Smyth, F. (1980) *I'm Jack: The Police Hunt for the Yorkshire Ripper*. London: Pan

Kirchoff, G.F. (1988) The Unholy Alliance between Victim Representation and Conservatism and the Task of Victimology. Paper presented to the Tenth International Conference on Criminology, Hamburg, 2–6 September

Kitsuse, J. and Cicourel, A.V. (1963) A Note on the Uses of Official Statistics. *Social Problems* 2 (2): 131–9

Kleckner, J. (1978) Wife Beaters and Beaten Wives: Co-conspirators. *Crimes of Violence* 15 (1): 54–6

Klein, D. (1981) Violence Against Women: Some Considerations Regarding its Causes and its Elimination. pp. 64–80 in *Crime and Delinquency* 27 (1)

Klein, D. and Kress, J. (1981) Any Woman's Blues: A Critical Overview of Women, Crime and the Criminal Justice System. pp. 152–86 in Tony Platt and Paul Takagi (eds), *Crime and Social Justice*

Lambert, John (1986) *Police Powers and Accountability*. London: Croom Helm

Landau, S.F. (1981) Juveniles and the Police: Who is Charged Immediately and Who is Referred to the Juvenile Bureau? *British Journal of Criminology* 21: 27–46

Landau, S.F. and Nathan, G. (1983) Selecting Delinquents for Cautioning in the London Metropolitan Area. *British Journal of Criminology* 23: 128–49

Langan, P.A. and Innes, C.A. (1986) Preventing Domestic Violence Against Women. *Bureau of Justice Statistics*. Washington, DC: US Department of Justice

Law Commission (1987) *Binding Over: The Issues*, Law Commission Working Paper 103, Criminal Law. London: HMSO

Law Reform Commission of Australian (1986) Domestic Violence Report 3. Canberra: Australia Government Publication Services

Laycock, G., and Tarling, R. (1985) Police Force Cautioning: Police and Practice. *Howard Journal* 24 (2): 81–92

Lea, J. and Young, J. (1984) *What is to be Done About Law and Order?* Harmondsworth: Penguin

Lederer, L. (ed.) (1980) *Take Back the Night*. New York: William Morrow and Company

Le Doux, J.C. and Hazelwood, R.R. (1985) Police Attitudes and Beliefs Towards Rape. *Journal of Police Science and Administration* 13 (3): 211-24

Lewis, N. and Wiles, P. (1984) The Post Corporatist State. *Journal of Law and Society* 2 (2): 65-90

Lidstone, K. (1987) Social Control and the Criminal Law. *British Journal of Criminology* 27 (1): 31-6

Lock, Joan (1979) *The British Policewoman: Her Story*. London: Robert Hale

Loeb, R. (1983) A Programme of Community Education for Dealing with Spouse Abuse. *Journal of Community Psychology* 2: 241-51

Logan, F. (1986) *Homelessness and Relationship Breakdown*. London: National Council for One-Parent Families

London Strategic Policy Unit (1986) *Police Response to Domestic Violence*, LSPV Briefing Paper no. 1. London

Lord, L.K. (1986) A Comparison of Male and Female Police Officers' Stereotypes and Perceptions of Women and Women Police Officers. *Journal of Police Science and Administration* 14 (2): 83-97

Lustgarten, L. (1987) The Police and the Substantive Criminal Law. *British Journal of Criminology* 27 (1): 23-30

McBarnet, D.J. (1978) The Police and the State: Arrest, Legality and the Law. pp. 196-215 in G. Littlejohn, B. Smart, J. Wakeford and N. Yuval-Davis (eds), *Power and The State*. London: Croom Helm

McCabe, S. and Sutcliffe, F. (1978) *Defining Crime: A Study of Police Decision Making*. Oxford: Basil Blackwell

McCann, K. (1985) Battered Women and the Law: The Limits of the Legislation. pp. 71-96 in J. Brophy and C. Smart (eds), *Women-in-Law*. London: Routledge and Kegan Paul

McClintock, F.H. (1963) *Crimes of Violence*. London: Macmillan

MacDonald, J.M. (1961) *The Murderer and his Victim*. Illinois: Charles Thomas

McGillivray, A. (1987) Battered Women: Definition, Models and Prosecutorial Policy. *Canadian Journal of Family Law* 6: 15-45

McGuigan, P.B. and Pascale, J.S. (eds) (1986) *Crime and Punishment in Modern America*. Washington, DC: Institute for Government and Politics of the Free Congress Research and Education Foundation

McHugh, P. (1980) *Prostitution and Victorian Social Reform*. Beckenham: Croom Helm

MacKay, A. (1985) Diversion from the Criminal Justice Process: A Viable Alternative for Cases of Domestic Violence. *SCOLAG Bulletin* (April): 53

MacKinnon, C.A. (1985) Pornography, Civil Rights, and Speech. *Harvard Civil Rights - Civil Liberties Law Review* 20: 1-70

MacLean, M., Jones, T. and Young, J. (1986) *Preliminary Report of the Islington Crime Survey*. London: Centre for Criminology, Middlesex Polytechnic

McLeod, E. (1982) *Working Women Prostitution Now*. Beckenham: Croom Helm

McLeod, M. (1983) Victim Non-Co-operation in Domestic Disputes. *Criminology* 21 (3): 395-416

Manchester City Council Police Monitoring Unit (1987), *Police Watch* (July)

Martin, D. (1976) *Battered Wives*. New York: Pocket Books

Martin, S. (1978) Sexual Policies in the Work-place: The International World of Policewomen. *Symbolic Interaction* 2: 44-59

Matza, D. (1964) *Delinquency and Drift*. Berkeley, CA.: John Wiley and Son

Matza, D. (1969) *Becoming Deviant*. Englewood Cliffs, NJ: Prentice-Hall

Mawby, R.I. (1985) Bystander Responses to the Victims of Crime: Is the Good Samaritan Alive and Well? *Victimology* 10 (1–4): 461–77

Maxfield, M. (1984) *Fear of Crime in England and Wales*. Home Office Research Study 78. London: HMSO

Mayhew, P., Clark, T.V.C., Sturman, A. and Hough, J.M. (1976) *Crime as Opportunity*. Home Office Research Study 34. London: HMSO

Meehan, E. (1986) Women's Studies and Political Studies. pp. 120–34 in J. Evans, J. Hills, K. Hunt, E. Meehan, T. ten Tusscher, U. Vogel, G. Woylen (eds), *Feminism and Political Theory*. London: Sage

Metropolitan Police (1986) *Working Party on Domestic Violence Report*. London

Metropolitan Police (1987) Strategy Statement. January. London

Metropolitan Police (1988) *Equal Opportunities: Guidelines for Police Managers*. London: Personnel and Training Department, Metropolitan Police

Metropolitan Police (1989) Strategy Statement. January

Metropolitan Police Crime Prevention Service (1986) *Positive Steps*. London: Metropolitan Police

Milton, C. (1972) *Women in Policing*. Washington DC: US Department of Justice

Ministry of Justice and Attorney General of Canada (1986) *After Sexual Assault - Your Guide to the Criminal Justice System*. Ottawa, Ont.: Department of Justice

Mishkin, B. (1981) Female Police in the US. *Police Journal* 54 (1): 22–30

Montgomery, P. and Bell, V. (1986) *Police Response to Wife Assault: A Northern Ireland Study*. Belfast: Northern Ireland Women's Aid Federation

Moody, S.R. and Tombs, J. (1982) *Constructing Prosecution Decisions: The Case of the Procurator Fiscal*. Edinburgh: Scottish Academic Press

Moore, D.N. (1979) *Battered Women*. Beverly Hills, CA: Sage

Morris, A. (1987) *Women, Crime and Criminal Justice*. Oxford: Basil Blackwell

Mott, Joy (1983) Police Decisions for Dealing with Juvenile Offenders. *British Journal of Criminology* 23: 249–62

NACRO (National Association for the Care and Rehabilitation of Offenders) (1988) Some Facts and findings About Black People in the Criminal Justice System, June (pamphlet)

Naffin, N. (1984) *An Inquiry into the Substantive Law of Rape*. Adelaide, South Australia: Women's Adviser's Office, Department of the Premier and Cabinet

National Crime Survey (1982) Washington, DC: US Department of Justice

National Swedish Council for Crime Prevention (1982) Report no. 9 Stockholm: E. Kuhlhorn and B. Svensson Research and Development Division, Council for Crime Prevention

Nelken, D. (1987) Critical Criminal Law. *Journal of Law and Society* 14 (1): 105–17

New South Wales Task Force on Domestic Violence (1981) *Report*. Canberra, New South Wales

New South Wales Task Force on Domestic Violence (1985). *Report*. Canberra, New South Wales

Newman, D.J. (1966) *Conviction: The Determination of Guilt or Innocence without Trial*. Boston/Toronto: Little, Brown and Co

Oakley, A. (1981) Interviewing Women: A Contradiction in Terms. pp. 30–61 in H. Roberts (ed.), *Doing Feminist Research*. London: Routledge and Kegan Paul

O'Brien, R.M. (1988) Explaining the Intersexual Nature of Violent Crime. *Criminology* 26 (1): 151–70

O'Donovan, K. (1985) *Sexual Divisions in Law*. London: Weidenfeld and Nicolson
O'Donovan, K. and Szyszczak, E. (1988) *Equality and Sex Discrimination Law*. Oxford: Basil Blackwell
Ohio Attorney General (William J. Brown) (1981) *The Ohio Report on Domestic Violence*. Ohio: National Graphics
Oppenlander, Nan (1982) Coping or Copping Out. *Criminology* 20 (3, 4): 449–65
Pagelow, M.D. (1981) *Women Battering: Victims and their Experiences*. Beverly Hills, CA: Sage
Pahl, J. (1978) *A Refuge for Battered Women: A Study of the Role of a Woman's Centre*. London: HMSO
Pahl, J. (1982) Police Response to Battered Women. *Journal of Social Welfare Law*. November, 337–43
Pahl, J. (ed.) (1985) *Private Violence and Public Policy*. London: Routledge and Kegan Paul
Parker, S. (1985) The Legal Background, pp. 97–109 in J. Pahl (ed.), *Private Violence and Public Policy*. London: Routledge and Kegan Paul
Parnas, R. (1967) The Police Response to the Domestic Disturbance. *Wisconsin Law Review* (Fall): 914–60
Parton, N. (1985) *The Politics of Child Abuse*. London: Macmillan
Pashukanis, E. (1978) *Law and Marxism*. London: Ink Links
Pearl, D. (1986) Public Housing Allocation and Domestic Disputes. pp. 20–33 in M.D.A. Freeman (ed.), *Essays in Family Law 1985*. London: Stevens and Sons
Pearson, G. (1983) *Hooligan*. London: Macmillan
Phipps, A. (1985) Radical Criminology and Criminal Victimization: Proposals for the Development of Theory and Intervention. pp. 97–117 in R. Mathews and J. Young (eds), *Confronting Crime*. London/Beverly Hills: Sage
Pibus, C.J. (1980) Civil Remedies for Interspousal Violence in England and Ontario. *UT Faculty Law Review*, pp. 33
Piliavin, I. and Werthman, C. (1967) Gang Members and the Police. pp. 56–98 in D. Bordua (ed.), *The Police: Six Sociological Essays*. New York: John Wiley
Pizzey, E. (1974) *Scream Quietly or the Neighbours will Hear*. Harmondsworth: Penguin
Pizzey, E. (1989) A Comparative Study of Battered Women and Violence-prone Women. *Victimology* forthcoming
Pizzey, E. and Shapiro, J. (1981) Choosing a Violent Relationship. *New Society*, 23 April
Pizzey, E. and Shapiro, J. (1982) *Prone to Violence*. Feltham, Middlesex: Hamlyn
Platt, T. (1981) 'Street' Crime: a View from the Left. pp. 13–29 in T. Platt and P. Takagi (eds), *Crime and Social Justice*. London: Macmillan
Police Foundation (US) (1976) *Domestic Violence and the Police Response: Studies in Detroit and Kansas City*. Washington, DC: Wilt Bannon
Policy Studies Institute (1987) The Policing of Domestic Disputes, draft paper
Potts, Lee W. (1981) Equal Employment Opportunity and Female Criminal Justice Employment. *Police Studies* 4 (3): 9–19
Powis, David (1977) *The Signs of Crime*. London: McGraw Hill
President's Task Force on Victims of Crime (1982) *Report*. Washington, DC: US Department of Justice
Radford, J. (1987) Policing Male Violence – Policing Women. pp. 30–45 in J. Hanmer and M. Maynard (eds), *Women, Violence and Social Control*. London: Macmillan
Radford, L. (1987) Legalizing Women Abuse. pp. 135–51 in J. Hanmer and M. Maynard (eds), *Women, Violence and Social Control*. London: Macmillan

Radzinowicz, L. and King, J. (1978) *The Growth of Crime*. Harmondsworth: Penguin

Reiner, R. (1985) *The Politics of the Police*. Brighton: Wheatsheaf

Rittenmeyer, S.D. (1981) Of Battered Wives; Self-defence and Double Standards of Justice. *Journal of Criminal Justice* 9: 389–95

Rock, P. (1973) *Deviant Behaviour*. Oxford: Oxford University Press

Rock, P. (1986) *A View from the Shadows*. Oxford: Oxford University Press

Rock, P. (1988) *A History of British Criminology*. Oxford: Oxford University Press

Roy, M. (1977) *Battered Women: A Psychosociological Study of Domestic Violence*. New York: Van Nostrand Reinhold

Royal Commission on Criminal Procedure (1981) *The Investigation and Prosecution of Criminal Offences in England and Wales: The Law and Procedure*, Cmnd. 8092-1. London: HMSO

Royal Commission on the Police (1962). Cmnd. 1728. London: HMSO

Russell, D. (1982) *Rape in Marriage*. New York: Macmillan

Russo, P., Engel, A., and Hatting, S. (1983) Police and Occupational Stress: An Empirical Investigation. pp. 89–106 in Bennett R. (ed.), *Police at Work: Police Issues and Analysis*. Beverly Hills, CA: Sage

Sacks, H. (1972) Notes on Police Assessment of Moral Character. in D. Sudnow (ed.), *Studies in Social Interaction*. New York: Free Press

Sanders, A. (1986) The New Prosecution Arrangements: (2) An Independent Crown Prosecution Service. *Criminal Law Review*, pp. 16–27

Sanders, A. (1988a) Personal Violence and Public Order: The Prosecution of Domestic Violence in England and Wales. *International Journal of the Sociology of Law* 16: 359–82

Sanders, A. (1988b) The Limits to Diversion from Prosecution. *British Journal of Criminology* 28 (4): 513–32

Sanders, W.B. (1977) *Detective Work*. New York: Free Press

Scarman (1981) *The Brixton Disorders 10–12 April: Report on An Inquiry by the Rt. Hon. Lord Scarman*. Cmnd 8427. London: HMSO

Schechter, S. (1982) *Women and Male Violence: The Visions and Struggles of the Battered Women's Movement*. Boston, MA: South-End Press

Schwendinger, J. and Schwendinger, H. (1974) Rape Myths in Legal, Theoretical and Everyday Practice. *Crime and Social Justice* 1 (Spring–Summer): 18–26

Scutt, J.A. (1981) Sexism in Criminal Law. pp. 1–21 in S.K. Mukherjee and J.A. Scutt, *Women and Crime*. Sydney, London, Boston: George Allen and Unwin

Scutt, J.A. (1982) Domestic Violence and the Police Response. pp. 110–20 in C. O'Donnell and J. Craney (eds), *Family Violence in Australia*. Melbourne: Longman Cheshire

Scutt, J.A. (1985) *Even in the Best of Homes*. Victoria, Australia: Penguin

Scutt, J.A. (1986) Going Backwards: Law 'Reform' and Woman Bashing. *Women's Studies International Forum* 9 (1): 49–55

Scutt, J.A. (ed.) (1980) *Rape Law Reform*. Canberra: Australian Institute of Criminology

Select Committee on Violence in Marriage (1975) *Report 1974–5*. London: HMSO

Shainess, N. (1979) Vulnerability to masochism: Masochism as a process. *American Journal of Psychotherapy* 33 (2): 174–89

Shapland, J., Willmore, J. and Duff, P. (1985) *Victims in the Criminal Justice System*. Aldershot: Gower

Sherman, L.W. and Berk, R.A. (1984a) *The Minneapolis Domestic Violence Experiment*. Police Foundation Reports. Washington: Police Foundation

Sherman, L.W. and Berk, R.A. (1984b) The Specific Deterrent Effects of Arrest for Domestic Assault. *American Sociological Review* 49 (2): 261-72
Simpson, W.B. (1983) *Pornography and Politics*. London: Waterlow Publishers
Skogan, W. (1984) Reporting Crimes to the Police. *Journal of Research in Crime and Delinquency* 21 (2): 113-37
Skogan, W. and Maxfield, M. (1981) *Coping with Crime*. Beverly Hills, CA: Sage
Skolnick, J. (1966) *Justice Without Trial*. New York: John Wiley
Smart, C. (1976) *Women, Crime and Criminology*. London: Routledge and Kegan Paul
Smart, C. (1984) *The Ties that Bind*. London: Routledge and Kegan Paul
Smart, C. (1986) Feminism and the Law: Some Problems of Analysis and Strategy. *International Journal of the Sociology of Law* 14: 109-23
Smith, D.A. and Klein, J.R. (1984) Police Control of Interpersonal Disputes. *Social Problems* 31 (4): 468-81
Smith, David J. and Gray, J. (1983) *Police and People in London*. vols 1-4, London: Policy Studies Institute
Snell, J., Rosenwald, R.J. and Robey, A. (1964) The Wife-beaters. *Archives of General Psychiatry* 11: 107-12
Soetenhorst, J. (1989) Sexual Violence: A Challenge to the Legislator. *Victimology* forthcoming
Sonkin, D.J. (1987) *Domestic Violence on Trial*. New York: Springer
Southgate, Peter (1981) Women and the Police. *Police Journal* 54 (2): 157-67
Stanko, E. (1985) *Intimate Intrusions: Women's Experience of Male Violence*. London: Routledge and Kegan Paul
Stanley, L. and Wise, S. (1983) *Breaking Out: Feminist Consciousness and Feminist Research*. London: Routledge and Kegan Paul
Steer, D. (1981) *Uncovering Crime: The Police Role*. Royal Commission on Criminal Procedure, Research Study 7. London: HMSO
Steinem, G. (1980) Erotica and Pornography. pp. 21-5 in L. Lederer (ed.), *Take back the Night* New York: William Morrow and Company
Stith, S.M. (1986) The Relationship Between the Male Police Officer's Response to Victims of Domestic Violence and the Personal and Family Experiences. Paper presented to the World Congress on Victimology, Florida, July
Storr, A. (1968) *Sexual Deviation*. Harmondsworth: Penguin
Strategic Policing Unit, *Policing London*, monthly publication, 1985-
Straus, M. (1977) Sexual Inequality, Cultural Norms and Wife Beating. pp. 59-77 in J.R. Chapman and M. Gates (eds), *Women into Wives*. Beverly Hills: Sage
Straus, M.A., Gelles, R. and Steinmetz, S. (1980) *Behind Closed Doors: Violence in the American Family*. New York: Doubleday
Straus, M.A. and Hotaling G. (eds) (1980) *The Social Causes of Husband-Wife Violence*. University of Minnesota
Street, R. (1988) Women and Policing. Address to Howard League for Penal Reform, September
Sudnow, D. (1965) Normal Crimes: Sociological Features of the Penal Code. *Social Problems* 12: 255-76
Sudnow, D. (1972) *Studies in Social Interaction*. New York: Free Press
Sumrall, R.O., Roberts, J. and Farmer, M.T. (1981) *Differential Police Response Strategies*. Washington, DC: Police Executive Research Forum
Taylor, I. (1981) *Law and Order: Arguments for Socialism*. London: Macmillan
Tchaikovsky, C. (1985) Looking for Trouble. pp. 14-58 in P. Carlen, D. Christina, J. Hicks, J. O'Dwyer and C. Tchaikovsky, *Criminal Women*. Cambridge: Polity Press

Temkin, J. (1987) *Rape and the Legal Process*. London: Sweet and Maxwell
Thomas, T. (1988) The Police and Criminal Evidence Act 1984: The Social Work Role. *Howard Journal of Criminal Justice* 27 (4): 256–65
Thompson, E.P. (1980) *Writing by Candlelight*. London: Merlin Press
Timrots, A.D. and Rand, M.R. (1987) *Violent Crime by Strangers and Non-Strangers*. Bureau of Justice Statictics Special Report. Washington, DC: US Department of Justice
Tomes, N. (1978) A 'Torrent of Abuse': Crimes of Violence Between Working-Class Men and Women in London 1840–1875. *Journal of Social History* 11 (3): 328–45
Tong, R. (1984) *Women, Sex, and the Law*. Totowa, NJ: Rowman and Allanheld
Townsend, P. (1979) *Poverty*. Harmondsworth: Penguin
Unsworth, C. (1984) The Riots of 1981: Popular Violence and the Politics of Law and Order. *Journal of Law and Society* 9 (1): 63–85
US Department of Justice (1983) *Statistics*
US Department of Justice (1984) *Statistics*
Vandall, F.J. (1976) *Police Training for Tough Calls*. Emory University, Birmingham, Alabama
Vega, M. and Silverman, I.J. (1982) Female Officers as Viewed by their Male Counterparts. *Police Studies* 5 (1): 31–9
Vennard, J. (1985) Decisions to Prosecute: Screening Policies and Practices in the United States. *Criminal Law Review*, pp. 20–8
Waits, K. (1985) The Criminal Justice System's Response to Battering: Understanding the Problem, Forging the Solutions. *Washington Law Review* 60: 267
Walker, L.E. (1978) Battered Women and Learned Helplessness. *Victimology* 2 (3–4): 525–34
Walker, L.E. (1979) *The Battered Woman*. New York: Harper and Row
Walker, L.E. (1984) *The Battered Woman Syndrome*. New York: Springer
Walker, L.E. (1985) The Psychological Impact of the Criminalization of Domestic Violence on Victims. *Victimology* 10 (1–4): 281–300
Walker, L.E. (1987) When the Battered Woman becomes Defendant. Paper presented at the Fourth International Institute of Victimology, NATO Advanced Research Workshop, Tuscany, Italy, 9–15 August
Walker, L.E. (1989) *Battered Women Who Kill*. New York: Harper and Row
Wallington, P. (1987) Some Implications for the Policing of Industrial Disputes. *Criminal Law Review*, pp. 180–91
Walsmley, R. (1986) *Personal Violence*. Home Office Research Study 89. London: HMSO
Walmsley, R. and White, K. (1979) *Sexual Offences, Consent and Sentencing*. Home Office Research Study 54. London: HMSO
Walter, J.D (1981) Police in the Middle: A Study of Small City Police Intervention in Domestic Disputes. *Journal of Police Science and Administration* 9 (3): 243–60
Wasik, M. (1982) Cumulative Provocation and Domestic Killing. *Criminal Law Review*, pp. 29–37
Wasoff, F. (1982) Legal Protection from Wife-beating: The Processing of Domestic Assaults by Scottish Prosecutors and Criminal Courts. *International Journal of the Sociology of Law* 10: 187–204
Wasoff, F. (1987) Prosecutor's Discretion in Court Allocation in Domestic Violence Cases. Paper presented to the British Criminology Conference at the University of Sheffield, 12–15 April
Webb, D. (1984) More on Gender and Justice: Girl Offenders on Supervision. *Sociology* 18: 367–81

Weis, K. and Borges, S. (1973) Victimology and Rape: The Case of the Legitimate Victim. *Issues in Criminology* 8: 71–115

West, D.J. (1961) *Murder Followed by Suicide*. Harmondsworth: Penguin

Whitaker, B. (1982) *The Police in Society*. London: Sinclair Browne

White, S.O. and Straus, M.A. (1981) The Implications of Family Violence for Rehabilitation Strategies. in S.E. Martin, L.E. Sechrest and R. Redner (eds), *New Directions in the Rehabilitation of Criminal Offenders*. Washington, DC: National Academy of Sciences

Whitehouse, M. (1982) *A Most Dangerous Woman?* Tring, Herts: Lion

Whyte, W.F. (1943) *Street Corner Society: The Social Structure of an Italian Slum*. Chicago: University of Chicago Press

Wigmore, J. (1970) *On Evidence*. Boston: Little, Brown and Chaney

Wilbanks, W. (1983) The Female Homicide Offender in Dade County, Florida. *Criminal Justice Review* 8 (2): 9–14

Wilbanks, W. (1984) Murder in Miami. Miami: University Press of America

Williams, B. (ed.) (1981) *Obscenity and Film Censorship*. Cambridge University Press

Williams Committee (1979) *Report on Obscenity and Film Censorship*. Cmnd. 7772. London: HMSO

Williams, J. (1984) Marital Rape: A Time for Reform. *New Law Journal* (13 January): 26–8

Williams, K.R. and Flewelling, R.L. (1988) The Social Production of Criminal Homicide. *American Sociological Review* 53 (3): 421–31

Willis, C.F. (1983) *The Use, Effectiveness and Impact of Police Stop and Search Powers*. Home Office Research and Planning Unit Paper 15. London: Home Office

Willis, C.F. (1985) The Use, Effectiveness and Impact of Police Stop and Search Powers. pp. 94–106 in K. Heal, R. Tarling and J. Burrows (eds) *Policing Today*. Home Office Research and Planning Unit. London: HMSO

Wilson, J.Q. (1968) *Varieties of Police Behaviour*. Cambridge, Mass.: Harvard University Press

Wilt, G.M., Bannon, J.D., Breedlove, R.K., Sandker, D.M., Kennish, J.W. and Sawtell, R.K. (1977) *Domestic Violence and the Police*. Washington DC: Police Foundation

Wolfenden, J. (1957) *Report on Homosexuality and Prostitution*. Cmd 247. London: HMSO

Wolfgang, M.E. (1958) *Patterns in Criminal Homicide*. New York: John Wiley

Women's National Commission (1985) *Violence Against Women*. Report of an Ad Hoc Working Group. London: Cabinet Office

Worden, R.E. and Pollitz, A.A. (1984) Police Arrests in Domestic Disturbances: A Further Look. *Law and Society Review* 18: 105–19

Worrall, A. (1981) Out of Place: Female Offenders. *Court Probation Journal* 28 (3): 90–2

Wright, R. (1980) Rape and Physical Violence. pp. 100–13 in D.J. West (ed.), *Sex Offenders in the Criminal Justice System*. Cropwood Conference Series no 12. Cambridge: University of Cambridge Institute of Criminology

X, Laura. Clearing House on Marital Rape, Women's Herstory Research Center, 2325 Oak Street, Berkeley, CA.

Young, J. (1985) The Failure of Criminology: The Need for Radical Realism. pp. 4–30 in R. Matthew and J. Young (eds), *Confronting Crime*. London and Beverly Hills: Sage

Young, J. (1988) Radical Criminology in Britain: The Emergence of a Competing Paradigm. *British Journal of Criminology* 28 (2): 159–83.

# Index

For Product Safety Concerns and Information please contact our EU representative GPSR@taylorandfrancis.com Taylor & Francis Verlag GmbH, Kaufingerstraße 24, 80331 München, Germany